MEMORIES I CAN'T LET GO OF

MEMORIES
I CAN'T LET GO OF

Life Stories from Tontitown, Arkansas

EDITED BY

SUSAN YOUNG

Farther Along Books
2012

ISBN: 978-0-9829455-9-9

Designed by Liz Lester

Farther Along Books

CONTENTS

PREFACE

In 2002, the Tontitown Preservation Project was formed by a group of volunteers who wanted to assist the Tontitown Historical Museum in its efforts to document and preserve the community's Italian heritage. Part of the project involved a series of oral history interviews conducted with Tontitown elders. A standard set of questions was created, covering topics such as memories of grandparents and parents, home life, foodways, school years, community life, marriage, and raising a family. Likely candidates for interviews were identified. Then, the project took off. From 2002 through 2005, 48 interviews were recorded and transcribed. In most cases, the interviewee was photographed at the time of their interview. Volunteers who conducted the interviews were Andy Franco, Brenda Pianalto, Ruth Ann Roso Ritchie, Nova Jean Fiori Watson, and Mary Maestri Vaughan. To help get the project underway, a few of the first interviews were conducted by Bob Besom, director of the Shiloh Museum; Dr. Michael Pierce, professor of history at the University of Arkansas; and myself. The bulk of the grueling task of transcribing hours and hours of recorded interviews was done by Pauline Fiori Franco. Nancy Maestri Baker, Frances Verucchi Franco, Beverly Cortiana McEuen, and Brenda Pianalto assisted with the transcribing. The typed transcriptions were then housed in the Tontitown Historical Museum archives.

A few years ago, as I was working on a book about the early history of Tontitown, I had the chance to read the oral histories, and I was struck by the wealth of information they contained. Taken separately, they told the life story of an individual. Collectively, they told the life story of a unique Italian-American Ozark community. It's a story that deserves to be shared, hence this book.

My goal was to weave the transcribed interviews into a narrative format while at the same time staying true to the interviewee's responses. I combined similar discussion threads together. For example, if the interviewee talked about school recess games at one point in the interview, and later talked about what he or she took to school for lunch, I grouped those into one section of the narrative focusing on school days. I didn't want to clutter up the dialogue with distracting footnotes and editorial commentary. In other words, I wanted to get out of the way and let the interviewee's voice come through. When I did feel the need to insert an explanatory word or two, I tried to keep it brief. Those insertions are in brackets, [like this].

Having said all that, there are a few items that I do find myself wanting to explain a little further, so I'll do that now.

How Tontitown Came to Be

The Italian families who founded Tontitown in 1898 began their lives in America as tenant farmers on the south Arkansas plantation of Sunnyside. Groups from northern and central Italy arrived there in 1895 and 1897 and soon found themselves battling poor sanitation, disease, unfamiliar farming methods, language barriers, and contract disputes. In early 1898, some 40 families chose to follow Father Pietro Bandini, the plantation's resident priest, to the Arkansas Ozarks, where the climate, terrain, and small-scale agriculture were more similar to northern and central Italy. They settled on a parcel of rocky land west of Springdale. Abandoned cabins and outbuildings provided shelter until homes could be built. Horses and plows were bought on credit; land was cleared; and vegetable gardens, vineyards, apple and peach orchards, and fields of strawberries were planted.

With Tontitown, Father Bandini hoped to create a model of successful immigration. He believed that if the Italians were given the opportunity to own their own land, and farm it in the way they knew how, they could become productive citizens in their adopted country of America. Tontitown's hardworking Italian families did not disappoint; between 1898 and 1901, the majority of the original Tontitown settlers purchased a total of some 800 acres of land.

Bandini's emphasis on community productivity, education, family, and faith, combined with the work ethic of the Italian immigrants, were the cornerstones of Tontitown's success. As you read the narratives, you'll see that these cornerstones continue to play an important role in the lives of the descendants of the first Tontitown Italians.

Consider the Interviewees

They range in age from 56 to 93; most are in their late 70s and early 80s. Most of them relate their memories with a refreshing candor that often comes with age. Most of them are first generation Italian Americans. Their everyday lives still contain many direct ties to their Italian roots. Most of them grew up during the Great Depression. They describe the hard times experienced by most all rural Ozark families during those years.

A Few Specifics

Many interviewees speak of the time "when the school burned." The school was St. Mary's Academy, which opened in 1906 and was operated first by the Ursuline Sisters, and later by the Sisters of Mercy. The lovely two-story frame building, quite a contrast to the typical one-room rural Ozark schoolhouse of the era, was destroyed by fire in 1927. Until a new school building was finished (which still stands in 2012), classes were held in the old Smith schoolhouse, which was located on the northwest corner of present-day U.S. Highway 412 and Barrington Road. The Smith schoolhouse and grounds are also mentioned by many interviewees as the location of the early grape festivals.

Another incident recalled by many of the interviewees is the time when "a tornado blew the church down." The church was the original St. Joseph's Church, dedicated in 1900. Strong winds, perhaps a tornado, demolished the church in 1934. Parishioners built a new church, which was dedicated in 1944. In 2012, that building still stands on the northeast corner of U.S. Highway 412 and Barrington Road.

Some Italian words are sprinkled here and there in the narratives. Some were spelled phonetically in the original interview transcriptions. I tried to confirm the correct spelling of all Italian words, with mixed results. There are different dialects throughout Italy, so consulting a standard Italian dictionary didn't always prove successful.

Why the Title?

I knew I had found the title for this collection of life stories when I read this lovely passage from Francis Pianalto's interview: "There are a lot of memories I can't let go of. I do a lot of dreaming. When I was in the hospital one time, I dreamed I saw Jesus, Mary, and Joseph. They weren't 12 feet away from me. I thought I was dead, because they were coming after me with their arms stretched out, facing me, with a heavenly blue sky, and it was so beautiful. I have never seen anything more beautiful than Jesus, Mary, and Joseph reaching out to me and saying, 'Let's go.' I said, 'There is so much to be done here yet,' and they disappeared. Then I woke up. There was a reason for that. God wasn't through with me yet."

ACKNOWLEDGEMENTS

It's both satisfying and humbling to come to the end of the work and look back on all the folks who helped make this book a reality. First and foremost, the willingness of the interviewees to share their life stories is a gift beyond measure. Many of the folks you'll meet within the pages of this book are gone now, but their stories remain as a beautiful tapestry of Tontitown history. To all the interviewees and their families, I offer my sincerest appreciation. It has been a real honor for me to work on this book.

I am grateful for the work of the Tontitown Preservation Project volunteers who conducted and transcribed the interviews. Their love for Tontitown and their dedication to the community oral history project has produced a wealth of local history that is now preserved for future generations in the archives of the Tontitown Historical Museum. Thank you, Nancy Maestri Baker, Jim and Peggy Borden, Andy Franco, Frances Verucchi Franco, Pauline Fiori Franco, Beverly Cortiana McEuen, Brenda Pianalto, Ruth Ann Roso Ritchie, Danny Watson, Nova Jean Fiori Watson, and Mary Maestri Vaughan.

Thanks to the Tontitown Historical Museum board of directors for giving me permission to use the oral histories to create this collection of narrative stories. I am grateful for the work you do to make sure the history and heritage of Tontitown is preserved, recognized, and remembered.

Mark and Paula Bariola Zulpo provided an idyllic spot—their screened-in porch overlooking rolling green fields—to work on proofreading and editing. Pody Gay, Liz Lester, Beth Lowrey, and Susan Raymond listened patiently over many dinner conversations as I fretted about seeing the work through to completion. Liz not only went through all of that, she also agreed to be the book designer, for which I am so grateful. Thank you, Liz, for caring about this book.

Lastly, mostly, thanks to Frank Maestri, Mary Maestri Vaughan, and Nova Jean Fiori Watson. You make my heart full.

Irma Taldo Ardemagni

IRMA TALDO ARDEMAGNI

*Irma Taldo Ardemagni was born in 1912 in Tontitown,
Arkansas, to Giacomo (James) and Clementina Costa
Taldo. She was 90 years old when she was interviewed
in 2002.*

My parents never said too much about their parents. They had a hard time [in Italy], I know that. My dad lived about 15 miles from where Mama lived. He used to walk to visit her, to begin dating. Over there it wasn't anything for them to do that, there just wasn't any other way.

Mama had nine children. Emilia, Blanche, and Joe Jack [Joseph] came from the old country; Edward, Argie, Irma, Olivia, Rita, and Margaret were born in America.

When I was a child, we lived on a farm south of the cemetery [near present-day Taldo Loop]. I always milked two or three cows before we went to school. Then we walked a couple of miles to school. We walked, rain or shine, because there was no other way to get back and forth. Lots of times we were plenty wet when we got there.

At home, my parents spoke Italian all the time. We had to speak Italian with Mama and Daddy at home because they didn't understand or talk English. Then we go to school and had to learn to read and write English, and that was really hard.

[In Italy], every few miles they talk a different dialect. [In Tontitown], there were three or four different dialects. The Morsanis down the road, they talked different than us, and the Bastianellis talked another dialect. If I hear somebody talk real Italian, I don't understand them. I can speak a little Italian, if I try hard to find a word or two. Josephine Piazza is about the only one [in Tontitown] who still speaks Italian.

I didn't go to high school. After grade school I went to work. I helped my dad on the farm for one year, and then I went to Fayetteville to work at the City Hospital. I waited tables for the nurses, aides, employees, and students learning to be nurses. I worked there for a year or a little more. I was between 17 and 18 years old, so it was the late 1920s and early 1930s.

We never had a doctor in Tontitown. There was no hospital in Springdale, so we had to go to Fayetteville to the City Hospital. I had a brother die there. He had a ruptured appendix. He was 35 years old. It was awful.

Springdale was the only place we ever bought anything. We went in a horse and wagon. We started early—it took all day. When you couldn't speak English, it was worse than ever. You had to go down there and try to speak. One time somebody went to town and wanted to buy a dishpan to make bread in, and they didn't understand what she was trying to say. She said something about, "Sometime to wash-a the baby, sometime to make-a the bread."

As a child, I never was hungry. The older children might have been hungry, but in my time I was never hungry. Maybe we didn't have what we ought to have had, but we always had milk and butter and cows and cheese and pasta. My dad would go to town and buy 40- and 50-pound sacks of flour at a time. Then Mama made bread in the outdoor oven. We used to help her. I helped a lot, carrying bread to the oven, putting wood in the oven.

Mama always had chickens. She'd set the hens with eggs, and then raise her own chickens. [To catch and clean a chicken to eat] was easy. To begin with, Mama had a long wire with a hook at the end. She'd just grab a chicken by the foot, catch it, and pull it up. To kill them, she'd wring their neck. I got to where I could do it too. Just stretch it a little. Catch it by the feet and the neck and stretch it till it pops. Nothing bothered us—when you were hungry, you could eat after doing anything.

You mean you don't know how to pick a chicken? Heat about a gallon of water and dip [the chicken] down in the bucket, then just pull out the feathers. They come out easy. Then you get a newspaper and roll it up long and set it on fire, and with the newspaper you singe the entire chicken to get rid of the pin feathers. You could do it over a gas flame, but years ago we didn't have gas.

In other words, if you want to have chicken for dinner [the noon

 IRMA TALDO ARDEMAGNI

meal], you had to start about 7:00 a.m. You boil the water, catch it, kill it, pick it, gut it out, and cut it into pieces. Dip it into cold water a few times to chill it as much as you can. Then about eleven o'clock, start cooking. We had chicken about three times a week and always for Sunday dinner.

People used to come around to peddle meat at 25 cents a pound. We would buy a couple pounds of veal or beef. When you had four or five cows and they have their babies, then you keep them three or four weeks, there was no market for them. You had to get rid of them, so you'd butcher them and peddle the meat around the parish. I remember we would put [the butchered meat] in a bucket on a rope and drop it down the well to keep it cool a day or two. After that, it spoiled.

Whenever we made cheese, seven or eight people had more milk than they could use, so they'd carry their milk to one house, and they'd make a big old cheese. Sometime they'd bring it for a week to one house. I remember walking from our house south of the cemetery to Mary Maestri's house north of us. They had a little place where everyone brought their milk till they got enough to make some big cheeses. There was no cheese factory, it was just a little place where they had a big kettle and would put a little fire under it and heat the milk. Everybody would bring two or three gallons of milk, and every so often they would work it down. Pour all the milk in the big kettle and add rennet [an enzyme] to make the milk hard. Then you mix it all up and it settles. The cheese begins to crumble, then you take the whey out, and you have a big pan of cheese. You pour the cheese into a wooden form. It dries and gets hard.

We made pasta about every day. I still make pasta. I never have bought a package of spaghetti. [To make pasta], I just get a bowl—it depends how much you want to make. Get a gallon bowl, put flour in, then 12 or 14 eggs, stir it up, and first thing you know it's in a ball. Mix the dough with your hands. We use to roll it with a *miscoula* [rolling pin]. We even did that for the grape festivals. Everyone brought their own miscoula and we'd make a big sheet. You cut off a handful from the ball. Roll it to a big sheet about 18 inches round or more. Let it dry a little, then roll it, or fold it into a roll, and cut it. Shake it out on a table and let it dry, or drop it into a pot of boiling water. Hold one hand clenched near the edge of the pasta roll, and with the other hand use a large butcher knife and just cut small slices as you move your hand on the pasta back slowly. Every time you cut off a little bit, back up your fingers.

We would make sauce each time we had pasta; we did not have freezers to make ahead and freeze. My mother started hers with salt pork, onions, and garlic. Brown that good, then add tomatoes or ketchup. The ketchup we made at home didn't have all the spices in ketchup today. We're talking just regular tomatoes. To make the ketchup, we get tomatoes by the bushel and cook them. Then put them through a bag, like a flour sack or pillow case. Drain all the liquid, then hang this sack on a broomstick between chairs and let it drain several hours. Then empty the bag into a pan and run it through a colander to remove seed and skins. This will be thick. Place it on the fire again, boil it, and add some salt if you want to. We canned it, and then when you wanted spaghetti, there it was in the cellar. Some put oregano into the sauce, but I don't like it.

To make *polenta* [thick cornmeal mush] and *umido* [sauce], we used meat of any kind—rabbit, chicken, squirrel, quails, birds, anything we had. I prefer chicken. Put the polenta in a double boiler and do the best you can. Mama used an iron kettle. She put water to boil, added corn meal, and she'd cook and stir, cook and stir. It would stick to the side of the pot. When it was cooked, she would dump the polenta on a bread board, let it set a couple or 30 minutes, and then it's ready to eat. Make it pretty stiff. The umido sauce is about like spaghetti sauce, without salt pork.

Gene Ardemagni and I were married in 1931. At one time we had 25 acres of vineyards. We had an apple orchard and strawberries. Oh, we worked hard the first few years. First you put in a spring garden, then in the fall you put in a fall garden so you have vegetables year 'round. You name it and we had it. Peas, tomatoes, okra. I didn't really sell okra; I traded it for apples at fruit stands on the side of the road. Corn, yes, we raised corn. Raspberries. One year we planted sunflower seeds for the redbirds.

[There was an apple dryer] by the old Ardemagni place. Gene's father, Felix Ardemagni, owned the apple dryer. They'd buy a bunch of apples. They peeled the apples—I still have one of the apple peelers. They had six ladies who would peel them and slice them and lay them on a rack with air holes and place them in the machine. They would build a fire in bottom of the apple dryer and the heat would go up and dry the apples. They would sell them for dried apples. We had the railroad at that time.

There wasn't very many grapes when they first started. We used to sell them in those little baskets. After they got going, Welch's came in and bought [grapes] by the tons. We picked them in lugs. There was money in grapes then. We always had a pretty good-sized family and we picked our own [grapes]. Some people went to Oklahoma and brought Indians over to pick for them. Later, my nephews, Bob and Richard Pianalto, had a big mechanical machine to pick the grapes. Sometimes truckers would come buy a load of grapes. After Welch's closed, everything went to pot. Now there are very few grapes. Very few eat jelly now anyway. Everybody's on a diet.

Richard Ardemagni Jr.

RICHARD ARDEMAGNI JR.

*Richard Ardemagni Jr. was born in 1945 in Tontitown,
Arkansas, to Richard and Nettie Mae Solomon Ardemagni.
He was 56 years old when he was interviewed in 2002.*

My paternal grandparents were Felice or Felix and Enrica Pianalto Ardemagni. Both Felix and Enrica came through Sunnyside [a plantation in south Arkansas], and they were among the original settlers that came with Father Bandini to Tontitown [in 1898]. Felix and Enrica were married in Tontitown, and had the following children: Michael, Gene, Beato, Lucy, Rosalia, Richard, who was my father, and Agatha.

I remember Mom and Dad talking about the first two winters after [the original settlers] came to Tontitown. Those first two winters were really tough. I think it's been said by a few people, "Thank God for the rabbits." They don't know what they would have eaten had it not been for rabbits. Polenta and rabbit was about all they had to eat. I think some of them even went over to Oklahoma and worked in the coal mines, to get enough money to start with, and to be able to feed their families.

Dad never said much about the work he did as a child. I'm sure he helped with the farm, the vineyards, and everything that Grandpa Felix was involved in. Grandpa Felix was skilled at several things. He started a winery. He also had apples, and an apple press to make cider.

Dad graduated from Subiaco Academy [a Catholic boarding school for boys in Subiaco, Arkansas] in 1928. I feel sure it was because of John and Robert Lazzari that Dad went to Subiaco. The Lazzaris were from Tontitown. John went to Subiaco and became a monk in the Benedictine order, and Robert eventually went and joined the monastery there too. Dad was good friends with the Lazzari family.

Dad and his brother Beato, or Uncle B., went into business together in a general merchandise store on the southwest corner of the Highway 412 and Barrington Road intersection. It was the building that Mr. and Mrs. Frank Perona owned. I think the Peronas lived upstairs and Dad and Uncle B.'s business was downstairs. Mr. Perona operated a feed mill adjoining the store.

Dad was a hard worker. He lived for his business. In 1950, he and Uncle B. moved directly across the street [from their first store], where they built a new 10,000-square-foot building. I would think that it was one of the biggest buildings in Northwest Arkansas at the time. He had a general merchandise store: farm supplies, hardware, groceries, you name it. Dad's motto was, "If I don't have it, I'll get it." The name of his business was the Tontitown Mercantile Company. A few years later, he bought out Uncle B.

Dad devoted his life to that business, and trying to provide a very adequate standard of living for us. He worked all the time. If we ever took a trip, it was Mom and us three kids; Dad always stayed home to work. In 1965, I believe it was, he had his first heart attack. It was a rough one, and the doctors told Dad that he needed to slow down—that if he continued working like he had been, he would have another one and it would get him. He was only 55 at that time.

He first came to me and my brother, Loyce, and asked us if we wanted the store. See, we were raised in that store. From the day Loyce and I were old enough to do anything we helped out in the store, and the same way with my sister, Enrica. When she wasn't at home helping Mom take care of the household, she was working in the store. I told Dad, "What is most important to me now is getting my education. I only lack two years of college, and I know you can't hang in here, so if you want to sell the store that is okay with me." Plus, I was majoring in accounting, so I really wasn't inclined to be a merchant. Loyce was still in high school, so he was too young to even consider it. So Dad decided to sell the store. I think it was about a year later that his nephew, Felix Pozza, decided to buy the store from Dad. Felix and Bobby Pianalto bought the store.

After that, Dad did take it easy for a while. Having worked all those years so hard, he really didn't have any hobbies, so he went home and just sat. Dad passed away in 1977, only about 12 years after he retired.

　　　　RICHARD ARDEMAGNI JR.

I can't tell you the number of people who have come up and told me that if it hadn't been for Dad and Mom at one time in their life, they don't know if they would have made it, because Dad either extended them credit to get groceries, or he gave them food. They were always very generous with the nuns and the priests that were here. I don't know how many times they would come in the store and fill a cart with food and never pay a penny for any of it. I would haul the groceries down to their house. The Bastianelli sisters—when they got pretty well up there in age—I don't know how many sacks of groceries I hauled down to their house. Of course, they would always pay for the groceries and give me a quarter for delivering them. I remember that they would never lime their outhouse, and it would stink really bad. About once a month, Dad would send me down there with a bag of lime to lime their outhouse. The lime killed the odor. You went inside and took the lid off and scattered that lime all around in there.

My mom, Nettie Mae Solomon Ardemagni, wasn't from Tontitown. She was born in Gainesville, Texas. The Solomons moved from Gainesville to a farm in the Round Mountain community [east of Fayetteville]. Mom and her sister Leona were nurse's aides at the Fayetteville City Hospital when Dad's dad, Felix, was in the hospital. Dad went to see Felix, and he stumbled into Mom and her sister, because they were helping take care of Felix. That is how my parents met. Mom was 10 years younger than Dad. They were married in Tontitown in 1944. Once they were married, Mom started working in the store with Dad.

Mom was not Catholic when she and Dad got married. The first year they were married, when she was pregnant with me, Mom went to the nuns and started taking instructions [to become Catholic] without Dad knowing about it. Once she had me, I am almost sure we were baptized at almost the same time. She surprised Dad by telling him that she had been taking instructions and was ready to be baptized.

After Mom and Dad were married, Grandpa Felix moved in with them, and after about a year, she told Dad that Felix had to move out and go somewhere else or their marriage was not going to last. I think Grandpa was a very gruff old man. His routine in the morning, first thing in the morning, he had to have a clove of garlic and a glass of wine, and then he was ready for breakfast. Mom always said as soon as Grandpa would chomp down on that garlic he was in your face the rest of the day breathing on you, and as she was pregnant with me, it was more than she could take.

Mom was very much a believer in trying to make sure that as a family, we stayed close and did things together, since Dad worked so much and so hard. He kept the store open six and a half days a week. It was only Sunday afternoon that he would close. When we were smaller, Sunday afternoon was the time for the family to be together. Most often the thing we would do, especially in nice weather, we would go down to Brush Creek on a picnic, or swimming. Most generally, Uncle B. and his family, or Aunt Lucy and her family, or Buck Brunetti and his family, would go with us. Buck was one of the employees that worked for Dad for years. That was our routine. Work all week, and play on Sunday. Once the three of us kids were old enough to move around on our own some, the law of the land was that we all had to be home for Sunday dinner. The store would close Sunday at noon and we would have a big meal together. We all had to be there, because that was our family time together. We could not go anywhere on Sunday until after Sunday dinner.

Mom could cook like the devil, she could sew, and she could run the household. Even though she only had an eighth grade education, her handwriting was very beautiful. You could read and understand everything she wrote, and her math skills were excellent. She kept track of all the accounts at the store. She would follow up on collections, and would file all the tax reports for the store. All of our family seems to have pretty good math skills, and I think we got those from Mom.

Our house was small. Loyce and I shared one bed in one bedroom, and Enrica had a bed to herself. When it came time to go to bed, a line was drawn right down the middle, and Loyce and I dared each other to sleep on our side. We had our share of fights. Yet let someone else try to hurt me or hurt him or hurt Enrica—we always stepped up and defended each other. There was never any doubt about our love for each other.

I remember when we were around the dinner table and would ask Dad to teach us Italian and talk to us in Italian. He would say, "No, we are Americans. Our family immigrated here to be Americans and we have to speak English." Now, when he was with his cronies, they would always speak Italian to each other, but I think he experienced enough discrimination, and he wanted to fit in, so he always talked to us about being Americans and having to speak English. That is what I remember most about him. When he would get excited the English went away, but we always knew what he was telling us.

I went to school in the old school building that is still there, east of the Highway 412 and Barrington Road intersection. We had nuns as teachers. Sister Jovita [Zarnoski] was my first grade teacher. She is the one I remember as being the nicest. When it came time to start first grade, Mom had to drag me to school, because I did not want to go. Sister Jovita deserves some credit for getting me to go to school. I probably had her for first and second grade, and then for third and fourth grades, probably Sister Eugenia Pellin and Sister Winifred [Favre]. They were good disciplinarians, let's say that.

My best friends in grade school were Clarence Ceola, Billy Green, Claudie Penzo, Louie Perona, and my cousin, Bill Ardemagni. At recess, we played marbles, baseball, football, played on the swings. We walked home for lunch because we lived so close, but eventually we had a lunch program. Catherine [Hess] Taldo was cooking in the kitchen.

We went to Mass every morning before going to school. First Friday [a traditional devotional day in the Catholic Church, observed on the first Friday of the month] was a special day to go to Mass, and we would always have hot chocolate and sweet rolls at school before school started. I remember Catherine Taldo bringing out those fresh rolls and hot chocolate. We were not allowed to dunk.

I went to high school at Subiaco Academy. Loyce and I both went there and Enrica went to St. Scholastica Academy in Fort Smith. Mom and Dad were determined that we were going to get a Catholic education. Mom and Dad had taken us to Subiaco before, so it wasn't like we were going to an alien place that we had never been to before, and to be honest with you, after the first month there you get over your homesickness, because you make friends with your classmates.

I was in grade school when we got our first TV. Before that, radio was all we had. We would sit around in the evening and listen to the radio. We never had a phone in the house. The phone was in the store. That was one of the peculiar things about Dad—he worked so many hours at the store, and when he locked the store and went home he didn't want to be disturbed. He said if we had a phone in the house it was too easy for people to call and disturb him. He said if it was a real emergency they would drive up here and find us. And a lot of times at night, somebody would come by and say, "I really need this," or "I have a sick cow," and Dad would always go get them what they needed.

Our family Christmas tradition was to go to Midnight Mass and open our presents after Mass. Compared to today's Christmases, I guess you could say ours were bleak. We would always get some clothes, and we were allowed to ask for one thing that we wanted Santa Claus to bring. If you wanted a bicycle, you got a bicycle, but that was it. If you want a BB gun or a doll, that was it. There was no asking for several things.

Easter, of course, started with Lent. It was a given that we would go to the Stations [of the Cross] on Friday night, and it was a given that whatever went on during Holy Week, we were there. Back then we had 24-hour Adoration during Lent, so our family had an hour, and it was a given that we were going to go for that hour. As young boys in grade school we were expected to be altar servers. My mother made *fugassa* [Easter bread]. I remember bringing food to the church on Saturday to have it blessed. It was also a given that Mom would bake something for us to bring over to whatever priest was there.

I graduated from the University of Arkansas in 1967 with a commission as a second lieutenant in the army. I had a degree in accounting. I married Bernadette Balest (shortened from Balestreri) in 1968. She graduated from St. Vincent's School of Nursing. We have three children, Cara Marissa, Nino Matteo, and Ricco Michele.

I got out of the service in 1969 and began my career as an accountant. I retired in 1998. Now, Bernie and I travel. We like the outdoors. I like to fish. As a boy we used to hunt a lot. A bunch of us boys would gang up and go together and walk the vineyard rows, hunting rabbits, squirrel, deer, or whatever. I hunted until I went into the Army and then I saw so much violence, when I came back I put the guns up and never did hunt any more.

 RICHARD ARDEMAGNI JR.

LLOYD BARIOLA

Lloyd Bariola was born in 1934 in Tontitown, Arkansas. His mother was Adele Bariola Penzo. He was 69 years old when he was interviewed in 2003.

My grandparents, Joseph and Lucy Bariola, came from Italy to America in the early 1900s with three children: Louis, Columbus, and Kate. After they were in America, they had two more, Adele and Florinda or Frindy.

My grandfather was a farmer and he also butchered for different people. Butchered hogs mostly. He didn't butcher a lot of cattle. They traded labor. They would repay him by pruning [grape vines] or whatever.

When they first moved to Tontitown, the family lived in a log cabin. Then about 1910, *Nonno* [Grandfather] Joseph and his two brothers, Anthony and Dominic, built the big rock house. I think Cesare Mantegani did a lot of the rock work. I was told they got the rock just east of the house. It's got about 23 rooms. It was divided up into three sections. Nonno had the southeast corner, Anthony had the northeast corner, and Dominic had the southwest corner. It was two stories and then an attic that's more or less open. Two entrances are on the east. One entrance is on the south. The north was more of a storage cellar. Each family had their own private entrance. There are three staircases in each of the living quarters, and each of the living quarters had a staircase to the attic. So there are six staircases in the house.

My mother worked at Perona's canning factory. She was a good cook, and she sewed quilts and clothes. We had a garden. We canned tomatoes, greens, and fruit. We made jelly. Most of that work was done outside. When they cooked the ketchup, they had a big copper

Lloyd Bariola

pot. They would put it on the fire outside. They would grind up the tomatoes, cook them down, run them through a sieve and get all the peelings and seeds out, then cook it again. For canned tomatoes, they just put them in a quart or half gallon [jar] and cooked them over a fire outside in a washtub like a water bath, instead of pressure cooking. There weren't any pressure cookers then. Anything that needed a water bath—tomatoes, beans, swiss chard, whatever—it was all done outside.

To butcher a hog, they first would shoot it in the head with a .22. That didn't kill the hog, that just stunned it. As soon as it hit the ground they would stick a long knife in and cut the throat. Usually got into the heart. But anyway, it bled to death more than anything. They would raise the hog up and let him drop down in a barrel of boiling water, or hot water, and that would loosen the hair. You would get a knife, or Nonno used to have a little deal like a hoe. You would scrape the hair off the hog. You didn't cut it off, you scraped it. He had a vat that was about a foot and a half deep and two feet wide at the bottom and went out to three feet on top, about six feet long. You would put the hog in there; they were big hogs, about 600 or 700 pounds. They would put them in there and dump this hot water on them. They had a big kettle where they would keep water almost boiling. You get it too hot, and the hair wouldn't come off. It would be like not having it hot enough. They would scrape one side, then roll him over and scrape the other side, trying to get it all. Then they would scrape the feet because they kept the feet and the rind. They pickled the tail, the snout, the ears, and the feet. It was good. They let it hang all night outside. How they kept the dogs away, I don't know. The next day, they would carry it inside.

By this time, Anthony's family had moved out of the big house, so they used what had been Anthony's living room and kitchen to cut these hogs up. They usually just butchered one at a time, but it would be 700 pounds—that would be a small hog. They would have a couple big tables in there and there would be two, three, four people, working to cut the hogs up and to separate the meat as they wanted it. That night—this is the second day—they would debone the meat and grind it up. They would separate the fat from the meat, grind all the meat up, and put it into a big vat. It was a different vat from the one they butchered the hog in. It was clean. They put the meat in one end of it, and it would be 300 pounds, maybe more. They would tilt it up on one end and the blood would run down to the other end. The next day they would grind all the lard up and get it ready to cook. Some of it they just put it in a crock. They used the small entrails out of the hog [as casings] to make *salsiccia*—the little links [of sausage]. They put cinnamon and nutmeg in it. You had to eat those fresh. There wasn't any way to freeze them. They would hang them up on a pole and keep them as cool as they could. There would be strings of them 10 feet long. They would eat them for breakfast mostly. You just slice them down the middle and fry them. If they molded, it would ruin them.

They would make about a six-pound sausage. They used cow

guts for the sausage casing. They perforated the casing, after they got it packed. They would hang them up in a warm room for about two days. Not real warm, I'm talking about where it wasn't freezing. Every hole that they punched in [the casing]—they punched at least 100 holes in each sausage—the fat and the liquid out of the meat would seep through that. Then it would harden up and seal it tight. You would put those in the cellar and they would mold over. It looked like it was ruined, but all you had to do was wipe the mold off and start slicing it up. That meat was just as red as it could be. They put in salt and pepper, saltpeter, and garlic. They always had to add garlic. The pepper was whole black pepper. One day they butchered, the next day they cut it up. The next day they ground the lard and made the salami.

They would get all the lard and grind it up, like they would sausage or salami. They would put it in a big kettle, render it, and then dip all the lard off it. The cracklings go to the bottom. When it melts down, it separates. The gristle and the fat would separate and go to the bottom. They would dip that out and put it in jars or in a crock. Then they would have to seal it up. They would dip it out and use it to cook with. When they wilted a salad, it was always with lard. It is good, but it will kill you.

After they got through dipping off all they could without getting into the cracklings, they would save some of the cracklings. They would use it for different things, maybe for starting umido. They would always get the lard and put it in a five- or ten-gallon crock. Just put in lard and some salt, and pack it down real hard. Then when they got through, they had a board that would fit down in there that they would put on it. There were feed sacks they used for towels, and put it over that. They sealed it as good as they could. Left it down in the cellar where it would be cool. It would stay good almost all summer, unless it got real hot.

When they butchered hogs, they didn't throw anything away out of the hog. Blood is the only thing. One time I carried a dishpan full of blood to the house and got chewed out because I spilled it on the way. When I got to the house I got chewed out again for even carrying it over there because they didn't want to make any blood pudding out of it. They would cook the blood and it would harden up kind of like pudding. It was supposed to be good, but I can remember tasting it and it wasn't too good. I think the dogs ate most of it.

My mother also cooked quail, doves, and blackbirds. The blackbirds she cooked in umido. She fried the quail and doves. Blackbirds, starlings—they don't sound good, but they will eat.

On washday, they would heat the water outside. Then, I don't know when, they got a Bee-Vac washing machine. It looked like a Maytag. They had it over in the cellar. There was a well by the cellar where they heated the water. You would carry the hot water and put it in the tub. It would wash the clothes. It had a wringer on it. The white clothes, they would put in a tub of cold water with bluing. It was supposed to lighten up the whites. They would rinse them in that, and then they rinse them in another one. It was a lot of work. We hung them out on the clothesline.

The three Bariola brothers had a little building north of the house where they made cheese. I think the Sbanottos and Ardemagnis made cheese there too. Each one had a day to make cheese, say from eight in the morning until noon was one family, and the other would be in the afternoon. They would take their milk up there. They had a big kettle with a fire built under it. I don't really remember that. I do know that they kept it pretty busy. Somebody would be there most of the time. They made two or three different kinds of cheese. It all depends on how much rennet you put in it. They would come up with what people called *ricotta* now, they called it *puina*. It was mild. It didn't have a lot of taste.

Andy Penzo and I started trapping when we were in high school. We would set out steel traps and catch 'possums and skunks, skin them, and sell the pelts to individuals who came by every month or so. They would give you a dollar or so, whatever it was worth.

We hunted rabbits and squirrels. We set rabbit traps. A rabbit trap is a wooden box about eight inches wide, ten inches tall, and two and a half feet long. It's solid on one end, with a door on the other. You have some sticks that hold the door open in front. You put a few grains of corn in the back of it. When the animal went to the back to get the corn, they would trip the stick and that would let the door down. When you run them, usually in the morning before school, you would stand it up and open the door to see whether you had a rabbit or a skunk or a 'possum in it. Or a cat. You didn't want to catch a cat. You didn't want to get hold of a skunk either. We caught a few rabbits. The only one that I knew that would buy them was Mrs. Mary Ceola. She lived by the old railroad tracks. She would buy them for 10 cents.

I completed the twelfth grade. My best friend in school was Lester Ceola. I remember two of the nuns who taught in Tontitown—Sister Quintilla [Halter] and Sister Bernadine [Lake]. They were pretty rough. For lunch, I usually took a sandwich of whatever they had, usually peanut butter and jelly. Sometimes just jelly. Homemade bread; my mother baked bread about once a week.

After I graduated, my first job was setting tile for Joe and Earl Mussino. Then I drove a truck for B and H Canning Company, and then went to work for Payne Produce. After that it was Willis Shaw, and then Jones Truck Lines. I retired from there in 1991. I married Inez Nix Overton in 1999.

Now that I'm retired, I spend my time doing the least I can. We have 38 acres here. We sold the cattle about four years ago and I sold the hay equipment last year. We have a fifth-wheel travel trailer. This winter we'll be in south Texas for three months. In the summer we go fishing for a month at Broken Bow, Oklahoma. This year we went up in New York. Next year we're going up to Montana, and maybe into Canada. You might as well do it now, before you get too crippled up and can't go.

LEO BAUDINO JR.

Leo Baudino Jr. was born in 1934 in Cairo, Illinois, to Leo and Helen Beland Baudino. He was 69 years old when he was interviewed in 2003.

My grandparents were Frank and Maddelena Mollar Baudino. Frank lived in the village of Garzigliana, Italy. Maddelena was from Cumiana, Italy. Maddelena had two brothers who lived in Garzigliana: Luigi, who was a priest, and John, the church choirmaster. Frank Baudino sang in the choir, and every now and then, Maddelena's brother John would take Frank home for dinner with the Mollar family. That's how my grandmother and grandfather met. They had four children: my father, Leo, was born in Italy; Armando or Herman, Vicki, and Pauline were born in America.

Grandfather Baudino was the first in our family to come [to America]. He came for economic opportunities, I guess. He first settled in Westboro, Wisconsin. He got a job in a shoe shop there because he was a *calzolaio,* a shoemaker, in the old country. He was living in Wisconsin when he sent for my grandmother and my dad, who was seven years old at the time. Uncle John Mollar decided to come with them. He wasn't invited, he simply decided to come. He was a very integral part of our family.

The Baudinos were living in Wisconsin in 1911 when they saw some of Father Bandini's flyers advertising for people to come to Tontitown. Wisconsin was too cold for my grandmother, so they decided to come down here to Tontitown to see what this was all about, and here they stayed. My grandfather came with the idea of opening a shoe store. When they got here, Grandpa found out that he would never make a living just as a shoemaker, so he decided to open Baudino's General Store. They lived in an apartment above the store.

Leo Baudino Jr.

Most of the store's goods came by railroad to Springdale, and Grandpa would either take his wagon into Springdale and pick stuff up, or some of his friends who had motorized vehicles would help transport the goods to Tontitown. If they had to go to Springdale with horse and wagon, it was an all-day affair. It was almost eight miles from Tontitown to Springdale. My grandparents never owned a vehicle that wasn't horse-drawn. They had a wagon and a two-wheeled cart. Grandpa always farmed with a horse.

Later my grandfather bought a vineyard west of town [at the corner of Highway 412 and Harmon Road] and started farming. Uncle

John Mollar ran the store while Grandpa took care of the farm. My grandfather and Uncle John were as different as they could be. Grandpa was a nose to the grindstone, get the job done, get organized type of person. Uncle John was very much an artist, a man of very regular habits, and was very religious.

After Uncle John took over the store, it took on his personality. It was one of the most curious places. Only Uncle John understood his lighting system. He had a string going to each light, all over the store, and the strings were arranged on the ceiling so he could stand almost anywhere in the store and turn on any given light. The ceiling of the store looked like a big spider lived there. The store was built on a concrete slab. I remember Uncle John oiling the floor, then sweeping to keep the dust down. He always had more than one cat at the store. There was a yellow cat that would sit on the grocery scale, and Uncle John would have to move the cat to weigh out bologna. There was a piano in the store. Sometimes in the evening, Uncle John would play the piano, and people would come in the store just to hear him play. He also played the organ at church every Sunday.

Uncle John also had a unique way of stocking the store shelves. He didn't have all of the same items located in one place. He had a little bit of everything here and a little bit of everything there, so no matter where he was in the store, he could reach up and get practically anything the customer asked for. He never had to walk very far. And Uncle John spoiled the town kids rotten. He gave away a lot of candy!

It was not unusual for Uncle John to be seen wandering the streets of Tontitown at two or three o'clock in the morning. Just walking. I don't know the motivation for this, but he often walked around at night. Joe [J. T.] Taldo told me that his parents said, "If you hear something rattling in the yard at three o'clock in the morning, don't get excited. It's just Mr. Mollar getting a drink of water."

Uncle John was an educated man. In Italy, he had studied for the priesthood, and he also studied medicine. For years, Uncle John was kind of the town doctor in Tontitown. He set broken bones if the person didn't want to be transported all the way to a doctor in Springdale. You know, farm folks are always having accidents, and kids always have accidents. Uncle John was evidently pretty successful as a doctor.

I have only the vaguest memories of my grandmother, Maddelena.

She never spoke English, so I never really exchanged any words with her except, "Hi, Grandma." She died in 1937. Grandpa Frank and Uncle John both died in 1951, within a month of each other. Uncle John was still running the store, and Grandpa still working the vineyard, up until they dropped.

Growing up in Tontitown, my father lived only a block away from the church. He served Mass for Father Bandini practically every day. My dad's two jobs in the morning before he went to school were to milk the cow, and go serve Mass. He went to school in Tontitown until the eighth grade, and then he was sent to Subiaco [a Catholic boarding school for boys in Subiaco, Arkansas] to high school. He graduated from there and went to business college in Fayetteville for six months or so. Then he went to Fort Smith and got a job with First National Bank. Right after that he married my mother, Helen Beland, a Fort Smith girl. After they got married, my father decided the bank was never going to pay him a whole lot of money, so he went to work for the railroad. He was transferred to Springfield, Missouri, then to Memphis, Tennessee, and eventually to Cairo, Illinois.

I have two sisters. Sarah Ann was the oldest. She was born in Fort Smith. Mary Kathleen, the middle child, was born in Springfield, Missouri. Then I was born in Cairo, Illinois. In my childhood, we came to Tontitown every summer; usually it was the end of June or sometime in July. I remember following Uncle John around in the store. I enjoyed going out to the vineyard with Grandpa Baudino. He would give me little chores to do—hand him stuff, tie up a vine, that sort of thing. On our way back from the vineyard, much to my mother's chagrin, we would always stop at Granata's Winery and have a glass of wine. Even when I was a little bitty person. There, the men would visit. A lot of times they spoke in Italian, so I didn't know what they were visiting about. They didn't always speak in Italian, but a lot of times they did.

People in Tontitown were pretty darn self-sufficient. Most of them were farmers to begin with. They had their own cheese factory. It was a communal thing. As I understand it, each family had a month in which they were in charge of the cheese factory and making the cheese. The amount of finished cheese you received was based on how much milk you brought in.

Butchering was pretty much each person for himself. Practically

     LEO BAUDINO JR.

everybody butchered a hog and made salami. Grandpa never kept hogs, but he bought a hog every year to make salami.

I graduated from St. Joseph's High School in Cairo, Illinois, and then I went to the University of Illinois at Urbana. I got a degree in English and became a teacher. I've been married twice. My three children, Frank, Wynona, and Leslie, are from my first marriage.

For a while I dropped out of teaching and was in the restaurant business in Decatur, Illinois. Then I decided to go back into teaching. We moved to northwest Arkansas in 1979. I taught English at Springdale High School from 1983 until I retired in 1999. Then I moved back to Cairo, where I teach one course at the local junior college. I come back to northwest Arkansas every two or three months.

Lenor Brunetti

LENOR BRUNETTI

Lenor Brunetti was born in 1918 in Elm Springs,
Arkansas, to Eugene "Jim" and Louise Taldo Brunetti.
He was 84 years old when he was interviewed in 2003.

My Brunetti grandparents did not ever come to this country. My mother, Louise, was born in Italy. I faintly remember her father, John Taldo. He was a farmer, that's all I remember him doing.

The Taldos came to Tontitown in 1898 [with the original settlers]. Their home place was about one-eighth of a mile north of the center of Tontitown [the intersection of Highway 412 and Barrington Road]. I still own part of that property.

My parents had seven children: Mary, Ida, Inez, Clara, Rose, Isadore, and me, Lenor. My father worked in the Oklahoma coal mines, and my mother stayed here in Tontitown with us children. She was a good mother and a good housewife. She did lots of cooking and sewing. That, along with us kids, kept her busy. She did not work out on the farm to speak of.

We had a two-bedroom home. One of the bedrooms also served as the living room. We doubled up in the bedrooms. My brother and I slept in one bed and my mom and dad in another bed in one room, and my sisters slept in the other room. We used wood for our cooking stove and for the heater. The bedrooms were not heated, and they were cold in the wintertime. We didn't bathe a lot in the wintertime when it was cold.

I was 12 years old when my mom passed away. By that time, my dad had quit working in the mines. The only children at home at that time were my sister, Rose, and my brother, Isadore, better known as Buck. Rose became like a mother to us. She took care of us, and did a real good job of it.

I remember my mom, and then my sister Rosie doing lots of canning. We canned all our vegetables and fruit. Seems like we always had enough to eat. The only thing we tried to keep cool was milk. We would drop our milk down in a dug well and it would keep cool for a day or so. Other products we kept in a cellar. That kept the food fairly cool.

The main source of our meat was pork. We butchered hogs and made most all of it up in sausage put in casings, and then we would keep it in the cellar year-round. The Ardemagnis—Felix and two of his sons, Gene and Beato—used to go around the neighborhood and butcher hogs for people.

My Taldo grandparents had an outside oven where they baked bread. There was a cheese factory; I believe it was operated by Tony and John Costa. It was about one mile south of the Highway 412 and Barrington Road intersection. People would bring their milk there and have it made into cheese.

A typical breakfast back then was what we called *caffè latte,* which was milk and coffee and sugar, and bread or crackers. Mostly homemade bread.

We had a vineyard, and we made wine all the time. We made it in the cellar. We had a good cellar that kept the wine cool. We always had wine at home.

My dad never did own a vehicle. Horse and buggy and wagon were the only things he owned in the line of transportation. When we went to Springdale, we went in the wagon.

There were two stores in Tontitown, as I remember. Frank Baudino owned one store which also had a drugstore within. It was located about one-eighth of a mile south of the [Highway 412 and Barrington Road] intersection. Mr. Mollar worked in the store. It was a dungeon, a spooky place. It had dark places in the back where you went for dry goods. The other store was owned by E. P. Pianalto. It was on the southwest corner of Highway 412 and Barrington Road. We also did a lot of shopping at Elm Springs.

We walked to school, a mile and a quarter. A pretty good walk, especially in the wintertime when it was real cold. First through third grades were in one room, fourth and fifth grades in another, and sixth, seventh, and eighth in another, if I remember right. We attended Mass in the morning and prayers in the afternoon. After school we would go to the church and say prayers there.

We had nuns as teachers. One of the kindergarten teachers was Sister Barbara [Mattingly]. I can still picture her. She was a very good teacher and we liked her very well. The ones I did not like were Sister Aloysius [O'Neill] and Sister deChantal [Devine]. Sister Loyola [Ryan], the music teacher, I liked her very much. If a teacher had a problem they called Memo Morsani. He would come down to the school and straighten things out. He had kind of a rough voice and everybody was scared of him.

I was in the school choir. The sister got mad at me because I wouldn't sing out. She reprimanded me for that. She never did slap me, but I did get hit on the knuckles with a ruler a few times.

At recess and lunch period after we got through eating lunch, we would play out on the playground. The boys and girls did not play together. We played baseball and marbles. When the weather was cold, we played in the basement.

Bread, butter, and jelly was one of the main lunches we took to school. We also had sausage sandwiches. That was about the extent of it. We didn't have much of a variety. There was a pump outside the school building where we would get our drinking water.

The only time I ever remember missing school was when I played hooky. It was a rainy day. The Ardemagnis had an evaporator—a building where they dried apples—one-eighth of a mile north of Tontitown, and that's where we played hooky with some of the neighbor kids, whose names I'd rather not mention.

The school burned down [in 1927], and while a new school was being built, we attended in the old school building [Smith schoolhouse] on the northwest corner of Highway 412 and Barrington Road. There was hearsay about how the school burned; I never did know anything definite about it. It was said that one of the students placed some newspapers in the bottom of a downspout, and this paper was lit and fire went up to the roof and started a fire. I was in school that day. I remember the fire. The first thing I remember is grabbing my lunch pail and running outside. I don't remember too much after that. It was kind of a sad day, really. We stood there and watched it burn.

One of my best school friends was Francis Finn. The Finns lived farther out than we did, but we would sometimes meet not too far from my house and walk to and from school together. We would play marbles on the way home. We would just throw the marbles a long ways, and whoever hit the other one's marble got to keep the marble. We played for keeps.

I remember a prank that I pulled once. We were in reading class in about the fourth grade. Francis Finn was reading out loud and he came to the word "sweater." He did not know that word, and he asked me what it was. I told him it was "sweeter," even though I knew better. I recall the teacher coming over and slapping him and putting him in the corner for saying that.

Lawrence Pianalto was one of my school friends. Virgil Sabatini, my first cousin, was also one of my good friends. The Sabatinis at one time lived south of Tontitown about a mile or so and later moved north of Tontitown close to where I lived. We would get together and play a lot on their farm. They owned a big farm. I remember going ice skating on their pond when they lived south of town. We had a pond on our place, too, where we skated in the wintertime when the ice was hard enough.

We did not have a lot of free time living on the farm. Seems like we always had some kind of chores to do. We would get together on weekends and play baseball. In the summer our entertainment was swimming in Brush Creek. It was real cold water, but we didn't seem to mind. In the evenings in the summertime, we would get together with our cousins, the Sabatinis, and play games at their house. The Francos lived close by, and we would also play games at their house.

Sometimes in the wintertime we would go squirrel hunting. We ate a lot of squirrels. We also did a lot of rabbit hunting. We set traps for them, or we would shoot them, and in the wintertime when there was lots of snow we would go out with a club and get them. They wouldn't, or couldn't, run in the deep snow. The way we fixed squirrels and rabbits back then was in a stew, an Italian dish called umido.

The first Grape Festival I recall was held where the old [Smith] school was, on the northwest corner of the Highway 412 and Barrington Road intersection. Vendors came in and had different kinds of games, and our people served ice cream. Best I remember, they had hamburgers too. I don't recall them having spaghetti dinners then. It wasn't a very big festival, but people seemed to enjoy anything at that time. It was enjoyable for the kids.

At Christmastime, we went to Midnight Mass and sometimes,

Morning Mass. We looked forward to Christmas because it was the time we would get candy and small gifts of some kind. Santa Claus came on Christmas morning at our house.

For Easter, we would make fugassa, or Easter bread. Easter bread is sweet bread made with a lot of eggs and raisins. I remember my mom making me a small loaf of Easter bread and then putting a boiled egg in the center of it. I really enjoyed that.

I was 18 years old when I left Tontitown. I went to California, worked there four years, and then came back here. Shortly afterwards, I was drafted into the Army and went off to war. I trained in Alabama, and then went on maneuvers in Tennessee and Arizona. We went to California for amphibious training. From there we went to Hawaii for jungle training. Then we proceeded to the combat zone, which for us was the Carolina Islands in the South Pacific. I was not on the front lines because I was a code operator. They kept me on the rear lines. I was in the service three and a half years.

When I got out of the Army, I returned to Tontitown briefly before I went to Detroit, Michigan to work for Chrysler Corporation. I had a cousin in Detroit, Dominic Sabatini. I stayed there six months. I did not like the city. I came back to Tontitown and lived with my sister, Rose, who by then was married to Premo Franco. Then I moved to Tulsa, Oklahoma, and attended the L. P. Gas Institute.

I met my wife, Betty Murdock, when I was working in Muskogee, Oklahoma. We were married in 1949. We stayed in Muskogee for four years, and then moved to Woodward, Oklahoma, for a time before we decided to move back to Arkansas. I went to work for Hatfield Pontiac-Cadillac in Fayetteville as parts manager, and then went to work for Freez-n-Stor. I worked there a great number of years, and then transferred to Campbell Soup Company. From there we moved to Broken Arrow, Oklahoma, then back to Tontitown. We have two children, Rick and Lisa, and four grandchildren.

All of us Brunettis had good singing voices. I have lost some of my voice because of a problem I had with the dust from working in the hay. It affected my vocal cords somehow and I can't sing like I used to. There is a Mexican love song that I like quite a bit. In English it says, "I'd like to lift you with my heart."

Cletus Cigainero

CLETUS CIGAINERO

Cletus "C. J." Cigainero was born in 1924 in Texarkana, Texas, to Giovanni (John) and Blanche Bash Cigainero. He was 79 years old when he submitted a written interview in 2003.

My paternal grandfather was Giovanni Batista Cigainero. He came to America in 1883. My paternal grandmother was Metilde Tondolo. My paternal grandparents' first home in America was in Nashville, Tennessee.

My maternal grandfather was John Bash. He was born in America. He worked as a miller. My maternal grandmother was Mary Welty. She was born in America. My maternal grandparents' first home was in Paradise Ridge, Tennessee.

My father was born in Italy. He did not attend school. He worked as a blacksmith. His siblings were Joe, Gus, Flore, Mitch, Louis, Annie, and Vince. My father did not talk much about his childhood. I remember him telling me once he was riding a horse and was chased by a bear.

Special skills my father had were gardening, blacksmithing, and woodworking. He built wagons.

My mother completed the sixth grade. She did not ever work outside the home. Her siblings were Victor, Flavius, John, Peter, Sarah, Louis, Mary, Mary Patsie, Clement, Mary, Bertha, Charles, Linus, and Anna. Mother played the guitar at Tontitown dances. She also crocheted and knitted.

I completed the twelfth grade in Texarkana, Texas. My siblings are Mitelda, Lawrence, Frances, Edward, and William.

Listed below are the names of our children and grandchildren:

Cecilia—Nicole, Sol
John—Sharel, Katie
Mary—Astrid, Gabril, Bill
Donna—Shannon, Aaron, Laura
Loretta—Jacob, Hanna, Calab, Jemma
Mark
Dolores—Olivia, Adam Emily, C. Y.
Mitchell—Sean
Raymond—Elsa, Lucy, Paul, John
Blanche—died 1988
Joseph—Aiden, Jerrit, Logan
Cynthia—Rachel, Sara, Benjamin
Frances—Shea, Kristopher
Celeste—Mariah, Devaon
Keith—Rheena, Corbin
Justene—Jonathan, Camron
Marshall—Jessica Horton, James Horton
Dennis E.

OLIVIA PIANALTO CIGAINERO

Olivia Pianalto Cigainero was born in 1928 in Tontitown, Arkansas, to Leo and Lucy Ceola Pianalto. She was 75 years old when she was interviewed in 2003.

My paternal grandfather, Dominic Pianalto, was a teacher in Italy. He came first to Sunnyside, then to Tontitown [in 1898, with the original settlers], where he was a farmer. His first home in Tontitown was about one and a half miles west of Tontitown and one mile south, on what is now Pianalto Road.

My father, Leo Pianalto, was born in Italy in 1889. He completed the third grade. He talked about his childhood many times to us, but I don't have a lot of memory of a lot of things he talked about. He didn't want to go back to Italy, that was for sure. He talked about his trip over here on the boat. He was one that didn't get quite so sick. But many people did. His mother, Catherine, passed away in Sunnyside.

Dad was a farmer. He also built many buildings around here, and he was in the chicken business.

He raised hogs. We slaughtered them on the back porch, where we had the table set up and the machines to make salami.

We had cows for milk and Mom made butter. We had a well, and when we needed to, Daddy arranged it so that we could let the milk down into the well to keep it cold. He had it fixed where we could raise it back up when we needed it.

My mother was a busy mother. She had a big family and I helped her lots with the cooking. Mom made polenta and homemade spaghetti. Homemade bread. She canned peaches, tomatoes, vegetables if she had them. We used to pick what is called *radicchi* in the field, bring

Olivia Pianalto Cigainero

it in, and clean it thoroughly to make salads. It is a form of greens that you can eat if you pick them when they're very young.

After school, I helped my mom lots because there was seven brothers older than myself. I would tend to some of their clothes if I had to. I'd put the buttons on if needed.

My mother liked to get out and walk down the road from our home to meet her sister, my Aunt Alice [Ceola Mussino]. Daddy would wonder where she was and I'd say, "Daddy, there she is."

My brothers and sisters in birth order are: Eugene, Lawrence, Gabriel, Olivia, Oliver, Francis, Leo Junior, Leonard, Lillian, Edward, Juanita, and Raymond. Growing up, we would get into mischief every once in a while. We liked to throw rocks because we had lots of rocks around here. I threw one, one time, and I didn't mean to hit my brother but I did. After that I never threw any more. We had a good time together. There was a lot of music in our family. My brothers got into the instruments. They would have a banjo, guitar, harmonica, violin, and we would all go to the yard in the evenings and the music would flow. And we sang. I'll never forget that because that was one of the beautiful things in our family life. I very much enjoyed it.

We lived two miles from the school. My brother Francis would take us to school on the bicycle. If someone was still walking, he would come back and pick them up and bring them to the school. He made more than one trip until we were all there. Mr. Bersi lived down the street from us. He had an old car, and he would give us a ride sometimes. Other than that, we walked to school and walked home.

My best friends in school were Imogene Ardemagni, Beatrice Taldo, and Zelma Zulpo—she was one of my very best friends. Also Annabelle Pozza, Sarah Ann Taldo, all the Taldos. I loved all the Taldos.

I completed the ninth grade here in Tontitown. I remember Sister Agnes [La Bounty] was one of the nuns who taught us. At recess, we played a lot of jacks. We used to go down to Mr. Mollar's store because he was such a wonderful man. He loved all of us very much. We would get a piece of candy from Mr. Mollar and run back to school quickly so we would be on time.

I used to go in Mr. Mollar's store just to see him, just to be in his presence. He would walk to church from his store. He was dressed in solid white. Sometimes he would tell me about how he washed his clothes with a cleanser. He'd tell me things like that.

I remember Ardemagni's store. We loved going there. Then there was another store down a ways, Claude Morsani's. That's another special person.

I remember the tornado that destroyed the church [in 1934]. We were in the cellar. It took the roofs off of the chicken houses here on the farm. The next morning, Daddy said, "I need all of you to help me." We gathered the chickens up and salvaged all we could. That was a big day.

We didn't get lots of oranges through the year, but at Christmas, we always got oranges. That was wonderful. When we were young, we would go to Mass in the morning. As we got older, we went to Midnight Mass. For Christmas dinner, my mother would serve the best rabbit you ever ate. We had stewed rabbit, polenta, chicken, spaghetti, salads.

During Lent, we did without meat on Fridays. We gave up candy, saving it until Easter Sunday, putting it in a container. We wanted to take some out but we never did. We would wait for Easter Sunday.

Easter dinner was celebrated as big as Christmas dinner. Easter bread was one of our favorites too. The Easter bread Mama made, I always loved that. I make Easter bread. I have some in the refrigerator right now. With my bread machine I made it this time.

When I was young, one of my first jobs outside the family farm was to work for mothers that had new babies, like Norina Stolfi. And as kids, we were sent off to pick strawberries in other people's strawberry patches. We would get up early in the morning and we would have a certain place that we would go to pick that day. We were on our knees a lot.

I met my husband, C. J. [Cletus] Cigainero, through my cousin, Lillian. C. J. and his brother would come up [from Texarkana] to work in Fayetteville. When we first met, he didn't have a car. His brother Lawrence had the car. So we were never alone when we went out. We drove around to Springdale and back. We would go to Lake Frances [near Siloam Springs] sometimes. There was some wonderful memories there.

We were married in Tontitown. C. J. and I moved to Texarkana, Arkansas where he worked at Decker's Meat Packing Company. Then he worked at 24-hour service stations. He had different jobs.

Our children are Cecilia, John, Dennis E., Mary, Donna, Loretta, Mark, Dolores, Mitchell, Blanche, Raymond, Joseph, Cynthia, Frances,

     OLIVIA PIANALTO CIGAINERO

Celeste, Keith, Justene, and Marshall. I was a busy mom. I worked almost all the time. Slept when I could. It was a continual process with the family and that's how we lived. C. J. did his job, and I did mine.

Is the world a better place now than when I was young? Well, I say yes and no, but mostly yes. I believe it is. We have access to different things now that we didn't have when we younger. I'm thankful that our children have all grown and got their own occupation and they are all doing well, so far. We have 39 grandchildren.

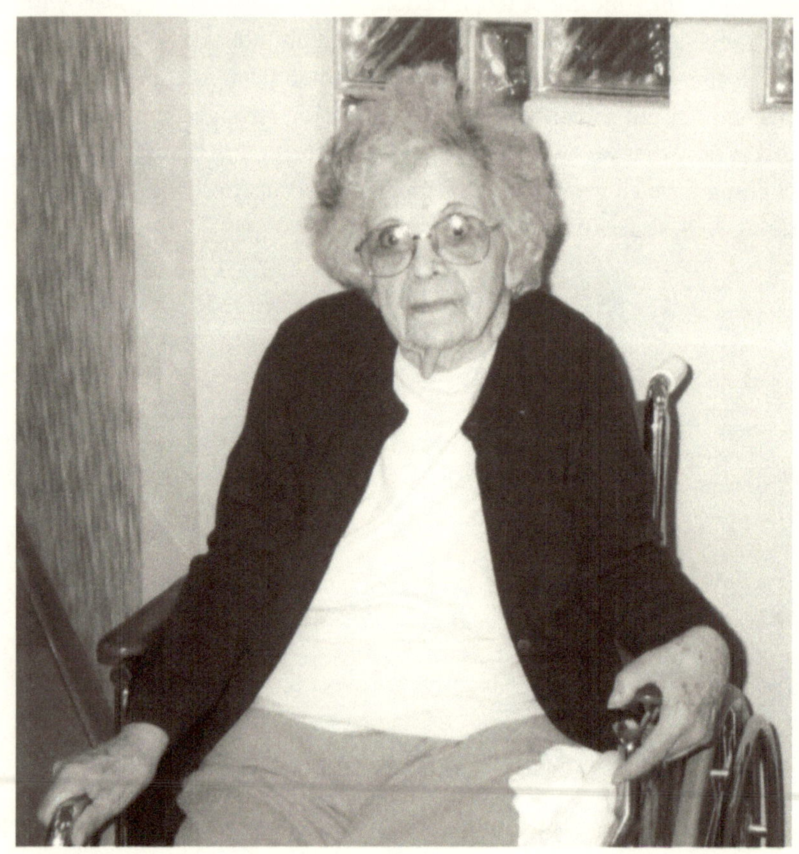

Candida Morsani Crane

CANDIDA MORSANI CRANE

Candida Morsani Crane was born in 1911 in Tontitown, Arkansas, to Emedio and Adele Papili Morsani. She was 92 years old when she was interviewed in 2003.

My grandfather and step-grandmother, Patricio and Annunciata Papili, had three children when they came from Italy to America: Adele, Emily, and Anthony. My mother, Adele, was in a convent in Italy, but my grandfather didn't want to leave her there, so they brought her with them when they came to America.

My brothers and sisters are Clementine, Amerigo, Anna, Elizabeth, and Agatha. I was born at home. Virginia Morsani delivered me. I went to school in Tontitown, and then went to Mena [Arkansas], where I stayed with the sisters and finished my education. I completed the tenth grade.

When I was growing up in Tontitown, we kids helped my mother do the washing. We had a garden and we canned stuff. I remember canning turnip greens. We butchered hogs and hung sausage in the cellar. Mama and several ladies would get together and make cheese.

We had an oven outside where Mama made bread about once a week. We lived across the road from the Fletchers. They made bread in the oven in their house. We traded bread with them. [The Fletcher's son, Albert, went on to become Bishop of the Archdiocese of Little Rock.]

We ate a lot of bread and cheese, and my mother made a kind of pizza, but it was different than what they make now.

We didn't have a car. We had a horse and buggy. Our light was from a coal oil lamp.

I married Frank Crane in 1939. I was 28 years old.

James Finn

JAMES FINN

*James Finn was born in 1915 in Elm Springs, Arkansas,
to Giovanni (John) and Mary Piazza Finn. He was 87
years old when he was interviewed in 2002.*

Mother came to America on a ship with a lot of immigrants. Many of them went to live in Sunnyside, Arkansas. About one-third of them died from malaria down there. I don't have any living or deceased down there. Then Father Bandini came along and moved them [to Tontitown, in 1898].

My father was not at Sunnyside. What group he came here with, I don't know. He escaped [serving in] the Army in Italy and went to South America. They brought him back [to Italy], and he had to serve two years in the Army. Then he came to America.

My parents met here in Tontitown. My father was 10 years older than my mother. When I was a child, I remember my dad had straight black hair and a mustache. Mother had dark hair. She kept it rolled up in a knot or a pigtail.

I was one of 16 children: Lawrence, Eugene, Albina, Palma, Angelina, James, Rose Emma, Luciano, Josephine, Benny, Virginia, Floyd, and four infants that died.

My parents spoke Italian at home because they couldn't talk English. If we wanted to eat, we had to talk Italian. If we got in an argument and Dad wanted to know what it was about, we had to talk Italian.

Our home had four bedrooms. Us boys slept in one room and the girls in another room. Each room had two beds. Dad and Mother had their room, and there was another bedroom. We ate our meals at a long table that sat 12 people. Against the wall it had benches, and the other side of the table had chairs.

For breakfast, we ate oatmeal, milk and bread, hot cocoa, whatever they had. For noon and evening meals, we had mostly spaghetti and sometimes, chicken. Vegetables, all homegrown. My mother was a good cook. She made her own spaghetti on a hand-cranked machine.

Dad was a farmer. He grew tomatoes, beans, corn, grapes. Us kids had to get out and do chores. It was either that, or we didn't eat. I plowed with a team of mules. I had to feed the cattle. I never did milk. I couldn't stand the odor of milk. We made cheese. Five or six families would get together and we would carry the milk to Dick Franco's. Whoever had the most milk got the cheese that day. We butchered and cured our own meat. We were pretty self-sufficient. We didn't go to the store for very much.

For fun I liked to go fishing and hunting. My favorite fishing spot was along the Elm Springs Creek. We caught catfish, bass. For bait we used worms, corn, chicken livers.

During the winter I got up at 3:00 a.m. to run my trap line. It was on the bluff at Elm Springs, just below our house. I had maybe 15, 18 traps. I checked the traps every morning. I was trapping for the hides. I trapped 'possums, skunks, civet cats. A civet cat is just like a skunk, only it stinks a little worse. You just find their dens and set a metal trap there at night. I'd take the animals home and put them in the barn, then skin them after school. Just skin them, stretch them on a board, let them dry out, and sell them. A good fur would bring about $2.

One time they run me out of school. The schoolhouse had benches. There were seven or eight kids to a bench. I was in the middle of the bench in the middle of the room. Sister Peter, she always took a nap in the morning. These girls kept hollering, "Sister, Jim stinks of skunk," but Sister Peter never did smell it, because she had gone to the convent. When she came back and walked up and down that aisle she said, all excited, "What is that?" "Sister, we keep telling you, James stinks of skunk!" I hadn't noticed, but when I dressed a skunk, it dripped on my shoe. Sister Peter put me on a bench outside on a long porch.

I walked about two and a half miles to school. For lunch, I took a sandwich—sausage or ham or jelly, depending on the season. I carried my lunch in a tin lunch pail.

I liked school. My best friends were Albert Pellin, Ernest Bariola, Floyd Maestri, and Delmo Sabatini. Ernest and I used to chop all the wood for the nuns during recess and carry their water. The nuns were strict. One of them was. I learned a lot from her, Sister deChantal [Devine]. My dad was strict too. She knew my dad, and boy, she was strict like he was. I mean, you had to toe the line. I got a lot of whippings in school. I don't remember what I did to get them, but she used a ruler on your hand.

We had religion first thing in the morning, and then we went to regular books. I liked arithmetic. We had recess in the mid-morning, and again in the afternoon. We played baseball or shinny stick. It's like golf, only we used a tin can, and just a limb or stick to hit the can.

I remember when the school burned [in 1927]. At the side of the front steps were some gutters. At recess, two boys were playing and lit some papers and put them in the gutter. About 15 minutes later, Memo Morsani came up hollering that the school was on fire, and to get out of there. I fought my way in and got my books but I lost my arithmetic, the best subject I had. Coats were hanging in the hallway, and I grabbed my sister's and others and threw them outside. I made three trips to throw clothes out. Memo Morsani came and threw one armload of clothes outside. Then the bell tower came down and burned the pile of clothes, and there went my sister's coat. After the fire, school was held in a building [Smith schoolhouse] located on the northwest corner of Highway 412 and Barrington until the new school was completed.

One funny story I remember that happened in school—I had a friend who said we were going to make some whiskey. We needed a part for the still, and we went to find Angelo Bersi, who was supposed to have the part, but he wasn't at home. Then we saw him coming up the road in his pickup. We walked to his house and knocked on the back door. He was sitting there, and as soon as we knocked he ran in the bedroom. We asked Mrs. Bersi, and she said Angelo wasn't home. A few days later, the priest came to the school and said to Sister deChantal, "Sister, you have bootleggers in here." She asked who it was. She grilled one guy but he didn't know anything, because she had the wrong guy.

I quit school after the eighth grade. Dad had told me if I wanted to be a lawyer, he would pay my way to the university; otherwise, pick a trade. I went to work on the farm. I guess I was about 15 years old.

The first Grape Festival I remember was in the old [Smith] school where Tontitown Mercantile is now [the northwest corner of Highway

412 and Barrington Road]. They had a lot of games. We threw rotten eggs at a guy's head sticking out of a tent. Some guy had a two-by-four and you paid to drive nails in it, but the nails wouldn't go in. One guy noticed that the nails were bent on the end. So he beat the hell out of the guy running the nail game and ransacked the whole thing.

We were building the new church, it was about 1940, I think. I was working with the carpenter. We always went in to work at 7:00 a.m., and the rest of the people came in at 8:00 a.m. I climbed up on the scaffold and worked a little bit. I moved a little and the scaffold fell. I broke my leg bone and cut my head. I passed out. Then I looked up there at the carpenter. He could tell I wasn't on my scaffold, but he didn't know I fell. I didn't call [to] him; I just passed out two or three times, back and forth, back and forth. [They found me when] the rest came in to work at 8:00 a.m. They took me to the hospital in Fayetteville. They went and got my mother and dad. I heard them talking to the undertaker out there. They thought I was dead. I kept saying, "Don't tell Mother and Dad I got hurt."

I married Rosie Della Rosa in 1941. She lived out near Highfill, about 15 miles from Tontitown, but we always knew the Della Rosas. The family went to church here. And we all went to dances at Mantegani's. We grew up together.

We moved to Oakland, California, the year we were married. I worked in the shipyards there. Worked with the naval submarine— riveter, driller, and machine work. When the war ended, we came home. Well, first we went to Independence, Missouri, for about one and a half or two years, and then we came back to Tontitown. In Missouri, I worked on a little farm where a guy dressed chickens for a restaurant in Kansas City.

I farmed when we moved back to Tontitown, and Rosie worked as a waitress at Mary Maestri's for 16 years. We have four children: Richard, Frank, Barbara, and Larry. We have nine grandchildren, and four great-grandchildren. Rosie and I have been married for 65 years. I don't know the secret to staying married so long. I guess just by taking one day at a time.

 JAMES FINN

FLOYD FRANCO

*Floyd Franco was born in 1925 in Tontitown, Arkansas,
to Dominic and Teresa Piazza Franco. He was 76 years
old when he was interviewed in 2002.*

My grandfather was Giovanni Batiste Franco, and my grandmother was Rachele Turcato. They left Italy in 1920. They came through Ellis Island to Tontitown with their son Joe and his family. My grandparents lived with my parents until their death. I remember when my grandfather passed away. They laid him on a board and then they took a casket out there and put him in it. He laid there in the house until the funeral.

My father was born in 1894 in Italy. He came to the USA in 1913. He worked in the mines in Oklahoma, and from there he came to Tontitown. He married Teresa Piazza in 1920 in Tontitown. She was born in 1893 in Italy. She came to the USA in 1895 and went to Sunnyside, Arkansas, and then she came to Tontitown [in 1898 with the original settlers]. Their children were Angie, Jim, Johnny, me, and Gabriel.

My dad was a pretty good carpenter. He built chicken houses around here. He butchered hogs. My mother, well, all she done was, she took care of you. She did the cooking, the washing, and she carried water with a five-gallon bucket. They had what they called the *bigolo* [yoke] over the back, and carried two buckets at a time. She sewed some, patched all our clothes. It kept her busy doing that. She made cheese. She worked out in the field. One year, my dad was going to plant an acre of cucumbers. My mother told him, "If you plant an acre of cucumbers you better be ready to pick them. I'm not coming out there." Well, he didn't plant any cucumbers.

My mother canned a bunch. I remember when we canned spinach one time. We were outside and put the canning jars in a No. 3 washtub

Floyd Franco

and let them cook in there. Then we let the jars cool and set them up. The tub had 17 quart-sized jars in it. My dad said, "We'll wait till the jars cool off and then we'll take them out." So I went down to the well to get a bucket of water, and I told my dad, "I'll cool them off." I threw that bucket of water on there and busted every jar. Every one but three.

Mom was the disciplinarian in the family, 100 percent. We had a cross-eyed dog. When Mom whipped me, if I hollered at the dog, by gosh he'd be there and she didn't have a chance to whip me. That dog would take up for me. Boy, my mother would get mad.

My dad and his brothers owned a canning factory. All they canned was tomatoes. When tomato season come, my dad would get up in the morning and light the boilers, and then everybody else would come to work. Come down and peel tomatoes and can them. Then they hauled them to [the nearby community of] Johnson and labeled them there. Dick Ceola had an old Model T truck, and he hauled the canned tomatoes. I never did work in Dad's canning factory, but we'd go down and sneak around in there. They had an engine to pump water out of the well, and the engine was on a hot shot. Victor [Franco], he'd hook the hot shot up to the fence and have these kids go over there and get a hold of that fence and then he'd turn it up. Boy, when it buzzed, I'll tell you what! We had a hell of a time with that, but it wasn't too good.

How I got this scar on my chin? One Sunday afternoon, I was standing in the doorway of the old canning factory, and Uncle Jim Piazza was standing behind me. My brother Gabriel had a slingshot. It had a string about three feet long, and you would spin it around and turn it loose and see how far you could throw a rock. When it come time to turn it loose, it slipped out of his hand and that rock hit me right there on the chin. Hit me right there and that thing bounced plumb across that canning factory and half way back. Joe Franco and my dad took me to the doctor down at Elm Springs, Dr. Cooper. I was down there from five o'clock till midnight when we got home. I just had three stitches.

I completed the seventh grade at Tontitown. Gilbert and Gordon Cortiana were my best friends. The nuns were our teachers. I remember Sister Pius [Hourigan] and Sister Genevieve [Chafe]. I think Sister Genevieve was about the toughest nun they had. Lots of times I had to carry wood and throw it in the basement so we'd have fire for heat. At recess we played marbles. For lunch I took a bread and jelly sandwich, and sausage, we took that. We walked to school in the wintertime, and if there was snow and it was cold, we had to walk right back [home] because they didn't have enough heat to keep it going.

After school, Gabriel and I always got the wood in and the kindling to build the fire the next morning. Johnny and Jim was to take care of the cows and the mule. In our spare time, we played baseball a lot, played marbles and *bocce* [a game similar to lawn bowling]. Hide and seek. We went swimming a lot in the summertime.

For breakfast we always had caffè latte. At noon we'd have spaghetti or chicken and mush, or just whatever came handy. For supper the biggest part of the time we'd have soup.

Our family holiday traditions were for Santa Claus to come on Christmas Eve, until we caught him, and then that ended that. Christmas dinner was just a regular meal. For Easter, we made cookies and Easter bread.

The first grape festivals I remember were held right up there where the Mercantile is [the northwest corner of Highway 412 and Barrington Road]. We'd go to the Grape Festival and if we got a dime, that took care of us for that day. I think the festival run two days back then.

I remember when the church blew away in 1934. I helped work on the construction of the new church, making cement blocks and just doing whatever they needed me to do.

My first job away from the farm was working at the canning factory at Elm Springs. Lots of spinach. Then I worked for Crain Brothers as a chicken catcher. We'd leave home about six o'clock in the morning and maybe not get home till the next day. And when you got your check, you got $10. Then I hauled feed for them some.

In 1944, I was drafted when I was 18 years old. I was in the infantry for two and a half years. The day I was 19 years old, I was going on the front line down on the Rhine River. I was on the front line for 56 days straight. Then I got a piece of steel in my foot and was sent to a hospital in France, then back to my regiment. But by then, the war was over. I was discharged in 1946. I came home and went back to work for Crain, which was later sold to Quaker Oats. In 1954 I went to work at Heekin Can Company [in Springdale]. I was there for 36 years and 3 months, until I retired.

One Saturday after I came home from the service, I went to Springdale with my brother Johnny and Cleo Fair, the girl he was going with. That's when I met Cleo's sister, Bonnie, right there in front of Lichlyter's Department Store. After that, we dated every time I had a chance. We were married in Tontitown. Got married on Wednesday, and on Thursday we moved into our house, where we've been ever since. We have a daughter, Becky, and two granddaughters.

LENO FRANCO

Leno Franco was born in 1927 in Highfill, Arkansas, to Giuseppe (Joe) and Angela Schiavo Franco. He was 74 years old when he was interviewed in 2002.

My grandfather was Giovanni Batista Franco. He was short, had dark hair, and I think he had a mustache. My grandmother was Rachele Turcato. She was heavy and tall. They came to America [from Italy] in 1920. My mother, father, and oldest sister Raphael came with them. Raphael was six months old. My grandparents on my mother's side did not come to America.

Mother had 11 children, but she raised 10. Raphael was the oldest, then Elda, Frank, and Victor. Dick and I were twins. I had a brother, Marion, who died of whooping cough when he was six months old. I don't remember if he was born before Palmer or after Palmer. Then Palmer, Andrew, and another set of twins, Virgil and Virginia.

When my parents first came to Tontitown, I think they stayed with Uncle John Franco until they found a job milking cows in Highfill [a community north of Tontitown]. The fellow who owned the dairy furnished them a home. Dad bought a Model T, and they would commute back and forth to Tontitown to go to church, among other things. I don't remember living in Highfill, but I can remember that old Model T.

My father was mainly a farmer, but he was also a stonemason. He didn't pursue that work, but he did do a little of it at Lake Wedington for the WPA. I remember a funny story about when my dad worked for the WPA. The workers would ride back and forth to Lake Wedington in the back of a truck. My mother had two sets of twins—my brother Dick and I, and Virgil and Virginia. When Virgil and Virginia were born, this guy on the truck started kidding my dad, saying, "Hey Joe, how do you

Leno and Barbara Franco

do that? That must be fantastic. I don't know how you worked that out."
Finally my dad had enough of it and he said, "Okay, you really want to
know? When you get home tonight, have your wife change all the bed
sheets, take a bath, put on a nice robe, and then call me."

My mother never learned to read and write. As a child in Italy, she
worked in a silk factory where they had silkworms. She was a very good

cook. She made all the bread we had, all the spaghetti. She did it all as far as cooking. There was none of this package this or package that. Flour and eggs, and she was on her way.

We sat at a big table for dinner. Breakfast was not formal; we had caffè latte, which is coffee and milk with biscuits to put in it.

We raised our own food. We grew tomatoes, and there were always a lot of blackberries around. My mother canned all that stuff. She made juice, and she canned strawberries, and green beans.

Before and after school, we had to slop the hogs and milk the cows. In the wintertime we had to put some hay out for the cows and the horses, and feed the chickens. I can remember having as many as 49 hogs on the place at one time. My father would sell some of them. Back then, there were people who came by in a pickup with a stock rack on it, and they would stop and ask if we had any cattle or anything that we wanted to sell, and they would buy.

We butchered hogs. To butcher a hog, to begin with, you wouldn't feed him the day before, because you don't want to kill a hog with a bunch of feed in him. Then the next morning we killed him with a .22. We would shoot him between the eyes, and then stick him in the throat to bleed him. We would have scalding water ready, and put him in the scalding water, and then scrape him with a knife. Then we would take a singletree off a plow and hoist him up in a tree. We would split him, and then let him hang that evening. The next day, we would bring him in, lay him on the table, and cut the lard and the hams off. They had three different kinds of meat from different places on the hog. One of them they did for salami; that was the biggest stack. Then the next one was the little weenies. It was the red meat around the head and neck, stuff like that. That was called *luganega*. And then they had another one, I don't remember what kind of meat that was, it was kind of a gristle and even some skin that they put in there, and they would grind it up after they boiled it. They used it up right away, because it was cooked and it would spoil. It was about as big around as a baseball. It was something like head cheese. They made some bacon, but not much. Basically, it was just grind it all up, make sausage, and render the lard.

To make lard, we would cut it up in strips about an inch and a half wide, take the skin off of it, and grind it up in a meat grinder. Then you threw it in a big kettle and boiled it, and rendered it, and what you had left I guess you called chitlins. The Italians called it *ciccioli*. My mother would put it in jars. It didn't have to be processed; it had salt in it so it would keep. We had a cellar, but it wasn't a very good cellar. It was dark and damp but it did the job. We kept some meat there, but Uncle John was the one with the good cellar, so we put the salami there. About every three or four days, Dick and I would have to walk down there and get a salami.

We had a goat now and then. We milked her for one thing, and then we would get one once in a while and my father would hit it over the head, and we would eat it. I think my mother fried it like pork chops. It's a real red and lean meat. It's a whole lot like a deer.

My mother made this white cheese. She would let the milk sit until the cream came to the top. Then she would skim it off, take what was left, and do something to it to separate it from the other. During the process it looked like cottage cheese. She would put it in a mold to squeeze the water out of it. She put salt in it. I don't remember exactly what she did, but she would let it sit for quite a while. It was really good; it tasted like mozzarella that you buy now. They called it *cassata*.

In the winter, we went hunting for anything that came along. We didn't go quail hunting or rabbit hunting, we just went hunting, and what popped up got popped. My mom would fry rabbits, but she wouldn't eat one. She said it reminded her of a cat, so she would not eat it.

I had a bunch of rabbit traps. They were little box things with a trigger on the door. You put bait in there, corn or grain. I remember one time I had a bunch of these traps and I would get three or four rabbits every morning. You would set them in the paths that the cows walked in. You could tell from a distance if you had a rabbit, because the door would be down and you have to be careful because it might even be a skunk. You could tell by the odor pretty quick when you got up close. Anyway I would catch these rabbits and put them in a tow sack and Mrs. Ceola—Fred Ceola's mother—she would buy these rabbits from me, still alive, in a tow sack. I would take those rabbits by there in the morning and she would buy them for 10 cents apiece. I went by there one morning and she said, "Let me see here." She was a big woman. She ran her hand down in the sack and told me the rabbits were too small, and she would have to cut me back to eight cents. I got ticked off, but there was nothing I could do about it because I couldn't very well take the rabbits to school with me. So I let her have them.

I completed the sixth grade in Tontitown, and later I got my GED. My best friends in school were Albert Piazza, Jim Aimerito, and Francis Tomiello. I remember Sister Adrian [McGrath]. She taught me quite a while. She was a sweet woman. She would do anything she could for you. Anything you needed she was ready to do it. Then we had Sister Bernadine [Lake]. She was a short woman. She knew how to use a ruler. She held it loose, not tight like Sister Adrian did. A loose ruler would sting. You had to hold your hand out, palm up. This was done in front of the class [as punishment] for talking, throwing paper wads, or making paper airplanes, things like that.

At recess, we played tag or marbles, and we played a game called "come through." They had a line on either side, and a few people in the middle, and they would holler, "Come through," and somebody else would holler, "Come through," and they had to run from one line to the other without being touched. If you got touched, you were out.

We played a lot of ball, and we used to have a game they called shinny. You would get a stick and a can and the idea was to start in the middle to see which one could [hit the can] over his opponents' goal. Sometime that stick hit the shins pretty good.

We brown-bagged it for lunch at school—salami, or jelly and butter, or egg sandwiches. The Lazzaris had some Jonathan apple trees, and Gene Ardemagni had some, but I never did get any of his, because I had to go out of the way to get his. After the apple harvest was over—Lazzari knew I was getting apples—I would go through these apple orchards on my way to school and fill my satchel with apples. There was a place on the way to school where the road grader would make little banks on the side of the road. Well, I would dig me a hole as far as I could reach, line it with grass, and roll those apples in there. Then every morning, even if it was freezing, I would go by there on my way to school, reach back in there and get an apple, and put it in my lard bucket lunch box. They used to ask me where I was getting those apples, and I would never tell them, because that would have been suicide.

Once in a while we would drop by and visit my grandparents as we were walking home from school. They lived with Uncle Dick and Aunt Teresa Franco. My grandmother would give us *frittole,* which is a drop doughnut.

At home we [made a toy out of] a wheel about eight inches in diameter. It came off the hub of a wagon wheel. We would take a Prince Albert can and a stick about a yard long, smash the can and fold it over to make a kind of a cup, [and attach it to the stick]. Then we would roll the wheel around [with the stick].

We played cards. One game was *burraco* [a type of rummy]. Another game we played was *tressette*—three sevens, I guess it is. Those two games that were played all over Tontitown.

I never did make wine or home brew, but my dad did. He put it in the cellar. I remember him hiding grapejack [distilled wine] down in the woods. Not everybody had a still. There was one or two around. When somebody got ready to run off a bunch of wine for grapejack, they would get this guy, and he would come run it off for them. He brought his still to our cellar, and he would run it off, and he would take a certain percentage for his services and leave the rest of it. When the feds got pretty hot, they would carry [the grapejack] to the woods and hide it. I know that my dad had a five-gallon crock, and he would take it down in the woods to hide it. Many people liked to put some grapejack in their coffee in the morning. That is what they call coffee royale. That is very good.

As for the businesses in town that I remember, Richard and B. Ardemagni owned a store, and the post office was in that building. It was [on the southwest corner of Highway 412 and Barrington Road] across the street from where the old mercantile building is now. Perona owned the building. They had a general store and feed store in the same building, and the Peronas lived upstairs. Then there was Claude Morsani's general store, about a block down the road.

John Mollar also had a store, about a block south of the Ardemagni store. Mr. Mollar's store is one that will never be again. The aisles went everywhere. He kept the lights in the store off all the time, and there were strings that ran across the ceiling like a spider web. If you wanted to look at a shirt, he knew which string to pull so the lights would come on at the shirts. I don't think that I was ever in Mr. Mollar's store that he didn't give me a little piece of candy when I left.

     LENO FRANCO

After the old church was blown down by a tornado [in 1934], Leon Zulpo, Albert Piazza, Jimmy Aimerito, and my brother Dick and I chopped that church up for firewood for the nuns to use start a fire in the mornings, and to cook with. We got out of school for a while to go over there and chop kindling and take it to the convent.

When the new church was being built, everybody pitched in and worked on it, basically on the weekends. Some of it was built during the week. I remember that Jim Finn fell off the scaffolding. I don't know how high he was, but he got hurt when he fell off, and they had to take him to the hospital. I remember working on it myself. I carried rocks, and filled in here and there. I was too young to do any sawing or anything like that. I doubt that I could drive a nail then.

At Christmas, we went to Midnight Mass, and then we went home. Before going to church, we always went to the barn to feed the cows. See, that is when the Christ child was born, and the cows were around him to keep him warm, and so they needed something to eat. That was a tradition from the old country. The next morning, we had stockings full of apples and oranges.

For Easter, our main tradition was Easter bread. They called it fugassa. It was kind of sweet, but it set up like bread.

A common Halloween prank was to turn the outhouses over. I can remember one time when we were out pushing these things over. We were in a car—somebody had a car by then. My brother Virgil slipped and fell in one of outhouses, and they wouldn't let him back in the car, so he had to run alongside. One tradition at Halloween was there at the old [Smith] schoolhouse, there where Richard and B.'s new store is [northwest corner of Highway 412 and Barrington Road]. It had a porch about four feet high, and every morning after Halloween you could bet there would be a wagon sitting on top of that porch. A bunch of the older guys would go steal a wagon somewhere and roll it up there and lift it up there on that porch. One time it was on top of the building. I have no idea how they got it up there.

My first job away from the farm was working for a produce outfit, Crain Brothers. They had a store in Elm Springs, and they had one in Springdale. I was 16 years old. I was hauling 100-pound bags of feed at 16. I also went to the wheat harvest in Kansas and one year, Montana, during the summers when I was a teenager.

When I was 18, I volunteered for the Army. The war [World War II] was over by then; it ended shortly before I enlisted. I would have gone before, but my mother wouldn't sign for me. I wanted to go fight. I thought I was a rough guy. I went to Kentucky for my basic training and from there I went to Germany. Since I volunteered, I got to choose what I wanted to do, so I chose the armored division. I trained to fight in tanks. Since there wasn't any need for tanks, because the war was over, they put me in this constabulary [police force]. We were trying to run Hitler's SS troopers down. We set up check points and worked the borders. I was in the service about three years.

After the service, I went to work setting tile for Ernest Stolfi in Tulsa, Oklahoma. Then I got called back into the service, because of the Korean War. I was a mechanic in the reserves. We were on a ship headed for Korea, but they pulled into the harbor in Japan and let 19 of us mechanics off there. We stayed there in the harbor, getting ready to evacuate Korea to drop the atomic bomb. I even went to school to learn how to protect myself against the atomic bomb. I never could figure out how you could do that, but I got a diploma.

After Korea, I went back to setting tile. That is when I hooked up with Bill Fiori. I worked there for a while, and then in 1952, I married Barbara Avelene Beckford. She was a cousin to the Jaro family. I met her on a blind date. Marrying Barbara is surely is the best thing that ever happened to me. If it hadn't been for that, I would have been a bum by now. Our children are Stephen, Gary, Richard, Ronald, and Brenda. We have 12 grandchildren, and one great-grandchild.

After we were married, I signed up to go to auto mechanics school in Okmulgee, Oklahoma, at Oklahoma A & M. We went up there and stayed almost two years. The course was a two year course, but I got a job offer with Mid-Continent Oil Company in Tulsa, so I left two months early. I worked there in automotive research for 32 years.

About five years after I retired, Barbara and I moved to Pea Ridge, Arkansas. When we decided to move, Barbara's criteria was three bedrooms, two baths, a fireplace, and a big yard for flowers. I just wanted five acres so I could play.

RACHEL AND THOMAS FRANCO

Rachel Franco was born in 1919 in Georgetown, Illinois. Her brother, Thomas Franco, was born in 1920 in Tontitown, Arkansas. Their parents were Giovanni (John) and Theresa Zulpo Franco. Rachel was 84 and Thomas was 82 when they were interviewed together in 2003.

Our father came to America by himself when he was about 17 years old [about 1902]. His parents, Batiste and Rachele Franco, came to America in 1920. They [came to Tontitown and] lived with our parents for a while, until Uncle Dick Franco got settled in a home, then they went to live with him.

Our grandmother, Rachele, was large in stature, but our grandfather, Batiste, was just a little man, a small person. They were very gentle, especially our grandfather. Our grandmother was a little bit on the loud side.

Our mother was Theresa Zulpo. Her father was Tomaso Zulpo. They were among the first settlers to come to Tontitown in 1898. They came to America in 1896 when our mother was one and a half years old. She had a sister that died on the ship as they were coming to America. When they baptized this little girl, they picked up a collection—there was a shoebox of money [collected] on the ship. It was supposed to have been put in a trust fund in New York, in Father Bandini's care. Something happened to that box of money. We never found it.

Mother was only nine years old when her mother died. When she was 12 or 13 years old, Mother went to Eureka Springs and did housework. She didn't stay there long. She came back to Tontitown.

Dad met Mother here in Tontitown. He went to Dow, Oklahoma, to work in the mines and Mother went to Oklahoma and married Dad

Rachel and Thomas Franco

in 1913. *Zia* [Aunt] Teresa, Uncle Dick Franco's wife, remembered when Mother left Tontitown to go to Oklahoma to marry Dad—she had a big empty trunk, a dress under her arm, and what she had on.

From Oklahoma, our parents moved to Bauxite, Arkansas, for Dad to work in the mines. Down there they had malaria and everybody was sick. They had to leave there because of the malaria, and because if you didn't belong to the Odd Fellows, you could get killed or something. So they went to Cleveland, Ohio. Dad worked in the mines there. Mother did the cooking for the men that worked in the mines. Mother's brother, Uncle Ernest Zulpo, was there, and Uncle Dick Franco. They stayed there until the mines shut down or went on strike; they had to get out of town because it was dangerous. From there they moved to Georgetown, Illinois, another mining area. They were there 11 months, and then moved back to Tontitown.

Mother and Dad had eight children: Premo, Mary, Rachel, Thomas, Josephine, Lucy, Concetta, and Roy. We had to kiss Dad every night, and kneel in front of him and say our prayers in Italian before we went upstairs to bed. When he punished us, he didn't run after us. "Right here!" he'd say, and we [came and stood] in front of him.

We thought our grandfather, Tomaso Zulpo, was the best person in the world because every day he came to see us. He would walk to our house and come through our strawberry patch, pick our strawberries, and bring them to us. We thought he was so kind. He was bringing us our own strawberries. We really did like our Nonno. He was a good man.

Grandfather Zulpo died in 1927. His son, our Uncle Henry Zulpo, was in St. Louis and he came home for the funeral. Uncle Henry left here at a very early age and never came back until 1927 for his dad's funeral. Uncle Henry used to smoke. We stole cigarettes from him because he had the tailor-made cigarettes. In Tontitown we didn't have tailor-made cigarettes. We had grape leaves.

Dad was a farmer, and he also knew how to butcher a cow. We didn't have any refrigeration, so they would cut a calf up themselves and sell it. They would then go from home place to home place in a wagon and team of horses selling meat, three pounds for 25 cents. Three pounds went to Father Bandini and the nuns. That was first on the list. They got the best cuts of the meat. Three pounds always went to the Bastianellis, because they kept house for Father Bandini.

Mother was a very, very pleasant person. She was really family-oriented. She was with the family all the time. She didn't work outside the home after she married. She never missed a grape festival. She always made pasta. She went to Mass daily. She had eight children and that kept her busy. She had kids one after another.

We ate caffè latte for breakfast, spaghetti for dinner, and then *minestra* [soup] for supper. That was our menu every day. Dad used to always say, "On the farm, you had the egg, the chicken, or the potato." We always had those because we planted our own potatoes and raised our own chickens.

Mother made fresh pasta every day. We never dried any. Maybe she would make it at ten o'clock in the morning and we would have pasta at noon. We didn't often have a meat sauce. The spaghetti wasn't always made with just pure eggs either. We had to have one egg, maybe, and a cup of water.

On Sunday, she would maybe make frittole and *brustoli*. Frittole is a dessert made with raisins, eggs, flour, and milk. You mix it up to a consistency where you can spoon it and deep fry it. You take them out of the grease when they're done and put them into a pan and sprinkle some sugar on top of them. Brustoli is sort of a cookie. It's made with flour, milk, eggs, sugar, and vanilla. These have to be rolled out and cut into diamond shapes, then you deep fat fry them. They're easier to make than frittole.

We canned tomatoes on the wood stove. Mother would cook the tomatoes on there and put them in the jars. We canned peaches and green beans. Mother canned them in the water pack, that's how she canned all of her stuff. We canned meat, too, in a water bath. We had a cellar full of canned stuff. We used to make our own sauerkraut. We would put it in crocks and put a big heavy rock on top of the lid.

We raised our own hogs and made sausage. We used to butcher our hogs during the coldest part of the winter. It was never a dry day, it always had to be snowing or raining, so that we could bring all this mud in the house! We did all the making of the sausage in our living room.

Mother used to bring milk to the Ardemagni well house and they made cheese there. Several people would bring their milk there, put it together, and make cheese.

Dad used to go to Springdale and buy sugar and flour by the 100-pound sacks. That was at grape harvest time, when we would have money. We would also sell green peppers. We raised corn and put in a corn crib inside the barn. Dad would pick the best ears, take them to [the nearby community of] Johnson, and have them ground for [corn-meal to make] polenta. Mother made bread and polenta galore.

We ate rabbit, squirrel, birds, even those little snow birds. We would put a door out in the wintertime when there was snow and throw corn out there. These little birds would go under the door. We had a string attached in the window. We would pull the string and down went the door. We would then go out and step on that door to kill the birds.

In this part of the country there were apple orchards. The sage grass was real high. The snow would land on top of the sage grass, and the rabbits would nest in there. We would wrap our shoes with tow sacks and go into the orchards. These little rabbits would be sitting there. They couldn't run [because the snow was so deep]. We would take a club, hit them over the head, and come home with a sack full of rabbits. When you shoot a rabbit, the hair penetrates into the meat. When the rabbits were killed with a club, it was good, clean meat. The men of the parish used to congregate at our house and they would have polenta and rabbit umido. Tony Fiori, Cel Cortiana, Pete Tessaro, Uncle Joe [Franco], Uncle Dick [Franco]—Mother would fix that stuff for all those men. Well, Dad helped with the cooking too. The men would play cards and bocce, and drink wine.

We had gallon barrels of wine. That's one thing we always had plenty of. When it was a dry county and the sheriffs were out, Joe Lazzari had so many barrels, and somebody turned him in. They came out and pulled the spigot out. That wine ran all over the farm. We saw it. We saw that wine running out those barrels, and those cops standing there watching it. They had to do it. We never had trouble with anybody. But for some reason or other, they were watching us like hawks. Some of the people did sell. They did bootleg. They had to, to live.

The Elm Springs people never did like the Italians. They used to call us dagos. We would say, "If we're dagos, you guys are wops. We eat spaghetti and you eat slop." That made them mad. We weren't angels either, you know.

Rachel

I completed the eighth grade in Tontitown. I remember when the school burned [in 1927]. My new stocking cap got burned in it. That was a loss, because if you had a cap back in those days you were considered well-dressed. I remember Sister deChantal [Devine], Sister Peter, and Sister Loyola [Ryan] as our teachers. Sister deChantal was the mean one. Sister Peter was tough, you better believe it.

I was a tomboy. At recess, I played ball. We played with the boys, Margaret Taldo and I. At noon we would hurry and eat, then go play baseball with the boys, or hopscotch. My best friends at school were Margaret Natale, Genevieve Ceola, Rosie Sabatini, Beanie [Lavinia] Maestri, Grace Maestri, Josephine Fiori, and Chill [Cecilia] Ceola.

When I got out of school, I went out and did housework. I was a maid in Fayetteville. Then Father [Francis] Dollarton got me a job in Chicago doing housework. I got on the train and I went to Chicago, just a young girl. I was supposed to meet this lady at the train station. I was sitting there and saw a woman with about 10 kids with her. I said to myself, "I hope that's not the lady I'm going to work for." Sure enough, that was the lady. I don't know how long I was up in Chicago. From there, I came back home. By then I was old enough to work. I worked as a grocery store checker for two or three years. From there I went to beauty college in Tulsa. Then I came home and I had my own business.

Grace Maestri talked me into joining the Women's Army Auxiliary Corps during World War II. We went up to Iowa for our basic training with the idea that we could always stay together in the Army. We finished our basic training, and they sent me to Kentucky and Grace went someplace in Kansas. They put me in the cooks and bakers school. I was the only girl with I forget how many men. Anyway, I made the highest grade of the whole company. After I finished that, I got a furlough and came home. I wasn't going to stay in the Army. I quit, but Grace didn't.

Thomas

My best friends in school were Vincent Lazzari, Pete Pianalto, Raphael Bausinger, Catherine Taldo, Ann Aimerito, and Alda, Elizabeth, and Rita Bariola. I completed the ninth grade in Tontitown. That was the first year the ninth grade [was offered in Tontitown]. There was only two of us in that grade, Annie Aimerito and me, so we almost had private tutors.

I remember especially Sister Agnes [La Bounty]. Sister Agnes used to teach dancing and I was always one of her pupils. I remember her distinctly for that and she was good. And so was I.

The nuns didn't have electricity or running water, so at recess or noon, my activity was to carry all these dang tubs of water on the back porch and in the house [where the nuns lived], enough water to last them until the next day. We also chopped kindling for the nuns.

When we had Mass in the chapel, I had to set out the vestments for the priest. I learned how to do that in grade school. We went to Mass every morning. Then we would go to school and have an hour of catechism after Mass. You couldn't turn you head in church. You didn't dare, with the sisters sitting behind you.

We walked to school. Sometimes, if there was snow on the ground, Dad would hook up the team and take us to school in the wagon, or he would come after us in the wagon. We didn't like that because we were ashamed to ride the wagon.

We didn't always have shoes. We went to school sometimes barefooted. Eugene Pianalto tried stepping on my toes. That didn't set so very good with me.

We took mostly biscuits and jelly for lunch. Mother would make cocoa and put sugar in it and kind of make it into a paste, and put that in the middle of two slices of bread. Of course, we had sausage.

After I finished school in Tontitown, I went to St. John's Seminary in Little Rock. I studied for the priesthood for two years. Then I came home. I don't know what caused me to change my mind. I guess the good Lord had something else in mind for me. Then I was tied down more or less with the folks, because Mother had suffered a stroke. They didn't want me to quit [the seminary]. But I didn't want to go back anymore.

I didn't like farming. I worked at the canning factory in Elm Springs for just a short time, then I was drafted and spent three years in the Army during World War II. I was stationed in Mississippi, South Carolina, New York, and England. We went over into Germany. Germany, that was the termination of the war. When the war came to an end there we came back to the States to take island training because we were supposed to go fight the Japanese. While I was home on leave, the war with Japan came to an end, so I didn't have to go. After the war, I went to work at the VA Hospital in Fayetteville. I retired from there.

I remember Mr. Mollar. He had his store down a little bit from the southeast corner of the Highway 412 and Barrington Road intersection. He was a saint of a man. He played the piano, and the organ at the church. Every day at noon he came to the school and practiced.

The men of the parish built the church [dedicated in 1942]. We made cement blocks down by where the school stands now, in that area. We had this handmade thing that we would use to mix so many shovels of gravel, so many shovels of cement, so many shovels of sand, and then water. When we got done, we would form that into a brick. That is how the church was built, out of bricks. It was the men of the parish that did it. I helped make those bricks myself. I was grade school age. Dad used to go and work and sometimes he was unable or had to stay home for farming, so maybe my brother Premo or I would go and do Dad's work. We were sort of taxed with a day a week. Whoever was available was the one that went and worked. Angela Lazzari did some of the carpenter work inside. Joe Lazzari did the altars.

At Christmastime, it took Santa Claus all night to get to our house because we slept upstairs and Mother and Dad played Santa Claus downstairs. We went to bed early but every few minutes we would come to the top of the steps. When they were trying to put the few little candies that we got in the socks, there was a bunch of us at the top of the steps. Our Christmas never consisted of toys. We couldn't afford toys. But we always got an orange, and we always got a chocolate candy in our sock. Maybe they were melted by the time we got them, because the stocking was hanging by the stove. That was our Christmas. We always had a limb off of a tree and we would decorate it, or maybe a little Christmas tree. Inside the house, we would decorate with crepe paper.

Holy Week at Easter was the most peaceful time. It was wonderful. We went to all the church services. We never missed a bit of the services. We had Holy Thursday, Good Friday, and Holy Saturday until noon. All the services were in the morning then. We didn't dye Easter eggs, but we did have hard boiled eggs. Mother always made fugassa, a sweet bread made with raisins and nuts. You have to start your fugassa the night before and let it rise all night. The next morning, you make it into loaves. It took a day and a night to make fugassa. Each one of us took a fugassa and an egg to church and Father would bless them. This was on Good Friday. We would eat [the blessed food] first thing Easter Sunday. It was a tradition that never should have been dropped.

One time we were going to the church services for Lent, and we met Bill Fiori, and I think Jim Pianalto. Bill asked us, "Where are you all going?" I said, "We're going to church." He wanted to know what was at church. I said, "It's Lent." He said, "Well, who did you lend it to?" That embarrassed us half to death, because we weren't used to stuff like that.

I want to tell you about an Easter experience. It was Holy Week. I was going into Tontitown to get a gallon of coal oil for our lamps. As I was passing Dora Taldo's, the kids were out there pulling up grass. I said, "What are you pulling up grass for?" They said they were going to make a nest for the Easter Bunny who was going to lay eggs for them. Well, boy, that was something big. I had never heard of the Easter Bunny, because we were too poor, you know. Mother didn't talk about the Easter Bunny. So I went and got the coal oil and went home. We had this big rose bush in front of our house. So I pulled up all this grass and I made a nest all around the rose bush, and didn't say a word to anybody. I get up the next morning, went out there, and not an egg to be had. You talk about somebody who was disappointed. If I had told my mother about it, she probably would have boiled an egg or two. Anybody in their right mind knows that a rabbit doesn't lay eggs.

     RACHEL AND THOMAS FRANCO

MARY PIANALTO FUCCI

*Mary Pianalto Fucci was born in 1914 in Tontitown,
Arkansas, to Joseph and Annie Cigainero Pianalto. She
was 88 years old when she was interviewed in 2003.*

My paternal grandfather, Peter Pianalto, was a blacksmith and a
carpenter. He was like a commander. He told everybody what to do.
People say he was a farmer. He was not a farmer. He worked in Johnson
at the lime kilns. He also worked on some of the government buildings
in Fayetteville.

I remember that Grandpa sent money over to Italy to have Mass
said for his parents. My father tried to tell him that he could have Mass
said here, but Grandpa didn't want that. So my father mailed the money
to Italy.

My paternal grandmother was Maria Teresa Marigo Pianalto. I
stayed with her. She was sick a lot and my father would take me to
stay with her. She was the best grandmother in the world. When my
grandmother died, my father took Grandpa into our house. We kept
him until he died at the age of 92.

My maternal grandfather was John the Baptist Cigainero. His wife,
my maternal grandmother, was Metilde Tondolo. My mother was the
baby of 14 children. She was born in Tennessee, the only one of the
Cigainero children born in America.

My Cigainero grandparents never lived in Tontitown. My parents
met when my father went down to Texarkana, Arkansas, to work with
the trains. There, he boarded with my mother's Cigainero family. Dad
told his father that he found the lady that he was going to marry. They
got married, got on a train, and came to Tontitown.

I think my father worked over in Johnson [at the lime kilns] with his

Mary Pianalto Fucci

father at times. I remember him shoeing horses and mules in the shop
that Grandpa had near the Bastianelli home. Grandpa made horseshoes.
I remember I was so afraid he was going to get kicked by those mules
or horses. I would stand at the door and be so afraid.

My brothers and sisters are Matilda, Josephine, Gile, Pete, Philip,
and Louis. All of us were born at home. Aunt Iginia Cigainero and

Mrs. Virginia Morsani helped deliver me. We had a three-room house. I learned Italian before I learned English. Grandma and Grandpa Pianalto didn't speak English.

When I was growing up, in the summertime we had fieldwork to do. We had to get up at three o'clock to milk cows, and then we would get our breakfast. Then we would get ready to go out to the field and work. We planted tomatoes, strawberries, corn, and stuff like that. When it was hot, Dad would let us work until eleven o'clock, then we would rest or go down to the creek and swim until two or three o'clock.

We girls hoed grapes, pulled weeds, helped with the fertilizer. We never did the plowing, but I used to drive the harrow hitched to a mule. A harrow levels the ground to get it ready for planting. We could do the dragging because that wasn't hard. Dragging uses a big flat thing to level the ground so they could make rows for strawberries or corn. We planted corn with a little corn planter. You would put two or three grains in the planter, put it down in the ground, squeeze the handle, and it would plant the seed. Then you had to step on that to make sure the ground covered the seed.

We raised potatoes and beans. We cooked a lot of dry beans. We had beans all winter. We canned tomatoes to make pasta sauce. We had a big black pot outside and we cooked apples and made applesauce. Mama would always cook a lot of pasta. I always liked red beets with the pasta. She would cook red beets as a separate dish. She boiled them, put in a little vinegar, a little sugar, and a little salt, and stirred them up. They were warm from the stove. She would have green beans, potatoes, and onions. She put them together and boiled them with salt and pepper. We thought that was real good. Mama made about seven or eight loaves of bread a week. That would take care of us all week. For breakfast we had caffè latte, which is coffee with cream, milk, and sugar. We used stale bread and broke it up in the coffee.

We killed a chicken once in a while. We never had much meat. They killed two or three hogs once a year and they would make salami. There was all these salamis hanging in the basement and the cellar to cure. That was all the meat we had for the whole year. Mama would make some kind of pickled pig's feet. Sometimes when a butcher came by, Papa would buy a little meat, but not very often.

We didn't have cheese and we didn't have much butter either. We sold milk and cream. We didn't have any place to put butter. We didn't have an icebox or refrigerator. I remember Mother put it in the window-sill sometimes when it was cool in the winter.

My father would go to town once a month and buy flour and sugar and coffee. We didn't shop. If we needed a dress, [Mother] would tell him how many yards [of fabric] to get. He picked out the fabric. One time he picked out this white background with little yellow roses. At the time, Mama was trying to teach me how to sew. They were all out picking corn, and they left me home to clean up the dishes after dinner. Instead, I went and got the newspaper and cut out a dress. I had seen one in the newspaper and I liked the way it was made. It was low-waisted with pleats in the skirt. I had almost finished that dress, and Mama came home and the dishes were still on the table. She hollered at me about it, and my father said, "At least she's learning how to sew." It's hard to believe that my father would be interested. But I loved that fabric. I can still see that dress. I wore that dress a long time.

We went to school in a horse and buggy, and we would walk sometimes. It took a long time to walk four miles. I used to get so tired, I would sit down a while. We went to church in a surrey—a two-seated buggy with a roof on it.

I went to school until the eighth grade, in the building that burned [in 1927]. It was located where the school is now. There was the priest's house, the sisters' house, then the school. I don't remember what grade I was in when the school burned. They got everybody out but a Maestri. He was hiding in a closet. They finally found him. I remember that because everybody was so worried about him. I lost a new coat. We had picked strawberries to make money. Papa let us have the money when we picked strawberries. I used my money for a new coat, and then the coat burned.

I remember Mother Charles; she was one of the Ursuline Sisters. I had Sister deChantal [Devine]. She cracked fingers up and down the aisle, but we sure learned from her. Helen Sbanotto was my best friend in school. At recess we played ring-around-the-rosey. The boys would play ball. For lunch, we would take a salami sandwich. Alice Granata would always bring jelly and peanut butter sandwiches. I had salami, and I didn't like salami, so we would always trade. I didn't like the Italian salami that they made at home. I still don't like salami.

We didn't have any Christmas presents. Papa would go to Springdale and get oranges, apples, and maybe a little candy. That was our Christmas. We didn't know any different. Mama said our chimney wasn't big enough for Santa. We had our first Christmas tree when the boys came home from the Army. All of us went together and bought Mama and Papa a couch for the living room.

We didn't have toys. Mama would make us a doll out of socks that had the white heel and the white toe. Other than that, we didn't have any dolls. Grandma and Grandpa didn't want us to play with dolls. We don't know why. Mom would let us play with them, but if Grandpa was around he would take them away from us.

During Lent, we couldn't have candy. Of course, we didn't get candy anyway, so it wasn't too big of a sacrifice. We said the rosary every night. We fasted during Holy Week.

I remember going to Mr. Mollar's store. He carried writing paper, tapes to sew with, thread. He had stuff to eat, candies. I don't think he had fresh meat. When Grandma sent me over there to get something he would always give me a piece of candy. I wouldn't eat the candy until I brought it home and let Mama have some of it.

After I finished school, I started doing domestic work. I went to Washington, DC, to work for Senator [Claude] Fuller's daughter. I didn't want to go, but my father was so down in the dumps because he was going to lose his farm. [Fuller] said that if I went to work for them, he would see that Papa got [a job] on a road [construction project] with his team, and then Papa wouldn't lose his farm. That was how I got to Washington, DC. I made $8 a week and I sent my dad $6. Then I got a job in a laundry, and they paid me $30. I was so happy.

I was working in the laundry when I met Chuck Fucci at a service club dance. We danced together most of the evening. After the dance, we were walking to the bus and Chuck reached over and kissed my cheek. He said, "I'm going to marry you one of these days." He was transferred here and there. I moved back home to Arkansas. We married in Tontitown about four years later, in 1941. We didn't have any money. Chuck and I had $200 between us when we decided to get married. I didn't have a wedding dress. Chuck's sister-in-law had a sister who said I could wear hers, so they mailed me her dress. Papa wouldn't let me wear it. He said "You can't wear that. You're not going to go up there and show off with something that we can't afford." I pleaded with Papa and he finally gave in. I wore the dress.

Chuck was stationed in Michigan when we married, so we had to go back there to live. We stayed there for a while, but he was transferred so many times. When we were stationed in Germany, I wrote to my Pianalto relatives in Italy, and we went to see them as often as we could. They said they had never known what had happened to their relatives who left Italy and came to America. They didn't write back and forth to each other. It was like they were lost. I want to tell you how much meeting those Italians meant to me. I think those people made my life better because I met all of them. They were so wonderful, and so kind to me.

After 26 years in the Army, Chuck retired. We moved to Colorado, where he was city manager of Edgewater, Colorado, for 16 years. He died in 1994. We have two children, Claudia and Mark, and two grandchildren.

My hobbies? I've done a lot of sewing. When I first got married, Chuck would bring pants home for me to hem for the soldiers. I would only charge 50 cents a pair. I've sewn wedding gowns. I crochet. I've made braided rugs. I would go to shops and buy coats or something if they were all wool. I would cut them in strips, sew them together, and braid them [into rugs]. I've really got those down pat.

I love to garden. I like to work. I take care of my own house. I still drive my car, but only to church and the doctor, and they're all within a mile and a half of the house. I'm close to my family. I love them very much. I really and truly love my family.

     MARY PIANALTO FUCCI

HELEN FIORI GEORGE

Helen Fiori George was born in 1933 in Tontitown,
Arkansas, to Dominic (Dick) and Florence Granata Fiori.
She was 70 years old when she was interviewed in 2003.

My paternal grandfather was Pietro V. Fiori. He first came to America in 1895, then later returned to Italy, and came back to America in 1906. The best we know about why he went back to Italy, is that he had many depressing things happen to him and his family. His first wife, Maria, and two children died at Sunnyside from malaria. I have seen in a genealogy that he lost a child in 1899. We really don't have any accurate records or facts to determine what is correct. He was left with three children and no money, as he had used all he had taken to this country. We are under the impression he came on up to Tontitown [in 1898 with the original settlers], but decided to return to Italy where he still had family.

Grandfather Fiori was a farmer, but that included many other things. They had grape vineyards, apple orchards, and strawberry fields. They raised all their fruit and vegetables. We also had hazelnuts, hickory nuts, walnuts, and chinquapins. He raised tobacco, then dried the leaves and made snuff out of it. He sold this to people. He said inhaling the snuff cleared his sinuses because it made him sneeze. He also had some cotton in the garden area that he planted from seeds he brought from Sunnyside. There was also a rose bush there that he brought from Italy.

When Grandfather Fiori returned to Tontitown from Italy he made and sold *falce* handles. A falce was a hand-held scythe used to cut hay. He had regular customers who brought their falce blades to him to sharpen. He had cattle. He kept two goats for milk. He said the goat milk would keep his stomach healed. He loved to graft trees, vines, and anything he thought interesting. In later years he did a lot of basket weaving and

Helen Fiori George

sold those items in a roadside stand my parents had. Grandfather made several wooden things. I still have a set of bocce [balls] that he made, and a set my dad made. They were both quite crafty with wood.

My paternal grandmother was Judita Santa Guiliana. She married my grandfather, Pietro V. Fiori, during his return to Italy, and then came to America with him in 1906. She died in 1930. She and my dad were out milking the cows when she had a massive stroke.

My maternal grandfather was Leopold John Granata. He was from northern Italy. He was an orphan. We know nothing about any of his family. I understand that in Italy, he was quite a tailor of men's clothing. He came to America in 1908, when he was 21 years old. He was a farmer, but couldn't make a living at that, so in the winter months he, as well as others from the Tontitown area, would go to Krebs, Oklahoma, and work in the mines. My mother was born there before the Granatas made a permanent home in Tontitown.

[After they moved to Tontitown, Grandfather Granata] left the family here and went back to Oklahoma to work in the mines. He then ventured into other things. He made white lightning for a while during Prohibition and sold it for extra money to support his family. One time, the kids hollered at him that the sheriff was coming. They had a trap door in the living room that went down into the cellar, so they hurried and opened the trap door, shoved all their stuff down in there, put the trap door back, and moved the furniture on top of it before the sheriff got there.

In later years, Grandfather Granata established Bonded Winery No. 43. He had several different kinds of wine: grape, apple, strawberry, peach. He marketed in Arkansas and continued as long as his health let him. I worked in the winery under him.

My maternal grandmother was Mary Louise Fiori Granata. She came to Sunnyside with the Fiori family, probably 1895. There was her dad, John; her uncles, Joe, Tony, and Pietro B.; her aunt, Rosa; and her grandfather, Dominic. Mary Louise lost her mother when she was two weeks old. She was then raised by this group of men and her aunt, Rosa. Rosa was 11 at that time and always said, "Mary was my first child."

After I was grown, I took Grandmother Granata to the grocery store many a time on Wednesday. She was a diabetic and not supposed to have sweets, but after we canvassed all the grocery stores she would look at me and say, "I think it's time now for us to get the Papa Burger and the root beer float on the way home." She loved the floats from A&W Root Beer.

My father, Dominic Fiori, was born in 1908. He completed the third grade, and then he had to quit school to work on the farm to help make a living to feed the family. About his childhood, he told me they were poor, but they never went hungry. They worked in the fields. Their two-room house was quite primitive. His mother used to get real aggravated at him because when the chickens went under the house, he would try to catch them by their feathers through the floor. She didn't think that was very funny.

[Their house was so small], the children could not all sleep in the house. They constructed a very basic building on the top of the cellar, and some of the boys slept over there. Their beds were made of old shucks that were stuffed into ticking. They had no heat there. My father said many a time they would run to the house barefoot in the snow. I think they pretty much lived the same life as everybody did. They had no money. It was just a hard life.

Dad's older brother, Virgil, was kind of a rounder. One time Grandmother Fiori sent them to the store to buy a certain size of lamp globe. Virgil told the woman at the store that he needed the size of lamp globe that cost a nickel less, so that she would give him a nickel in change. He bought candy with it. My dad didn't know any better.

My mother, Florence Granata Fiori, was born in 1912. Her first year in school was at Woodlawn, near the Harmon community west of Tontitown. When she started school, Mother could not speak any English. Her teacher would write notes home, and my grandmother would interpret the notes and help my mother with her homework. Grandmother Granata is the one who taught my mother English, both speaking and writing.

After that first school year, Mother went to school at Tontitown. I think she went through the eighth grade. She was in the Tontitown school when it burned [in 1927]. She was in the middle grades, and was one of the ones that helped get the kids out of the building before it burned. She lost her only coat [in the fire].

Mother had to quit school because she had to go work in the fields. She worked in the fields with her dad a lot. She was the oldest child. Her father was very disappointed that she was not a boy. In later years, he expressed his regret that he had been so obstinate about it and acknowledged that he was quite proud of her.

During Mother's childhood, her family was like everyone else, quite poor. She and her mother had one dress between them. So Mother would go to Mass, come home and give her mother the dress, and then her mother would put on that same dress and go to church.

When Mother was 19 years old, she was working in the fields, cutting sprouts. A sprout went directly into her left eye and caused her to lose the sight in that eye. My grandmother removed the sprout from Mother's eye. Memo Morsani told my grandfather that there were doctors in Fort Smith that could probably save Mother's eye, if not her

                    HELEN FIORI GEORGE

eyesight. She spent six weeks in Fort Smith with Connie Pozza. Connie took her to the doctor each day. It was quite a deal, but at least she saved her eye.

Also when Mother was 19, she had pneumonia. Dr. Cooper from Elm Springs told her parents that she would not live. As a result of the pneumonia, the rest of her life my mother had asthma. She struggled to breathe the rest of her life.

I assume my parents both went to church in Tontitown, and that's how they met. They married in 1931. Grandmother Granata charged Mother's wedding dress at Wilson's [Department Store in Springdale]. It cost her $5.

I have two sisters, Mary Catherine and Pauline. I am the oldest. We helped on the farm, then we would come indoors and help Mother. I learned to cook when I was about five years old because many a time Mother would have to sit leaning over the back of a chair, struggling to breathe. I would bring the pans to her. She wouldn't let me peel potatoes because I peeled them too thick. I was wasting too much potato. Mother did a lot of canning. The only thing we ever bought was sugar, coffee, and flour. We always had homemade bread and homemade pasta. We made our own butter and cheese. Daddy made the cheese molds. Mother kept them in the house and she put oil on them till they got aged. Daddy made a box with a screen on the front that had three or four shelves, and he put that in the cellar. Mother would keep the cheese molds in there until we would use them. When the cheese was finished aging, she put a wax coating on it.

Breakfast was probably oatmeal. I remember eating a lot of oatmeal, because we got those green crystal-looking dishes, one piece in each box. We might have had some toast sometimes, enough to fill our stomachs, that was the main thing. I think they let us have a cup of coffee, or something like that. Sometimes a glass of milk. So much of the time our milk would get to where you couldn't drink it, so we would make our own chocolate syrup. We mixed two tablespoons of chocolate and four tablespoons of sugar in water and boiled it until it got thick. We would use that to try and smother the [soured] taste of the milk. Dad would have coffee with milk and bread in it.

We had hens for eggs. We had a hen house, but we never liked to go in there, especially when the hens were trying to set, because they would chase us. One old rooster really terrified us. He used to chase us every time we went near him. We thought he was a lot bigger than he actually was and we were really scared of him. He wound up in a pot of umido.

When we got into the broiler business in later years, they would deliver the chicken feed and we would run and see what pattern they had on the feed sacks so we would know what kind of dress we were going to have. We used the white feed sacks for sheets and dish towels.

We thought we had big chicken houses but they were quite small compared to other folks. Daddy had an offer once to be financed and build bigger houses but he could not give in to borrowing money to gamble on what the broiler business would do. He always said that was one big mistake he made.

We butchered hogs and made salami, bacon, and other meats.

One of the calves that Daddy kind of made a pet of didn't like Mother. The calf got out of the pasture one day and when Mother tried to get the calf to go back in, she chased Mother into the house. She was definitely Daddy's calf. She would come up to him and take his hat off and lots of funny things.

We girls always disliked storms but we also knew we would get some ice cream if we got some hail. Daddy would tell Mother to mix up the ice cream and he would go out and gather up the hail and use that for ice. We did the same thing when we had snow storms. One time we had a hail storm and my dad went and gathered the hail to make ice cream. Grandfather Fiori would not eat it, as he said it would give him a stomach ache because it came from the storm.

My dad did a lot of things besides farming. He fixed equipment for family and friends. One of his projects was sowing beds of tomato seeds. He would make many short rows, sow the seeds, and then cover them with sawdust. He found the tomato plants would break through the sawdust easier than the dirt. He then would sell the plants to people putting out tomato fields.

In the 1930s, Dad built a roadside stand where he sold grapes, grape juice, and apple cider. He made the juice and cider himself, with very primitive equipment. He also sold gifts, novelties, baskets woven by Grandfather Fiori, and wine from Grandfather Granata's winery. Dad

 HELEN FIORI GEORGE

was always trying something new. He made some musical instruments such as fiddles and mandolins, and in later years, he made and sold a lot of doll furniture.

Dad's equipment for making grape juice and cider was made from some of the castoffs from Grandfather Granata's winery. He used a grape grinder from there. He built a heating pit under a handmade tank that would hold 10 cookers. He put water in the tank, the cookers in the water, and heated the grapes until they were warm. He built a press, using four feed sacks sewn together and placed into a frame. He poured the warm grapes into the sack, then folded the cloth and placed a wooden separator above each layer. It was 10 layers high. He then pulled down on a long pole that was attached to the top of the stack, and that mashed the grapes. A wooden trough carried the juice into cookers. When one was full, he would dump it into a 50-gallon wooden barrel. From there we would bottle it into gallon jugs. That was our job. We always had purple hands for the Grape Festival. He bought the jugs from drug stores selling Coca Cola at fountains, took them home, removed the labels, and sanitized and washed them. After filling the gallon jugs, he put them into a second tank with water in it and heated the juice to 190 degrees to pasteurize it. He had to buy special lids with rubber seals to be sure it would seal to keep. He then stored it in a building and brought it to the roadside stand as needed.

One winter in the early 1940s, Welch Grape Juice Company was buying grape cuttings. After Dad pruned the vines, he brought the runners—snow, ice, and all—into the house. After our day's work was done, we would drag these into the kitchen where we sat around and made the cuttings. He would bundle them 100 per bundle and tie them with wires. We worked many nights doing this, and were so excited as all three of us girls [made enough money to buy] a new coat from Montgomery Ward. We thought we were the richest girls around. We actually had a new coat from a store!

I went through the ninth grade at Tontitown, and then I went to Springdale High School the last three years. Our teachers at Tontitown were nuns. Sister Bernaldo [Kaelin] was my first grade teacher. Sister Bernadine [Lake] was my teacher for four or five years. I remember Sister Isidore [Kirk]. She was one everybody was afraid of. Sister

Quintilla [Halter] tried to get a singing group together, wanting to teach us music. Sister Adrian [McGrath] was another one that everybody was afraid of. She was the one that used to have her yardstick handy.

When I started school, I was scared to death. I'd never been off the farm. If it hadn't been for Louis and Philip Pianalto, I would have never gotten to school the first two years. Daddy paid them 25 cents a week for me to ride with them. The first year Louis and Philip picked me up. They had to go real early so they could play ball before Mass, which was before school. I don't remember it, but I have been told that I would cry all during Mass, I was so scared. The second year, Louis dropped out of school, so I rode with Philip. The third year, my dad would walk with me to Tontitown. It was three miles. Then I would walk home with the Pianaltos and the Piazzas until we got to the M and M Tile corner [Highway 412 and Pianalto Road], where they turned north, and I would run like crazy to my grandparents' winery, which was another quarter of a mile [west]. My grandmother Granata used to cook for the family and the workers there, so she always had a snack for me. Gile Pianalto was working for my grandfather Granata, so I would ride home with Gile at five o'clock.

That went on until I was in about the sixth grade. Then I would drive Dad's old Ford to Tontitown, and haul Pauline, Mary Catherine, and Martha Granata. When I was 11 years old, I got caught in the snow. Sister Bernadine came to me and said, "I think you better gather up your bunch and get ready to head for home, because the snow is getting too deep." We got up there just below where Uncle Lawrence [Granata's] house is now and the snow was so deep that it drowned the car out. I walked down to Uncle Lawrence's house, which was just a little ways down the hill. We had a phone [system] that my dad had put together with grape wire as our phone line. It went to our house, our grandparent's house, and Uncle Lawrence's house. Each of us had a different ring. I called Dad and told him we were stalled. He walked down to where we were, but by the time he got there, the car had dried out and it started right off.

My best friends in school were Luellen Penzo, Rita Piazza, and Sarah Taldo. I started school with four boys, Vernon Taldo, Edward Pianalto, Frank Maestri, and Roy Franco. In later years, Barbara Verucchi, Nova Jean Fiori, and I sort of stayed in a group.

At recess, we used to play games like red rover, ring-around-the-rosey, things like that. In later years, somebody must have got enough money to buy a set of jacks. As we got a little older, if we ever got our hands on a nickel, we would save it, because at noontime if it was raining, we would go to the school basement where they had a jukebox. That's where we learned to dance to Bob Wills.

For lunch, we took bread and jelly. When they were rebuilding the church [that was destroyed by a tornado in 1934], my dad worked on Wednesdays on the church. He would bring his lunch, so Sister would let me go eat my lunch with him.

As soon as we got home from school, Daddy would tell us, "Hurry and eat a sandwich and get your overalls on. I turned out the potatoes today and you all have to go pick them up." Or, we had so many rows of vines to tie by night because he had pruned that day. He would have the work laid out so we could do our part when we got home. Then we would come back in and help Mother fix the food.

Our first car was an old Model A. When Mary Catherine was about six years old, about 1942, she was chosen to crown the Blessed Virgin [a traditional Catholic ceremony in which a statue or image of Mary, the mother of Jesus, is adorned with a crown]. Dad took us [to the ceremony] in that Model A. It was pouring down rain, and Mary Catherine was dressed in white. That car leaked everywhere. There wasn't a corner we could put Mary Catherine in. We tried covering her up to keep her dry until we got to church.

Daddy then bought a used Nash. It belonged to a man that ran the theaters in Springdale. He came out and showed it to Daddy and they took a ride. Mary Catherine and I were sitting in the car looking it over. We had never seen a car with a cigarette lighter before, and it also had a big plastic horn on it. By the time they got back to the car, we had heated that lighter and decorated that horn—we burned about four or five circles in it. Daddy wanted to know who did that. We said we didn't do it, but of course he knew we did.

Those old Nashes used to slip out of gear. You had to get out and lift up the hood, realign the shift, and slip the gears back in before you could move the gear shift. One time—I think I was in the sixth or seventh grade—I was sent to Tontitown [driving] that car. The shift slipped out, so I lifted the hood and got up there. I was barely big enough to get up on the fender. Anyway, I had the hood up and here came Gabriel Pianalto. He said, "Do you need some help to fix that thing?" I said "No, I believe I can make it." I lined up the shift, dropped the hood, and got back in the car.

We got electricity in 1943. We only had one light bulb in each room. I don't think we even had any plug-ins [electrical outlets]. At that point we had graduated to a kerosene cookstove that my grandparents had given us, so we were really uptown. One time Daddy won an Aladdin electric lamp in a drawing held by the Famous Hardware Store in Springdale. We had never seen such a bright light in our life. It was quite an adventure when we got electricity.

Our family tradition at Christmastime was to pop popcorn and string it up. We went to the woods and cut down a tree. We decorated our tree with a package of tinsel. We would save the tinsel and use it the next year. We went to Midnight Mass. For a while, when there was just the four of us, we used to go in a buggy that was drawn by a mule. I can remember going to church in that because Mother and Daddy used to sit me down right on the floorboard between them.

Daddy or Mother usually made something to give us for Christmas. I remember one year Daddy made me a little red wooden rocker. Mother would make a doll out of old socks. One Christmas, we got a catalog and our parents let us select something we really wanted. Mary Catherine and I decided on one of those typewriters that you turned the wheel and pressed a key to print. I was looking in the closet one day, and saw a box with "Typewriter" written on it. I got so excited, I went and got Mary Catherine and showed her. She was mad at me for telling her who Santa Claus was.

The first Grape Festival I remember was west of the second store that Richard and B. Ardemagni built [on the northwest corner of the Highway 412 and Barrington Road intersection]. Mother and Daddy gave us girls a dime apiece—a nickel for a ride and a nickel for a hamburger. *Nonna* [Grandmother] Granata managed to give us all another dime.

After high school, I went to work at Welch's [in Springdale] for 67 cents an hour. I met my husband, Luther George, when I worked in the offices of George's. Luther, his brother, Gene, and his dad, C. L., were owners of the family business, George's Incorporated. I also volunteered at Springdale Memorial Hospital for 30 years. I have two sons, John and Rick, and five grandsons.

Is the world a better place now than when I was young? Well, we've got a lot of things that make our life easier as far as living conditions. I think we've lost a lot of personal contact with our families and our friends. I still think we need people. I think we need our families. I'm very fortunate. Both of my boys live just a little over a mile from me. If I need them they can be here in about two minutes if the light is green. If it's red, it takes them about five minutes.

Lillian Cortiana Granata

LILLIAN CORTIANA GRANATA

Lillian Cortiana Granata was born in 1924 in Tontitown, Arkansas, to Celeste and Mary Ceola Cortiana. She was 78 years old when she was interviewed in 2002.

My paternal grandfather was Eustacchio Cortiana. He came to Tontitown with the original group of settlers [in 1898]. He raised five children: Dick, Joe, Virginia, Louise, Mary, and Celeste, who was my father. Everyone called my father "Cel." Dad used to say when he was a young man, before he was married, that he was a bum. He left home to look for work. Two or three or four of them would jump on the train going through Tontitown and go to different towns to do work.

My maternal grandparents were Santo and Maria Ceola.[1] They were also part of the original group of Tontitown settlers. My mother was a baby when she came over from Italy. The family came with three girls: Lucy, Alice, and Mary, who was my mother. Another daughter, Fausta, was born in America. The family story is that when Santo got sick enough to die, he wanted his wife, Maria, to marry his brother, because Santo would take care of the kids. She married him; they called him Santo also. They had eight children: twins Rinaldo [Nel] and Julia, Victor [Hi], Fred, Dick, Victoria, Cecilia [Chill], and Genevieve.

One time Nonna Ceola went to Springdale to buy supplies. She tried to make them understand that she needed a pan big enough to make bread. Nonna couldn't talk English and so she tried to describe it to them. She said, "Sometime you wash-a the baby, sometime you

---

1. Research by Jan McQuade Sturm shows that Maria Ceola's first husband was Domenico Ceola. He died, and Maria later married Domenico's brother, Santo. Jan McQuade Sturm, "The Original Settlers of Tontitown," *So Big, This Little Place* (Tontitown Historical Museum, 2009), 149.

make-a the bread." She went round and round and described it, and she finally got a pan.

I think my mother finished the fourth grade. When she was 10 or 11 years old, she went to work for the Reynolds family in Fort Smith. Mother said the Reynoldses were very wealthy people, and very good to her. She cleaned their house, cooked for them, and sewed their clothes for them. Mother sent money home to her family so they could live.

My parents met each other because their families were neighbors. Back then, nobody had anything to do with Tontitown. We were immigrants. Elm Springs didn't like Tontitown, Springdale didn't like Tontitown. And of course [the Tontitown Italians] couldn't talk English. I was brought up to speak English. The only time Mother and Dad talked Italian was when they said something they didn't want us kids to understand.

Mother was an extremely good seamstress. She made her mother's dresses, her sisters' dresses, and every dress I had. My underpants always matched my dress. When I got a little older and someone would show me their store-bought underpants, I thought if I could just get a pair of those, I'd be in seventh heaven.

Shortly after I was born, we moved to Hartshorne, Oklahoma, for Dad to work in the mines. When he came home from the mines, his face was pitch black and his feet were pitch black. Dad would kick his shoes off and say, "Come on, Chi Chi,"—he called me Chi Chi—"look at 'em." His feet were as black as his shoes. I'd go get a pan, warm some water, and wash his feet until they were clean. Dad worked in the mines for four years.

We sold beer in Oklahoma and it was a very successful thing. Dad also operated a restaurant. Every penny was saved. Mother had a leather pouch, and she said, "When this gets full, we are going to move to Arkansas." And we did. I was five years old when we moved back to Tontitown.

In Tontitown, Nonna Ceola lived in a two-story house across the field from us. I liked to be over there with them. My aunts were just like mothers to us. They helped take care of me and [my twin brothers] Gilbert and Gordon. That's when Gilbert and Gordon and I would take the silks off the corn and smoke it. We'd go out in the field, take some pieces of the Sears and Roebuck catalog to roll the silks in, and smoke it.

    LILLIAN CORTIANA GRANATA

When I stayed at Nonna Ceola's house, I slept in a bed with my aunts. The mattress was a big old fluffy thing about 12 inches high. The mattress had little pockets, and you could put your hand in there and shake up the corn shucks to fluff them up. You fluff the mattress up as much as you can, and then you go to bed.

Nonna cooked everything on a woodstove. She boiled coffee in a big old pot. Just fired the heck out of it and poured the grounds in there. When it was cooked, she would put a cloth over your cup and pour through it like a strainer. That was it. We always had coffee for breakfast at Nonna's.

They had a cow for milk. They had to buy flour to make bread. They grew their own beans, corn, and potatoes. They loved cornbread. They made beer in a log building. Behind the door in Nonna's bedroom there was a hole in the floor. After the beer was made, she would store it down in this hole. You see, it was against the law to make beer, and if they were to find beer in your house, they'd call it a raid and you could be fined or jailed. Uncle Hi [Victor] Ceola went to jail for awhile. I remember visiting him.

We grew grapes, tomatoes, and strawberries. What little grapes Dad had, he took down to Welch's [processing plant in Springdale], but he never really took that much. He had just enough to make wine and grapejack. He sold that on the side to make a little extra money. It got to where it was hard to raise grapes because of frost and bitter rot. Bitter rot was horrible.

Dad went into raising chickens. When he quit raising chickens, he started making wine in the chicken house. Angela Lazzari sold him her wine vat. It was about 20 feet in diameter and 5 feet tall. Dad and Harry Sbanotto owned a grape grinder together. When they needed to grind their grapes for wine, they'd just go back and forth.

Grapejack is made by taking wine and distilling it into whiskey— white, potent liquor, 150 or 160 proof. Dad even had some once that was 190 proof. He had to dilute it. It was so strong it would burn your tongue. They'd dilute it down with water to make it about 90 proof, then drink it and have a good time. My mother always put grapejack in her coffee. She lived to be 90 years old.

They had customers coming from Bentonville, Springdale, and everywhere wanting this grapejack. Nobody was making it but the

Tontitown people. They're the only ones who had grapes; nobody knew too much about grapes around here except the Italians. So they made this grapejack, and the American people really went for it.

Once in a while, Dad would raise calves to butcher. Henry Neal, who lived by Brush Creek, butchered a calf at least once month. They would come by your house [with cuts of meat] in the back of the pickup. They had a scale in the back end of the pickup, and you paid for whatever part of the meat you wanted.

Dad always raised his own hog. He had a hog pen right next to the house. We had sausage the whole year long. The harder it got, the better it tasted. You cooked all the fat off the hog and rendered the grease. They put the grease in a great big crock jar, and it would harden into lard. That lard was used to cook with all year long. If it got a little rancid on the top, you'd throw that away and work down to the fresher [portion]. And salt pork, you canned it in a jar. There's a certain part of the fat of the hog that you use to make salt pork. Dad would put a lot of salt in it and put it in a jar, and when you open the jar, the top would be a little brown, but underneath that it would be white. That's how you seasoned your food. They buy salt pork even now to make the spaghetti at the Grape Festival.

I finished the tenth grade in Tontitown. Of the nuns, I remember Sister Wilhelmina [Dower]. She was mean. During recess, we used to play drop the handkerchief or ring-around-the-rosey. My best friend in school was Grace Maestri. I'll never forget when Lawrence Pianalto came [to the school] with a [car] battery—you know, they were mechanics. They made everybody hold hands, and first thing you know, everybody hollered! He shocked the livin' daylights out of everyone.

I used to sing in the old church until the tornado tore it down [in 1934]. The night of the tornado, my dad had us all in our basement. My mother had a jar about half full of dimes, and we got in such a hurry to get to the basement, she dropped the jar and had dimes all over the place. We were shocked to death when we found out that our church was blown down.

I remember John Mollar [a storekeeper and the church organist]. He was my everything. I was in choir all my life. He always brought us lemon drops, and he'd say, "All right children, it's time to clear your throat." He gave us all a lemon drop and we'd sing, after we sucked our lemon drop.

Mr. Mollar taught me how to play the organ in church. I played a few times, but I didn't like that kind of music. I was a hillbilly girl from Tontitown. I liked all this western music. At the time, it was Roy Rogers. I knew every song, every word. After my piano lesson, as soon as Mr. Mollar would leave his piano—he was strictly a classical man—all his music would go to the side, and I'd play anything I could think of, by ear. He'd come back to me and say, "Oh no, no, no, my child. You don't do that, my child. You play this way." So, I'd have to play it that way. Every time I would leave, he would give me candy. He had a lot of candy in his store, and he was so generous. During Lent, I would go down to Mr. Mollar's store and he'd give me candy. But during Lent, you know, you don't touch candy. So I'd take the candy home and hide it in a jar. As soon as Lent was over with, I'd give the candy to my mother as a present. She loved candy.

Mr. Mollar also doctored everybody. If you were sick and not feeling good, he'd give you something to make you well. He was a saint if there ever was one in this town.

Close to Mr. Mollar's store was Perona's canning factory, there on the southwest corner of Highway 412 and Barrington Road. That's where Aunt Bessie and Aunt Jay [Julia Ceola Brunetti] and all of them went to make their money. They'd get a big old bucket and they'd fill that bucket up with peaches, and get paid a nickel a bucket. I'll never forget one time when I went down there with them. There were gorgeous peaches there, and oh boy, I thought, I've got to have that peach. I'll take it home to Mother. Mrs. Perona came by and told me not to ever come back, because she said those peaches were not to take home. She was mean. Mr. Perona was so good, but she was something else. Of course, being in that kind of business, you had to be that way, I guess.

I remember Strabala's blacksmith shop. He used to take care of your horses. He put shoes on them. One time we stole Mr. Strabala's wagon on Halloween night. It was Bill Fiori, Guy Bariola, Buster [Lawrence Granata], and I. We brought the wagon up to the old [Smith] schoolhouse on the northwest corner of Hwy 412 and Barrington Road and set it on that porch of the schoolhouse. And, don't you know, Mr.

Strabala came running out with his shot gun that night too! He did. He followed us with a shotgun.

The cheese factory was up near the old historic Bariola place. Everybody on that road—Dora Sbanotto Taldo, Nonna Ceola, us, the Sbanottos, the Penzos, and the Tessaros, would all pool their milk and bring it to the cheese factory. They had a great big copper vat in there. You weighed your milk in that vat. The more milk you put in, the closer the time come for you to make your cheese. When you got a certain amount of milk in there, then you made a cheese of your own. You're going to make a big cheese when the time comes, a big cheese. You skimmed that milk and you got the cream off the milk to make your butter, when it was your time. You would make your cheese, work it, put rennet in to make it clabber, and then stir it all up, warm it up. When it gets warm enough to clabber, then you take it out, strain it, and put it into a round wooden frame to drain and harden. When the cheese was cured and ready, we removed the frame and took the cheese home. My dad had a slanted board, so the cheese stays up here and all your whey drips out of the cheese. Every day or two you'd turn the cheese over, and then first thing you know, it would start drying and crusting on the outside. I remember my dad waxing the cheese.

On the weekends, we had dances downstairs in the hotel—the old hotel where Uncle Dick Cortiana lived. There was live music by the Lewis Haney bunch. They played guitars. Dick Fiori played the violin, and his wife Florence even played the guitar. Leonard Haney played too. We also had dances up on Gildo Mantegani's porch. He had a great big cement porch.

I was strictly a jitter-bugger—that was my life! When they had the armory in Springdale, Bob Wills used to play there all the time, and we'd go down there once in a while. Richard Ardemagni would load up Beanie [Lavinia] and Grace Maestri, me, Flossie and Virginia Fiori, all us girls, and he'd take us to these dances then take us home. He was our chaperone.

My brother Gilbert was a jitter-buggin' fool. He could throw me over his shoulder and land on the floor. Gilbert was so durn good, that the people would actually stop dancing and they'd make a great big circle and just watch. He was that good at it.

The first grape festivals I remember were held where Richard

[Ardemagni's] store is [on the northwest corner of Highway 412 and Barrington Road]. There was a hall [the old Smith schoolhouse] where we used to have our school programs. The nuns used to bring us over there and here came Santa Claus running all around the wooden building, shaking bells. He came inside, got up on the stage, and gave all of us little bags of candy. That hall is where the first grape festivals were.

My dad used to run the hamburger stand for the Grape Festival. The merry-go-round was in Aunt Mary Fiori's yard. Every picnic, if we were lucky, we would get a quarter. That was our spending money. If you bought a hamburger, it was a nickel. Pop was a nickel. I got in real good with the guy that run the Ferris wheel. He just loved me to death and I used to ride that Ferris wheel for nothing. Oh, it was great. I don't remember the spaghetti dinners at all. I don't think they really had spaghetti dinners then. These little carnivals used to come in and sell all the goodies and what-nots, things like balloons and little monkey things. Outside of the Ferris wheel, I don't know of any other activity.

I met my husband, Lawrence "Buster" Granata when I was 12 or 13 years old. He was six years older than me. He had this Model A Ford with a rumble seat in the back end of it. At that time, nobody had cars. He used to drive this Model A into the school yard, and then he kept on circling and circling, blowing his horn. Buster always wanted me to go with him to the show, but my dad was very, very strict with me. I mean, you're not going anywhere with anybody. And I played by the rules.

Buster wanted to know if he could take me home after school. There was no way I'd ride home with him. I walked home with the rest of the kids. All the Bariola kids and all of us walked home together. Agatha Morsani used to walk with me until I got to the railroad tracks. From there, I walked with Rosie and Josephine Bariola. I had my brothers with me too. Finally, Buster came to the house and talked to Dad and asked if he could take me home from school once in a while. It started that way.

After tenth grade, I went to Fort Smith to finish high school, because I was going to be a nurse. I was going to stay with the nuns down there, but they found this lady that wanted me [to work for her]. I stayed with her and she promised the nuns that she would see that I got to school and I got my education, and in the meantime, I could help her at home. She had two kids, I liked that. She was a beautician, and she dyed my hair platinum blonde. Buster came down to see me, and he kept circling the street, and didn't stop. He said, "I really didn't think it was you. You better get your other hair back. I don't like it like that." I said, "I can't do that, it's dyed." After a while, Buster said, "If you don't get that hair back the way it is supposed to be, I'm not going to come see you anymore." I took it serious. I was 15. He said, "I want you to come home and I want you to marry me." I said, "With my blonde hair?" He says, "No, you've got to change it." I was afraid he wasn't going to come back to see me. So I come back home and went to see Margaret Perona, who was a beautician. I asked her if she could dye my hair back brown again. She said, "Let's dye it an auburn red color." So, she dyed it red, really red. But at least Buster liked it better than the platinum blonde color.

Dad didn't like the fact that I was not going back to Fort Smith. He did not like that at all. But he said, "I'll tell you what. If you think you're serious enough and you love him that much, then I'm not going to make you go back to Fort Smith and stay there and go to school."

So, I married Buster in 1940 when I was 16 years old. Hey, anybody that married back then, they had a dinner that you would never forget. Everybody ate worlds of spaghetti and meatballs, and Buster's mother made a veal bird—beef that's rolled up with toothpicks in it.

Buster's dad, John Granata, owned Granata's Winery. Right before Buster and I got married, his dad was selling worlds of wine and whiskey to Fort Smith people. They were buying it by the barrels. And he sold wine to all different states, even Texas. He and Jack Burrows would load the truck up and deliver wine. There were little roadside stands at that time, where you could buy little souvenirs, and they sold wine too. Buster worked with his dad in the winery, delivering wine. I worked in the winery too. That thing was open 24 hours a day! His dad hired practically every young guy here in Tontitown until the war started. When the war started and all those guys had to go to the service, that really hurt John Granata, because he lost most of his help.

Dad [Cel Cortiana] became mayor of Tontitown [in 1949]. Once he remarked to me, "Boy, I tell you what, Lillian, I really made the money this year. They've raised my pay. I got $40 this year." Once in a while, when somebody would ask Dad to marry them, he'd ask me to come and be a witness. Sometimes I'd go do that, and also sing for them. Dad made many trips to Fayetteville [on behalf of] Tontitown. He was very, very good as city mayor.

Buster and I had five children: Martha, Carolyn, Darlene, Tommy, and Bobby. Martha was Grape Festival Queen in 1957. Three girls would run for queen, and the girl who sold the most chances [to win a prize] would be queen. In 1957 [the prize] was a Buick automobile. Alice [Granata] Leatherman and I would go one way and Minnie [Piazza] and Martha would go another way, and somebody else would go another way, hitting folks up to buy chances. Alice and I went toward Siloam Springs, and there were a bunch of guys on the side of the road with the big yellow hats, construction workers or something. We went over there, and by golly, we sold chances. Let me tell you another one. This is a dandy. We stopped at John Mitchell's junk yard. He bought two chances from us, and he won the car!

Carolyn was also a Grape Festival Queen. I think there was a period of time when the girls did not sell chances, because no one was willing to beat the streets selling chances. Instead, the parish voted for a queen. That didn't go over too well, and it didn't last too long. They went back to the way they do now. Of course, that means more money is made for the Festival.

My hobbies over the years? I've grown flowers. I did oil painting and ceramics for a while. I played the organ, but not since Buster passed away. My brother, Gordon, always said I was the best cook in the world. He said I made the best Easter bread of anybody. He loved it, and I made a loaf for him every year.

Josephine Bariola Green

JOSEPHINE BARIOLA GREEN

*Josephine Bariola Green was born in 1919 in Tontitown,
Arkansas, to Dominico and Theresa Roso Bariola. She
was 83 years old when she was interviewed in 2002.*

My father worked in the Oklahoma coal mines before he came
here to Tontitown. I don't remember him very well. I just remember
him being sick from working in the mines. He died when I was young.

My mother came [to America] when she was two years old. She
had two brothers. Louis was the oldest, then Albino. Her sister died on
the boat coming over, so she had no sisters. My mother knew nothing
about Italy, because she was just a baby when she came. Her childhood
was sad, because her stepmother didn't like her. Before she married, she
lived with her brother Louis to help take care of their little ones. She
was a good cook.

From oldest to youngest, the eight children in our family are Flora,
Lino, Alice, Henry, Guy, me, Rose, and Thelma. The kids older than
me were all born in Oklahoma. The rest of us were born in Tontitown.

I went to the tenth grade in Tontitown. I started school in the
[building] that burned down [in 1927]. I remember what caused it to
burn. The older boys would stuff their papers up the gutters, and one
morning after Mass we was all out playing, and the little ones, like me—
the first graders—they chased us with burning rags and stuffed them
up the gutter. Pretty soon, about ten o'clock, Memo Morsani and all of
them come yelling, "Get out! The school's on fire!"

The nuns were our teachers. I remember Sister Genevieve [Chafe],
Sister Wilhelmina [Dower], and Sister Vivian [McNally]. My best friends
were Grace Roso and Dorothy Fiori. At recess we played baseball.

That's all there was to play. I took bread and jelly for lunch. We walked to school.

For breakfast we had caffè latte with homemade bread. We was never hungry. To keep milk and butter cold, we hung it with a rope down in the well. Mother made cheese. We girls milked cows, fed chickens. The boys worked in the field. At night, we had no way of going anywhere, so we stayed at home. We would piece quilts with Mama and patch socks, do whatever. Once in a while she let us go out to play in the evenings, but not too often. She kept us close to her. She had a very rough life, because she had eight to feed and not much means of doing it.

At Christmastime, we always got a little something, but it wasn't much. I can remember we got a doll between the three of us [youngest girls]. That was it.

On Halloween, I didn't get to get out. [My mother] would say, "No ma'am, you're not going." So no ma'am, we stayed home.

After [I graduated] I went to work in the kitchen at Fayetteville City Hospital. I made $5 a week, with room and board. I gave some of my pay to my mother to help her out.

I met my husband, Johnnie Green, at a dance [at Mantegani's dance hall] across the street from the Venesian Inn. We married in 1941. Our children are Johnny Joe, Bill, Kenneth, and Sondra. We have eight grandchildren, and eight great-grandchildren.

I worked at a café in Springdale by the name of Chicken Little. Then I went to work at the Venesian Inn, then I went to the VA and worked in food [service] there. I retired from the VA. My hobbies are sewing and quilting. I crochet, embroider, and do hand work.

ALMA CIGAINERO HARTMAN

Alma Cigainero Hartman was born in 1919 in Tontitown, Arkansas, to Joseph and Iginia Pianalto Cigainero. She was 84 years old when she was interviewed in 2002.

My mother was born in Italy. Her parents were Dominic and Catherine Penzo Pianalto. They came to America [to Sunnyside] with their four children: Leo, Erlinda, my mother Iginia, and George. My mother was three years old [when she came to America]. She remembered the trip, how cold it was, how uncomfortable it was. My grandmother Catherine died in Sunnyside giving birth to twins. She and the twins are buried there.

When the family came to Tontitown [with the group of original settlers in 1898], they first lived in a log cabin on the old Fiori place just south of Highway 68 [today's Highway 412] on Barrington Road. Dominic and the kids, along with Dominic's brother and sister-in-law, Pete and Teresa—we called her Aunt Tracy—all lived in that log cabin.

A few weeks after they were here a tornado came. Pete, Aunt Tracy, and Dominic took all the kids around a bed in the southwest corner of their house. They were kneeling around the bed praying the rosary. The tornado took the top of the cabin off, took it all off except the bed that they were around. They said Father Bandini had said Mass in that corner several times. After all of that, they found a bottle of holy water in the debris that wasn't broken. That was a miracle.

Grandfather Pianalto came to Tontitown with four children and no wife. Aunt Tracy was taking care of his kids, plus three of her own. Dominic went back to Italy to find a wife who could come back and take care of his children. He left the kids with Aunt Tracy, and told them he would be gone just a little while. In Italy he wasn't having much luck, so

Alma Cigainero Hartman

he went to the parish priest there and told him his situation. Together, they walked to the Taldo home. The priest told them right away why he and Dominic were there: to find a wife for Dominic to take back to America to raise his children. They talked a while. Rose Taldo was 27 and had no prospect of marriage, so they decided she should do this. Dominic was old enough to be her father, but that didn't matter, because it was a matter of life and death. They got married that evening, and the next day left for America. She said he was an old man, but she would obey him and do what he told her to do. That's how they managed.

Dominic and Rose bought 10 acres west of Tontitown. Dominic built an outside oven to supply the bread for his family. After it was all talked about among the rest of the Italians [in the community], they all decided they would take one day of the week and take their bread to this oven and cook it. They had to do it on their day because each day there were different families. This went on for a long time, probably years.

Mama just went to the third grade. Her father, Dominic, had been a teacher in Italy so he did very well with teaching his own kids. As soon as she was 12 years old, Mama had to go out to work to help supply food for the family that was coming along—Kate, Lena, Dave, and Joe by that time. Mama went to work for the Faulkners in Eureka Springs. Mrs. Faulkner would send $3.75 home to Dominic every month. That's all she made, $3.75 per month. Mama worked really hard. She cared for five children, cooked, and cleaned. She had to carry water for their baths as well as household needs, two buckets at a time from the well. Mama said it was up such a steep hill, and lots of steps. Once Mama was told to tell the children to stop the iceman. Well, Mama forgot to do that and Mrs. Faulkner slapped her right in the face. So Mama said, "Well, that's it, I'm going to write to my father and tell him what happened." But Mrs. Faulkner would not let the letters go out. The seventh letter finally got home to Mama's father. Mama came home after that. Years later, when all of us kids were still at home, Mrs. Faulkner would come here every year and visit with Mama. She would bring everything she could think of, trying to ease Mama's pain. I don't think Mama ever forgave her. She never got over it.

My father, Joe Cigainero, came to Tontitown from Texarkana, Arkansas. The doctor in Texarkana told Papa's father that he had to be sent to the higher country because of his health. Papa had very bad asthma and was told he would not live six months if he stayed there. He came to Tontitown and stayed with Kate Neal, roomed and boarded there. That's how he met Mama. Papa was maybe 11 or 12 when he came to America. He was 15 years older than Mama. Mama was not quite 18 when she married; Papa was 33. They remained married 60-some years.

Papa bought land here and four of his brothers came before he got married and helped him build this house we are in today. This is where my parents lived until both of them died. My parents had five children: Catherine, Eileen, Alma, Madeline, and Lillian.

My father was a very good carpenter. He did not go to school one day in his life, but he could build the most beautiful things you ever saw. He could take lumber that somebody threw away and make something out of it. I know when he worked for B. and Richard Ardemagni [owners of Tontitown Mercantile], they would have bought [lumber] for him to work with. But Papa would go out back and find something and say, "This will do fine." He would take all these scraps and make shelves or whatever out of it.

We started first grade in the school that burned [in 1927]. We then went to school in the old [Smith] school that was on the northwest corner [of Highway 412 and Barrington Road]. When the school that is here now was built, I guess I was in the third grade. I finished school there. The Sisters of Mercy taught us all the way through. They had 10 grades. I went through tenth grade, then finished high school through the mail with the American School in Chicago.

We walked to school. When it rained, we went down to our knees in mud. Before school, we didn't have a lot of time. We had to fix our own breakfast because Mama and Papa went out to milk cows. When we came home we had our chores to do—chickens to feed, wood to carry in. We used a lot of wood [for heating] because our house wasn't very tight. In springtime we had to tie grape vines. We had acres of vineyards. We had to do all of our tying in the evenings. In summertime, we planted and hoed berries, and planted tomatoes for the canning factory. We picked tomatoes. We worked hard, but it was fun.

When we were growing up, we were never hungry. There was always enough food. Our meat was pork. We always had salami. We had cows, so we always had cheese. We all pitched in to help Mama in the kitchen, because she had been in the field most of the day. We peeled potatoes. We had vineyards, strawberries, and always raised chickens. We ate a lot of eggs.

We had grapes to sell. We didn't actually sell them, we traded for flour. There was no money exchanged. They took the grapes to the railroad tracks in Springdale. There was a walkway about chest high; you unload your grapes there and picked up your flour. We put the flour on a swinging table upstairs—seven or eight 100-pound sacks—so nothing could get to them. Of course, Mama covered them with cloth.

I remember going to Mr. Ardemagni's store with three eggs in my hand—because there was no paper sack to put them in—to trade for a one-cent pencil. We needed a pencil, and he could use the eggs.

We had a hard time during the Depression. We always ate, though. We always had plenty of food. All we bought was a little coffee, sugar, salt, and flour. We had salami that we kept in the cellar. We had bacon.

 ALMA CIGAINERO HARTMAN

Papa cured it, and all the meat was kept in the cellar. As far as chicken, if we wanted chicken for dinner, Papa would kill the chickens and hang them by the feet from a tree so all the blood would drain to the head. When the chicken was cold, he would take it down and chop off the neck and head. Mama would take it into the house and run it through scalding water, then cut it up and put it in some salt water. We helped pluck the feathers. There were a lot of pin feathers; we singed them off. Then Mama would fry the chicken.

Mama made a lot of pasta at a time. She would put it in sugar sacks. We bought sugar in 100-pound sacks at canning time. She put a sheet on the bed and laid the spaghetti on that to dry. When it was dry, she put it in the sugar sacks that she had ripped apart into squares. She gathered the four corners together and hung them upstairs where we kept flour and sugar. It was just four pieces of wire hanging from the ceiling holding a board, and we put these things on it. Everyone did that. It would get air, but no mice or anything could get to it.

We had no refrigerator or way to keep anything [cold]. We kept our cream and butter down in our well. Papa made buckets out of wire, with a lid of wire. Hooked it to a rope and let it down the side of the well so we could still draw water from the center. Mama made her own cheese right here in her kitchen. It would take a while for it to cure, and then whenever it did she kept it in the cellar.

When I was a child, all the people were poor. We were all poor. A lot of the American people—I know Mama helped a lot of them and their families. The Italians always had food, because they always had their own beef, chickens, pork. We canned vegetables and fruit. We canned at least 700 quarts of vegetables every year because that is what it took to feed our family.

Before we had electricity, we had an Aladdin lamp that we used when we all sat at the kitchen table and studied. It was hard, but that was all we knew. Whenever Eugene Pianalto and another fellow put in our electricity, it was heaven. Mama and Papa told us to keep the lights off except when we really needed them.

Mama used to go down to Mary Maestri's [restaurant] to work. From here she would walk down through that field. It's a long way down there. She would make spaghetti by hand. She cut it so fast; I don't know how she kept her fingers away from the knife. Then she would walk back home. One of us would probably have supper started—that was in wintertime. Mama always had a pot on the stove with a cooked chicken in it when we got home from school. We would take that broth and break up homemade bread in a bowl, and pour that broth over it. That is what we would eat to warm up. There wasn't a lot of heat in this house. Heat got away.

Mama always loved gardening. She had a rose garden out here bigger than this house. Papa had to help her with the rose garden. He would say, "Dad blame it, I always have to help you." The roses would stick him, you know how they do. Her peonies are still here, after all these years, on the north side of the house.

Mama, my sisters, and I made quilts together in the wintertime, when Mama saw we had the time to do it. We had to work till dark to get the wood in, get the chickens fed, and get the pigs fed. Then we had to study. Mama only had us quilt when she saw we had the time to do it. She would cut out the blocks, and in the evening, each of us girls would sew a block. When we finished one, she gave us another one. The quilts were six blocks by seven blocks, just large enough for covers.

Mama would go down to the Canup's house and buy the dirty wool they had took off the sheep they raised. We took it home and would wash it and re-wash it out in the backyard and put it on old sheets to dry. Then we'd wash it again because it wasn't clean enough. That is what we put in our quilts, instead of the cotton batting used today.

We made all of our clothing. All of our dresses [were made] out of printed feed sacks. If you don't mind my saying, our underclothes were made out of flour and sugar sacks. The outer clothes, we only had two apiece—one in the wash, and the other to wear to school. We had a treadle sewing machine, and we learned to make our own dresses.

When I was a child, the Grape Festival wasn't a festival; it was just something that we gave thanks for, a celebration for the families. We all got together. I think they cooked the spaghetti at home and brought it in. We walked in, nobody had cars back then.

After tenth grade, I went to California. Ernest Pianalto had married a Haney, and they had a store [in California.] They wanted me to work in their store. I went to California by bus. I went alone. After I worked [for the Pianaltos] awhile, I moved to Gilroy where Frindy [Florinda] Bariola lived, and worked with her, waiting tables at the Hecker Pass

     ALMA CIGAINERO HARTMAN

Inn. It was an Italian restaurant. Then I went to San José to work at the telephone company for three or four years. They had a big earthquake and I didn't stay there any longer. I transferred to San Bernardino and I lived with Aunt Linda [Erlinda Pianalto] Haney and her daughter, Martha. I worked long distance there. Then I came home.

I met my husband, George Hartman, when Louis Pianalto and his sister Mary were going up to this restaurant and dance place in Caverna, Missouri. I went up with them and met George there. Louis knew George; they were in the Navy together. At that time I was working at John Granata's winery, where I labeled wine.

George and I had four children: Duane, Patricia, Iginia, and Mary Nell. We had a café here in Tontitown. It was on the southwest corner of Highway 412 and Barrington Road. There were two apartments upstairs—the Peronas lived in the southwest corner, and we had the apartment in the northeast corner. George and I and the children were running the café. It burned. We lost everything, our home and our business. Everything.

After Papa passed away in 1967, Mama went to live in California with my sister Lillian and her husband, Bill Edwards. She stayed there for maybe 20 years, and then we brought her back here to Tontitown to live. She was 94 at the time. She was happy here, real happy. Mama had a really good sense of humor, all of her life she did. She worked hard, awfully hard, but she was happy.

When I was growing up, every night we all said the rosary together. We had to kneel down. If we didn't kneel down, we didn't dare go to sleep. Looking back on my childhood, as poor as we were, I wouldn't trade those days for any part of my life. Those were the happiest days of my life.

Catherine Taldo Hovey

CATHERINE TALDO HOVEY

*Catherine "Katy" Taldo Hovey was born in 1921 in
Tontitown, Arkansas, to Joseph and Dora Sbanotto
Taldo. She was 81 years old when she was interviewed
in 2002.*

My paternal grandparents were John and Maria Taldo. They were
born in Italy. Nonno was of medium build. Nonna was kind of husky.
She wore her hair in a bun. They didn't talk to us because they didn't
speak English. I learned very little [Italian]. The only words I heard were
words they wouldn't repeat to me. We used to listen and try to grab a
little bit now and then.

My maternal grandparents were Antonio and Pierina Tessaro
Sbanotto. Their children were my mother Dora, Theresa, Emma, Roy,
Helen, Connie, Harry, and Mabel. I don't know much about Mother's
childhood. They had to get out there and cut roots out to raise crops,
and they did a lot of work around the house.

My parents had eight children: Katy, Raymond, Fredie, Beatrice,
Patsy, Ida Mae, Sarah, and Joe [J. T.]. My father was a cutup, a jewel, he
was really good. He would take us to do work on the farm with him.
He was always in a good mood. I remember once Daddy wanted to go
to a dance at the school, and my mother said, "You can't go, because I
can't go." He said, "I will take Katy." My friends thought that was the
grandest thing in the world, to be taken to a dance by my daddy. They
all told me that.

My mother was a hard worker. She had to be. When my father died
in 1936, she was left a widow with eight children. My mother worked
her tail off. My brother Joe was born two months after my father died.
Uncle Dick Taldo lived with us and helped my mother. He took care

of the vineyard; he would prune and tie grapes. We had a winery at one time. All the family ran it, but Uncle Dick was the one who got the labels and stuff. Mother said that once they found me laying out flat on top of these rocks, and they thought I was dead. They picked me up to carry me in and smelled my breath and it was wine. I don't remember this happening to me, so I must have been pretty young. I think that is why I don't drink to this day.

I was the oldest child, and I'll tell you what, I washed diapers till I was blue in the face. Every time we got one [potty] trained, another one came along. We always had one or two in diapers. We didn't have washing machines. It was my duty to wash the diapers, rinse them, then wash them again and boil them. It went on like that all the time. I thought I never would get through washing diapers. I can just see myself standing on the back porch—it was screened in—washing, then hanging them on the line. In the winter we had lines in the basement.

I learned to cook by trial and error. Mother would say, "I'm going to such and such a place, do this, that, or the other. Now when a certain time comes, you start this, then start that." We didn't go by recipes. Mother made all the pies. I made all the cakes. We would go visit Nonna [Pierina] Sbanotto. She would bake us cookies. Now, I know they were just plain old cookies, but oh, they were delicious then.

We canned everything. I thought, "If I ever get married, I'm not going to can anything." In the spring, we hoed strawberries. I had to work on the farm too. We had three cows we milked. Well, [my brothers] Fredie and Raymond would get a bucket, go to the cow the closest to them, get one on either side of her, and the two of them would milk one cow. The other two cows were up to me. They would milk one cow and I would have to milk two. They were mean to me. I never did tell Mother, because it would have upset her.

Fredie used to tell our sister Beatrice, "When Mama starts to whip you, just yell real loud and she won't hit so hard." Beatrice used to pull a fainting spell on Mother, and she didn't know if she was faking it or what. Mother never had to discipline me. I was just afraid to hurt her feelings. I felt like she had already had enough. I would follow her around because she would say, "I just wish I'd die." So, when she would go to the barn, I would sneak down and check on her. That was just a manner of speech with her. I know that now, but I didn't know it then.

She dealt with sadness the best she could. She didn't let any of us know she was suffering, until she would make some remark like that. By then she was joking.

Mother used to do a lot of quilting. Quilting frames hung from the middle of the living room. All these women would come to the house one day a week and quilt with Mother—Aunt Theresa Zulpo, Aunt Emma Verucchi, Agnes Maestri.

The school was on the northwest corner of Highway 412 and Barrington Road. The old schoolhouse, they called it. [This was the Smith schoolhouse.] I remember Sister Albertine. I was an average student, I guess. Not anything to brag about. My friends were Beanie [Lavinia] Maestri, Virginia Fiori, Lillian Cortiana, and Madeline and Lillian Cigainero. The nuns wouldn't let us play with the boys.

For my first communion, I wore my mother's wedding veil—they cut the veil smaller—and my dress was made from her wedding dress.

I remember when the tornado took the church [in 1934]. We were all out in the yard, and several men kept saying, "Look at that cloud up there. It's going to be a bad storm." Sure enough, it took the church. Next day we went up to see what was done. It was ruined. It was awful.

During the grape festivals, I had to stay home and babysit so Mother could go up and work. She made pasta. Back then they would buy the chickens live and dress them. I got to go to the festival later in the evening.

Mother would let us have dances on Sunday night on our back porch—it was screened in and finished. Kids were always welcome at our house. I played cards with the older men like Uncle Dick Taldo, Dick Fiori, Tony Fiori, James Taldo. The men would come down on Sunday night and play cards. If one didn't come, then I could fill in and play pitch with them.

I had no idea of what I wanted to be when I grew up, because all I could think of was washing diapers. In the back of my mind, I thought I would like to be a nurse. But I never got that. We had no means for me to pursue this career. I dropped out of school when Mother's last kid was born. I went ahead and had other schooling, then worked as a laboratory technician.

My brother Raymond took me to California and I worked in a defense plant during World War II. I did riveting and stuff like that. I was happy. I made more money than I ever had in my life. That is where I met my husband, Charles Hovey. Charles was also working there, and then he got drafted. When I quit working at the defense plant, I came back home to Arkansas. When Charles got out of the service, he came here to see us. What attracted me to him? He was decent to me, for one thing.

After we were married, I always cooked too much. We could never eat all of it. I could cook for 10 people, but I absolutely could not cook for two. At first, we lived in a one-room apartment in Fayetteville. Charles started in pre-pharmacy school at the University of Arkansas. Then we moved to Clarksville, Arkansas, for pharmacy school. We lived in army barracks converted into apartments. Our kitchen sink was right there, our stool [toilet] was right there. You could sit on the stool and reach around the door to the kitchen sink to wash your hands. That was pretty small. Our first child, Cheryl, was born there. We later had a son, Ronnie. He was born in Springdale.

I used to play bridge as a hobby, but I've quit that. I still like to cook, but mostly, I just enjoy getting out of the way! Nonno Taldo used to sit on the back porch all day long, and just watch everything. When Charles and I got married, I took Nonno's chair and cleaned it up a little bit, and now I use it.

     CATHERINE TALDO HOVEY

ALMA ROSO HUNTER

Alma Roso Hunter was born in 1924 in Tontitown, Arkansas, to Albino and Catherine "Kate" Maestri Roso. She was 78 years old when she was interviewed in 2003.

My paternal grandfather, Giuseppe Roso, came to America in 1895. My paternal grandmother, Lucia—I don't know her maiden name— came that same year. They were [already] married when they came over. They went to Sunnyside, and then came to Tontitown [with the original group of settlers in 1898]. They died before I was born.

My maternal grandparents were Pietro Antonio Maestri and Melania Serri. They came to America in 1895 [to Sunnyside, then to Tontitown with the original group of settlers in 1898]. They died before I was born.

My father had one brother, Louis, and two sisters, Theresa and Angelina. Angelina died very young. My father went to the fourth grade in school. He was a farmer, and for some time, he mined coal in Oklahoma.

Daddy was very humorous. He loved to sing, but you couldn't get him to sing very often. He sang mostly when he was alone. When he was older, he sang more than when he was a young man. It was always fun to catch him singing when he really didn't want you to hear him. He would sing some Italian songs, and he talked about neighbors getting together and singing. He played the cornet in the [Tontitown] band.

I thought Daddy was very good at everything. He helped build his house and my brother Joe's house. I think he was a handyman. He really was. He made the concrete blocks for our house.

My mother's siblings were Aldo, Leo, Ciro, Grace, and Albano. I think my mother went to the sixth grade. I think she had a very happy

Alma Roso Hunter

childhood. She talked about things she and her mother did together, working in the kitchen. To me that's work, but to her that was an enjoyable event. Just before she married, she worked in someone's home in Fayetteville. Not for very long.

Mother was a great seamstress. She sewed all our clothes through high school. That was her main skill. Of course, I thought she was good at everything she did.

The funniest story I can think of about my mother was when she first had all her teeth pulled and had false teeth. She wouldn't let anyone see her. We used to chase her around the house trying to catch her without her teeth in her mouth. She would get very upset with us. We didn't catch her very often. She could run pretty fast.

I was born in Tontitown. My siblings are Richard, Joseph, and Grace. The main thing I remember about my brothers is catching them smoking and going in and telling on them. They would swear they hadn't been smoking, until I wondered if I really saw them smoke or not. Grace and I used to fight a lot, but we ended up being really good friends.

I don't ever remember being hungry as a child. We always had enough. Maybe not a variety, but we had plenty to eat—anything that could be grown in the garden or canned. Mother did an awful lot of canning. She would make grape marmalade. We would have to take the seeds from the grapes, and then squeeze from the pulp, from the rind, and separate them from the skin so she could make marmalade. That was a tedious, terrible job. After we grew up, Mother didn't make grape marmalade. We kids did the hard work. We peeled tomatoes. Mother even used to can spaghetti sauce. We ate lots of pasta. Our meat was mainly pork, from butchering. We always had hogs. We raised our own.

I think after the grape harvest, Daddy used to buy the flour, sugar, and other staples for a year's supply. Through the year we would charge things and then after he had his crops in he would go up and pay all his bills and buy all our staples for the following year. They were put upstairs in big sacks in one of the closets.

After school, I had to gather the kindling for the fire the next morning. When I was a little older, I did some milking. We had several cows. We made butter and all kinds of cheese. Mother used to put it down in the well with a rope. Then later on, I remember I wasn't too old, we got an icebox. We would put a sign out and the iceman would come and bring us so much ice. We always liked it when we could make home-made ice cream because then we got more ice.

To make cheese, several families got together. We had a cheese house on Joe Costa's place. One day a week, whoever had furnished the milk through the week took their turn making the cheese. I remember Mother stirring this in a big brass-bottomed kettle over an open fire. She had wooden molds that they poured it in. It was always good cheese.

For breakfast, we had oatmeal once in a while. Mother would make toast in the oven. Of course, we always had jelly. Eggs sometimes, but not every morning. Mother had lots of chickens, so we had plenty of eggs.

My first teacher in Tontitown was Sister Barbara [Mattingly]. I don't remember any others until I was in the upper grades and [had] Sister

Genevieve [Chafe]. I don't think anyone would ever forget her. I've had my knuckles whacked with the ruler many times. But I'm sure it was my fault. I was asking for it.

In one grade, several of us got together and I guess we formed what we thought was a club, for a short period of time. I can't remember who our teacher was, probably Sister Genevieve. She just put us in the back of the room and didn't teach us. She just completely ignored us. Apparently Mother never heard about it, or I would have really caught it. I don't remember exactly how long she did that, but we just weren't members of the class.

My best friends in school were Virginia Fiori, Beanie [Lavinia] Maestri, and the Pianalto twins [Virginia and Vivian]. At recess we played jacks, hopscotch, red rover, games like that. For lunch, we took jelly sandwiches and salami and cheese. We would have an apple, or if Mother had just baked, we would take a cinnamon roll. We always had a little something for dessert. We just went to the pump for water. We cleaned the chapel for the nuns. Also, after school, we had to clap the erasers and clean the blackboards.

We walked to school. In the wintertime I remember as a very small child, when it was snowing and the wind was blowing very, very hard, Daddy would carry me so I would be facing south, and he would take the wind and carry me to school.

I went to school in Tontitown until I was 13, then I went off to school at St. Anne's [Academy] in Fort Smith. It was very, very hard, being 13 and away at school. The first semester was really hard. But after that, it wasn't too bad. After high school, I went on to nursing school at St. Edward's [Hospital] in Fort Smith. I chose nursing as a career because I thought it was just the admirable thing to do, taking care of the sick.

As for businesses in Tontitown, I particularly remember Mr. Mollar's store because when it was real cold, we would stop there on our way to school and warm our hands around his big pot-bellied stove. Of course, he always managed to give us a little piece of candy or something. Regardless of how old it was, we thought it was pretty good.

I also remember the Perona store, the Ardemagni store, and the Morsani store west of town. The hotel building was there and the

   ALMA ROSO HUNTER

Cortianas lived in it, but I don't remember it as a hotel. We used to have dances there. I remember going to dances in that old hotel.

Before I left Tontitown to go to St. Anne's, I worked at Aunt Mary's [Mary Maestri's restaurant]. I worked in the evenings when she would have these dinners. I waited on tables in her restaurant in her home. I made 50 cents every evening. I thought that was big stuff back then.

At Christmastime, we always went to Midnight Mass. We used to have Santa Claus. One time I found a little set of dishes in a trunk in the attic. I ran down and told Mother that Santa Claus had hidden them. When Christmas came, it was a different set of dishes. I guess Mother took them back and exchanged them. For Christmas dinner, we probably had spaghetti, and maybe a baked chicken. We always had pies or cakes. Mother loved her sweets. We all did.

On Holy Saturday during Easter, Mother made hard-boiled eggs and Daddy took them up [to the church] to be blessed. I guess that tradition ended years ago, but it was a nice one. On Easter morning, after we came home from church and communion, the first thing we did was eat one of those blessed eggs. Daddy saved the shells so he could gather them up and burn them because they were blessed. We always had our blessed eggs first thing before we could have anything else from our Easter basket. We always did have an Easter basket. We had colored Easter eggs. We didn't color them ourselves. Easter dinner was same as Christmas dinner, spaghetti and a baked hen, probably.

The Grape Festival was always something to look forward to. I particularly remember that when Daddy would work in a booth, and any of our family would go to that booth to buy something, he never took our money. He always had someone else take it because he wanted to make sure that everybody knew that whatever we obtained had been paid for.

I met my husband, Howard Hunter, in Oklahoma City. We happened to both live in the same apartment house. Our landlord gave a Christmas party. I had never seen Howard until the party. That was the beginning of it all. We were married in Oklahoma City in 1958. I was a nurse at the VA. Howard was a contracting officer for the government. We have three wonderful children, Sherry, Allen, and Patti, and we have five grandchildren.

In some ways, I think the world is a better place now than when I was young. Young people are afforded many more opportunities. But we could do things back then that they can't do now. Kids can't go out and play without being watched constantly. There's always a fear that something may happen. We didn't have that when we were growing up.

ANNA AIMERITO LAZZARI

Anna "Ann" Aimerito Lazzari was born in 1923 in Dow, Oklahoma, to Giacomo (Jack) and Francesca (Frances) Marcangeli Aimerito. She was 80 years old when she was interviewed in 2003.

My father was born in 1886. His siblings were Jim, John, Jasper, Rose, and Dominic. My father completed the third grade.

My mother was born in 1889. Her siblings were Pepino, Dominic, and Theresa. Uncle Dominic lived in Dow, Oklahoma. Pepino went back to Italy and he died there. Theresa never came over [to America]. She spent her whole life in Italy.

My mother also completed the third grade. As a child, she did maid work. She cleaned houses for other people. Of her childhood in Italy, my mother said it was always hard work and no play.

My brothers are John Martin, John the Baptist, and James Adrian. John Martin died when he was nine months old.

My parents met in Dow, Oklahoma. My father was a coal miner there. I was born in Dow. We moved to Siloam Springs, Arkansas, in 1926, when I was three years old, and then we moved to Tontitown in 1936. We moved to Tontitown because my father's siblings Jim, Jasper, and Rose were living there. Aunt Rose married Camillo Morsani.

In Tontitown, my father farmed grapes and sold them to Welch's [processing factory in Springdale]. He planted tomatoes and sold them to Perona's canning factory. We had cows and we sold milk. They would pick up the milk cans in the mornings and you would milk at night.

In the summer, we had to work in the field. We picked strawberries. I never made a cent on the first day because I would eat strawberries all day. I love strawberries to this day. We also picked string beans. The

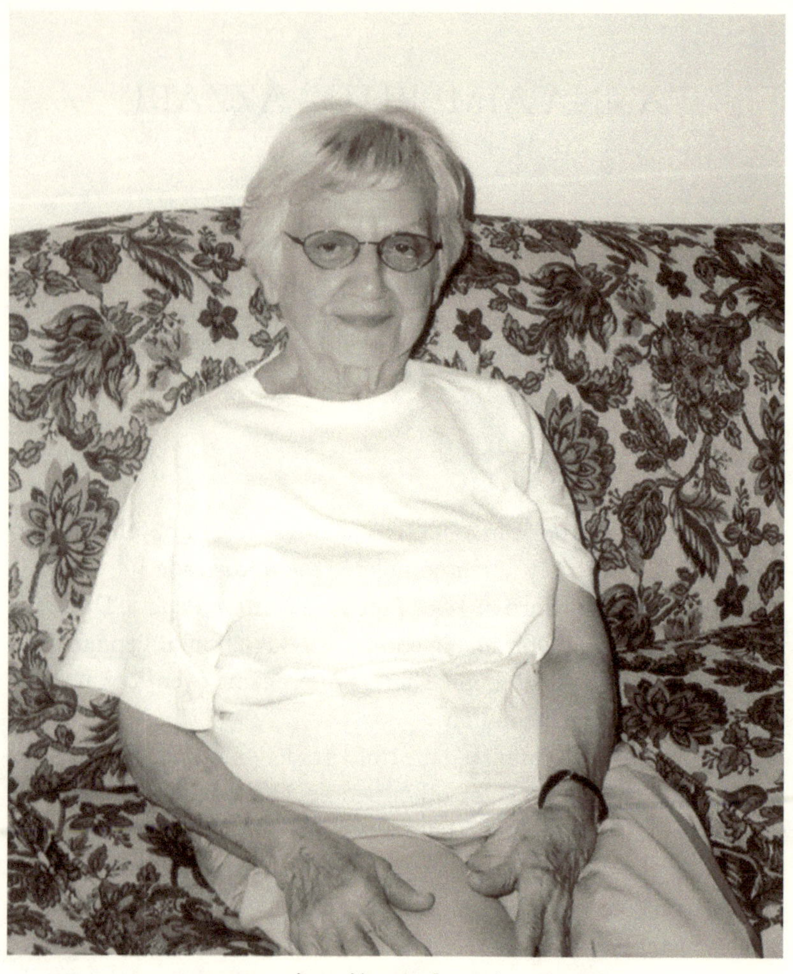

Anna Aimerito Lazzari

money we made we gave to my mom and dad. We weren't allowed
to keep any money. We did get to go to the theater in Springdale on
Saturday afternoon for 25 cents. Aunt Rose would drive us. She liked
movies. She liked Nelson Eddy and Jeanette MacDonald and so did I, so
we went to see Jeanette MacDonald and Nelson Eddy. Can you picture
kids going to see that now?

Mother made the best bread and lemon pie. She loved to make
bread and never measured anything, just a cup of this and a dash of
that. We had a woodstove, then we got a kerosene stove, then we got a

gas stove. She did real well with all of them. We had a gas refrigerator, believe it or not. We were wealthy in that respect. Before that, we had the old ice box that you had to buy ice for.

My mother did a lot of canning. She liked to work in the garden. She didn't spend her day out there, but she would hoe the vegetables that were growing. We raised hogs and chickens. My dad butchered, so we had sausage, ham, the works. We had a smokehouse. They used to dry the meat and then they would put it in a big old jar and pour lard over it. That was the way they kept the sausages. The sausages were in casings, and then you would lay it down at the bottom of a large jar, and then pour some lard over it. Of course, you had to eat the sausage before summer rolled around, because it would get rancid.

Mother made cheese. She had this big pot and whenever she had enough milk, she would pour all the milk in, bring it to boil, and put rennet in it to clabber the milk. Then she would take a beater and beat it and the solid part would all go down to the bottom of the pot. She just put her hands in there and put it in these round forms, and kept pushing it down until it was compact, then dried it. After it was dried, I think she put salt on the outside to preserve it.

We ate an awful lot of soup and beans, but I never was hungry. My mother made her own pasta—beat the eggs, rolled it out with the rolling pin, and then cut it either in little squares or thin or thicker. She'd make a supply for maybe two or three days. She would put it on the bed to let it dry.

We had kerosene lamps. I did not appreciate them because I was the one that had to keep them filled and cleaned, which you had to do almost every day. You had to put kerosene in the base or in the one that hung on the wall. You had to clean the glass chimneys. We washed them if they were black; if not, you could just wipe them out. Also we had one lamp, I forget what they are called, where you would pump something in and then you would turn it on and it really made a bright light. That's what we did our homework by. It was better than the kerosene.

Remember how people used to come by and sell things at your house? My mother could never say no to those people. She'd buy everything that came along. One day, a traveling salesman came to the house; I think it was in the middle of July. It was hot as blazes. Mother said to me, "I want you to get rid of him because I don't want to buy anything."

Mother went in the closet to hide, but she kept the door cracked. I got rid of the salesman and when he left, I said, "Mom, you can come out." She was soaking wet, drenched with perspiration. She said, "Couldn't you get rid of him faster?" I'll never forget that. She learned how to say no after that, rather than go in the closet.

We played a lot of dominoes and cards. Uncle Jasper would come down in the evening and play cards with my mom and dad. Uncle Jasper would have five or six sweaters on. As he sat down and played cards he would take one off at a time. By the time he got to the bottom sweater it was time to start putting them back on and go home.

I completed the eighth grade in Tontitown, and then graduated from high school in Springdale. In Tontitown, I had nuns as teachers. I remember Sister Loyola [Ryan], Sister Wilhelmina [Dower], and Sister Madonna [Hall]. Sister Loyola was my favorite. My best friends in school were Catherine Taldo, Rita and Elizabeth Bariola, and Madeline and Lillian Cigainero.

I can tell you some stories. Louis Pianalto and Stephen Maestri were in Sister Madonna's class. She was one who cracked your knuckles with a ruler. I'm not kidding you. One time, Louis was [pretending he was] the nun and Stephen was the student, and he said to Stephen, "Now if you don't behave yourself, I'll crack you across the knuckles." Stephen said, "Oh that's okay, go ahead and do it." While they're doing this, Sister Madonna was standing in the door. She took them into the library and did crack their knuckles. I don't know where she got the name Madonna because she was really strict. She didn't play around. She wouldn't get by with it today. That was so funny. I can still see the two of them in that classroom. Louis Pianalto also stands out in my mind because he and his brothers had an old Model T, and Louis always drove. It could be raining cats and dogs, and here they would come with the top down.

We got up and did our chores and then walked to school. For lunch, we took scrambled eggs and mustard on homemade bread, and fruit, if we had any. Sometimes leftover roast, cheese, stuff like that. At recess and lunchtime, we played hopscotch and ball. We had some swings, so we swung a lot. On the way home from school in the wintertime, we would ice skate on the ponds. One time we weren't home on time and my dad came up with the car and saw us skating on a pond. He made us get off that pond and we had to walk home. He drove right behind us. My father was very strict. But we did have a lot of fun with him. You toed the mark with him or else, but he was good to us.

After school, we had to carry in wood, feed the chickens, pick up the eggs, and bring in water for night. You didn't want to get up early in the morning and do it. We goofed off on Sunday afternoon. We could go play.

Our family Christmas tradition was to have a big dinner. We had pasta, chicken, vegetables, and fruitcake. That was our dinner. Santa came on Christmas morning, but there wasn't tons of gifts like you get today.

Our Easter traditions included a dinner with *risotto* [a rice dish], vegetables, and Easter bread.

The grape festivals were down in the school basement. Aunt Rose helped make pasta, so she got me involved. I'll never forget my first grape festival. I had to serve ice water at the tables. This man was sitting there eating, and I hit him on the head with a pitcher of ice water. I really soaked him. I felt awful. He was the nicest person and said, "Accidents do happen." That was my first experience of being a waitress.

I graduated from high school in 1941 and moved to St. Louis. My Uncle Dominic and Aunt Lena Aimerito lived there. They owned a tavern and restaurant. My oldest brother, John, was living with them and waiting on tables in the restaurant. He was due to go into service, so Uncle Dominic wanted me to come up and take John's place. But my uncle insisted that I also go to night school. I did, and got really smart. I took shorthand and typing. When I got good at it, Uncle Dominic said, "It's time for you to get out of here. Why don't you go find an office job?" So I went to work for Missouri Pacific [Railroad], in the freight office. I had fun. We were down by the river and the tracks were nearby. They were elevated, and whenever the war broke out we would always hang out the windows and the guys would wave at us and we would wave at them. It was our patriotic duty. Now you can see how ornery I was in my younger days!

I do want to tell you about a time when Louis Pianalto was in service and I was up here in St. Louis. He had stopped in to see my mom and dad back home in Tontitown. They said to Louis, "If you have a layover in St. Louis, maybe you could stop in and see Ann." They told him where I worked. I'll never forget this. It was after one o'clock, and I am at work, typing away, and all of a sudden I looked over to one side and I see this navy blue uniform. I looked up and it was Louis Pianalto. He had promised my mom and dad that he would stop in and see me, even if it was just for a minute. And it was just about a minute. He came in and said, "I told your folks I would stop in and see you. Here I am, I've got to go." He had to catch a train. Louis Pianalto was a good guy. There was some orneriness in him but he was a very good-hearted person.

My husband, Vincent Lazzari, and I went to grade school in Tontitown together. When we were little kids, I just didn't care for him. He teased me a lot. I went to Springdale High School after eighth grade, and he went to California to look for a job after he finished ninth grade. Later, he enlisted in the Air Force. In 1943 or 1944 I saw Vincent when we were both back home in Tontitown for a visit, and he said, "Why don't you give me your address?" We started corresponding. I saw him in Tontitown another time after that. Maybe we had one or two dates, that's about it. He got out of the service in April 1946, and in June, he came up to St. Louis to see me. He gave me an engagement ring on June 14. I was so happy. We got married in October. When they say fast engagements and fast marriages, we had it. They say that doesn't work, but we had the best marriage you could ever want. Everybody asked me, if you didn't like him in school, why did you marry? I fell in love with his uniform. I really fell for him. He was a super guy.

When we married, I didn't know how to cook, so Vincent cooked. One day I decided it was time that I start cooking. He said, "Well, okay, if you want to." So I did. The meat was raw, the potatoes were mush. Vincent finally said, "I think I better help you a little while longer." So he did, and I learned how to cook. Then when we had the little ones, he helped me. When they say "liberated woman," I was liberated from day one when I married Vincent, because he helped with everything. When the kids were born, he did all the laundry and all the grocery shopping, until I was able to do it again.

We've always lived in St. Louis. Vincent worked for Western Electric, then for Arsenal Map Company, then for Picker X-Ray. I kept working until we had our first child in 1948. Our children are Frances, Anthony, Margaret, Jim, and Paul.

     ANNA AIMERITO LAZZARI

Vince died in 1997. My life now involves a lot of church and volunteer work. Monday mornings, I tutor children who need help with
reading. I help with Red Cross blood drives. I belong to the Epiphany
Parish Ladies Guild. I make salads once a month for St. Patrick's, where
they feed the homeless.

I have three grandchildren. That's all I've got. All my girlfriends
have six or seven. But you know what? That's okay if that's all they're
going to give me, because they're real good kids.

Sister Teresina (Agnes) Lazzari

SISTER TERESINA (AGNES) LAZZARI

Sister Teresina (Agnes) Lazzari was born in 1915 in Tontitown, Arkansas, to Joseph and Josephine Lazzari Lazzari. She was 88 years old when she was interviewed in 2002.

My father was born in Italy. He was born up in the mountains in the Alps. He completed the fourth grade in school.

My mother was a Lazzari before she married. Her married name and her maiden name were the same. She was born in Italy. She completed the second grade.

My parents and my two older sisters, Angela and Mary, came to the United States in 1909. They came because they were quite poor, Papa's family especially. My mother's family was a little better off. There were so many people coming over because of the conditions [in Italy]. They were really having a hard time. The people that came [to America] made it sound like it was a real good way of living. I remember Mama working so hard. She didn't work that hard [in Italy]. She used to talk about taking the sheep into the higher mountains for grass.

Our first family home in Tontitown was on a farm north of the church about a mile and a half. My parents had five more children after they settled in Tontitown: John, James, Agnes, Francis, and Vincent. My father worked the farm, and was a carpenter by trade. When I was about eight years old, he built a great big house for the nine of us and then after a while, after all us children were grown and had left, he built another little bungalow closer to the church for him and Mama. The big house was quite a large thing and very, very plain. It had a downstairs, kind of a basement. I guess that's where the boys must have slept. The two girls and I slept together. Mama and Papa's room was real big.

Seems to me the kitchen was off Mama and Papa's bedroom. We had a Delco [generator]. We had electric lights. Electric lights were a lot nicer than having to light the lamps all the time, having to clean those mantles. We also had running water.

Papa was a good carpenter, but farming was what we made our living on. Our main crops were grapes and apples. We had lots of chickens and cows. I hoed the grapes, got the grass all cleaned out, tied the vines. We had a lot of fun. We started young, about seven or eight years old, I guess. No, we must have been older than that, I don't know, about ten or twelve. I remember when Papa was having trouble with his legs, he'd bring a stool along and he'd sit under a vine that had lots of grapes and cut the whole thing while sitting there.

I don't know if the Depression affected other people a whole lot, but we always had enough to eat because we had a big garden and lots of apples all through the winter. We ground our own corn to make cornmeal, and we made our own whole-wheat cereal. We never suffered. The only thing I remember missing was sugar. We bought sugar, flour, and other staples. We put sugar in the fruits that we canned. We did quite a bit of canning. We had calves, pigs, chickens. We kept milk and butter cold by putting them in the well. My mother made very good cheese.

We had a lot of fun as kids. When we picked apples, we'd get into apple fights. We had a lot of water fights. We used to go swimming in Elm Springs Creek on Sunday afternoons. Elm Springs was just about two miles from home. The Francos lived up on top of the hill and we lived down at the bottom, and we were together all the time on Sundays, almost always. They were like an extended family. One time we were in the creek in the water pretty deep and I was trying to dunk Tom [Franco]. I was really pushing him and his sister Rachel got a great big pole and she was going to hit me over the head. One night I went frog hunting with four boys and I tell you, they sure did some teasing. My brother and I and another fellow, a Bariola, got into a fight. I got in between them and tried to make them stop. I did not fight. But that's enough of that stuff!

My mother was a very gentle, quiet person. My parents were pretty strict, but I don't think I would call them disciplinarians. All Mama had to do was to say, "I'll send you to Papa, if you don't [do as you're told]."

But I don't ever remember being afraid of him, ever. Papa taught us a little bit of Italian at home. We'd get a penny, the one that did the best. And Papa liked to dance, but Mama and the rest of us never did dance.

I remember [Tontitown storekeeper] John Mollar. He never sat down. He walked all the time. He used to come over and see Papa quite a bit and he just pranced back and forth in the room all the time, instead of sitting down and visiting. I don't know what they talked about. None of us could hear. We were taught at that time not to listen in to grown-up talk.

I went in Mr. Mollar's store, lands yes! We'd go in and get candy. You'd get I don't know how many pieces for a penny at that time. He was kind; he'd give us some for nothing sometimes. He also played the organ at church.

When I was in first grade, I had a lay teacher. There was this one boy [in my class], Richard Roso. He was my pest throughout the school years. He was big at talking, and I never liked to talk. Anyway, the teacher said, "Now, if I put your name on the board, you are going to stay in at recess." Well, Richard talked, and talked again. His name got put on the board. When recess time came, we all went outside, and the teacher just let Richard go. I was just a little first grader, but I didn't feel it was right that he got to go out to play. And he was such a pest the rest of my school years. We were together through the tenth grade. He was all the time sitting in front of me and he'd turn back and write on my tablet and stuff. So I asked Sister privately—I had a Mercy nun as a teacher then—to please move me away from him. I just couldn't take all that pestering. But she didn't pay any attention to me. Then, one day she was putting a big geometry problem on the board, explaining it real fast. I was paying attention, but Richard was bothering me again. His hair was kind of long, so I caught him and pulled him way back over my desk, and the teacher turned around and caught me. She said, "Well, Agnes, and then you say you don't want to sit close to him." I was so mad at her I could have died. That was one time I was really mad at one of my teachers.

My best friends in school were Tom and Rachel Franco and Mary Louise Pianalto. When we were small, we played during recess, but in upper grades, some of us girls had to shine the church candlesticks a lot. At recess, we played steal sticks, red rover, jump rope, crack the whip, and all these ring games. Steal sticks is where there's a pile of sticks over here for that side and a pile over here for this side and one side would steal the other's and the one that got them all first would win. Crack the whip was dangerous. You'd hold hands in one big line and the last one's feet would go way up in the air. You went flying. We played baseball with handmade bats and balls. We played shinny. That's what they were playing at school one day when my brother got hit with a can, I think it was in the forehead. He was a little first grader and I must have been in third grade. I told Sister that they should not play that rough game on the playground, and they quit it. I influenced that.

Our school was a two-story frame building. The sisters lived upstairs and we went to school downstairs. I was in the fifth grade when the school burned in 1927. Some boys were playing with matches and paper in the gutter. We helped rebuild the new school—the school that's there now. We picked the rocks from our field [to use in the construction of the school]. I don't remember when it [the old school] burned, but by the next September they had the [new] school up already.

The community put on a lot of plays, and my sister Angela was in quite a few of them. Sometimes if they needed a little kid, I'd be in the play too. Otherwise I went to the neighbor's house right next to the hall. My classmate and I would study together until Angela got finished. But this is the important thing about that—we'd have a nickel. We'd go and buy a Milky Way candy bar, and then on the way home we'd nibble on it, as we walked in the dark.

I don't know that I experienced anti-Catholic prejudice from local people myself, but I know there was talk about it all the time. The Tontitown kids went to Springdale after the ninth grade to school. At first the Tontitown kids had a very rough time, I hear, but the Springdale schools were really happy to get the kids from Tontitown. I taught [in Tontitown] five years in the 1970s, and [the Springdale schools] just couldn't wait to get those kids from Tontitown because they were really good students.

Once, our family was caught making wine [without a license]. Mama was sitting on top of the cellar door—we had the wine down in the cellar—and [the officers] were trying to make her get up, because they wanted to get in and see what we had down there. Mama just would not move. She was right, but we kids said, "Get up, Mom, and let them in there." They took the barrels and just poured them all down the hill. All our hard work. We never sold wine. And we had the habit that, if anybody we knew would drink too much, we wouldn't give them but one glass.

I remember the 1934 tornado. Oh, it shook the house. I was scared. We just stayed in the house and prayed. It was in the night. The next day, the church was down. They rebuilt the church; my father made a lot of the beautiful woodwork in it.

Our family Christmas tradition was to go to Midnight Mass. At Easter time, we fasted for Lent, but did not dye Easter eggs. We kept the week religiously. During the grape festivals, we were so happy to get a few dimes and nickels to buy ice cream.

My first job away from home was at St. Scholastica [Convent, in Fort Smith]. My pay was God's generous love. It took a big knock for me to give in and become a nun. I guess the Lord couldn't get me. The Mercy Sisters wanted me because they were teaching [in Tontitown], and they were bound that I go to their community. I don't know, I just didn't want to go. Then my brother John died. He was four years older than me. He was going to Subiaco [Abbey Seminary, in Subiaco, Arkansas] to study for the priesthood. They took him to the hospital on Sunday night, and by Wednesday he was gone. They think it was a brain tumor. Whenever we got the call that John had died, I heard a voice saying, "You'd better take his place."

My older sister, Sister Rosaire [Mary], also became a nun. Our parents never did talk for or against our being religious. It was all our own decision. Sister Rosaire was an Ursuline. [The Ursuline Sisters were teaching in Tontitown] when she was in school and she used to stay with them quite a lot and do little chores for them. For Sister Rosaire, going to live with the Ursulines in Springfield, Illinois, was kind of like going home.

What does it entail to become a nun? Lots of things. Follow the Holy Rule. You're a postulant for six months, then you're a white novice for two years, and then you make your first vows. We didn't take many classes at that time. We mostly worked. We had big fields of vegetables. We even had cows and pigs and chickens. We used to put on big dinners and bazaars for money-making.

I really didn't decide to go into teaching. They decided for me. Once when I was in formation at the convent, Sister was sending somebody to work in the kitchen. That was going to be their job. So I said, "Sister, may I go to the kitchen, too?" She said, "You go on to [teach] school." Just like that. So I went to school and I'm glad now because I think teaching is more interesting. I got my degree in the summer months after teaching all year.

My first teaching assignment was in 1938, at St. John School in Fort Smith, an all-black school. You know what, I had never seen a black person, and I got two cold feet when I was told that I would be assigned there. But they were good kids. I was there nine years, the longest I was on any mission. Along with teaching, I did almost all the janitor work.

I also taught at St. Boniface School in Fort Smith, and in Fayetteville, Tontitown, Brinkley, and Moberly, Missouri. In 1987, I didn't really retire, I was rehired. Recycled. St. Scholastica needed somebody to run the laundry and they couldn't get anybody to run it. Most of them, I'm sure, had a good reason. But I couldn't run it either. I knew I couldn't. I was scared to death of machines. But Sister said, "Well, we'll just pray over it a while and see what happens." So I accepted it, and it was really hard work. We had to do the wash for the sisters, and we had quite a big infirmary then, and then we had the retreat center. We had all the wash from all those places. It was a hard job, but I made it. I didn't do too bad. For eight years I ran that, and now I'm working in the garden. That's my favorite.

One thing about [attending a Tontitown Polenta Smear] that really thrilled me was when Lenor Brunetti came up and said, "I want to show you something." He took out his wallet, and he had little picture of the Sacred Heart. It was really fragile, but it was still intact. He said, "Your brother James gave me this when we were in the Army in California in the Second World War." Lenor had treasured it all those years. Imagine!

FLOYD MAESTRI AND
LAVINIA MAESTRI ZULPO

Floyd Maestri was born in 1915 in Tontitown, Arkansas. His sister, Lavinia "Beanie" Maestri Zulpo, was born in 1922 in Tontitown. Their parents were Albano and Agnes Pierce Maestri. Floyd was 86 and Lavinia was 79 when they were interviewed together in 2002.

Floyd

Our father was born up in the northern part of Italy, near the Swiss Alps. He came to America around 1895 with his parents. When they first came to this country they went to Sunnyside, Arkansas. Our father was too young to really remember life at Sunnyside because he was between three and five years old. I don't think he remembered the trip from Sunnyside [to Northwest Arkansas] either.

Our mother's family came here from Missouri, near the Arkansas border. I think they moved to Arkansas because our grandfather Pierce was not a really religious man, but he had a lot of thought about that. He moved to Bentonville because a priest would come there once in awhile and say Mass. I don't know how long they stayed in Bentonville, but Grandfather found out they had a Catholic church in Tontitown. He wanted his family to be close to the church, so they moved to Tontitown.

Lavinia

It wasn't too long ago, I said, "Mother, when was the first time you saw Dad?" While her family was still living in Bentonville, our mother was sent to a Catholic school in Vinita, Oklahoma. They thought she

Floyd Maestri and Lavinia Maestri Zulpo

would get a better education there. She wasn't too acquainted with the girls in Tontitown, but she knew a few. She came home for the weekend one time. Tabby Pianalto, some of the Pozza girls, and Mother were in a crowd together. Tabby said, "I think Albano Maestri will be home this weekend. I'm going to marry him!" I suppose it was just like a joke or something. Mother said, "When Albano came home and I saw him, I went home and I said, 'Tabby said she is going to marry Albano, but I think I am.'" And sure enough, she did.

I think when Mother was a child, she worked in the home. One of her older sisters, Mae or Elsie, worked for some of the people in Bentonville as domestic help. Mother never did. She worked at home, but never did go into the fields. They had apple orchards. She had several brothers, so she always worked in the house, cooking and whatever. I know after she came back from Vinita, and probably before she was married, Mother did work at the apple drier [in Tontitown]. There was an apple drier on the Zulpo farm. There was another drier over by the Steele or Harmon communities, back in that area. She also worked there.

Mother was a good lady. She would do anything for anybody. When

Josephine Perona [Sister Xavier] went to become a nun, Mother sewed all of her underclothes. Sister Xavier would come down and take care of the kids while Mother sewed for her. She also sewed for Vicki and Pauline Baudino—aprons and hats they wore when they went to nurses training.

Floyd

Our Maestri grandparents had a log cabin just about a block southeast of the [Highway 412 and Barrington Road] intersection. Then they had property about a mile farther south of Tontitown on Barrington Road. They also had a log cabin there. I was born in that log cabin. I don't remember living there, but I do remember it later. The way I remember, it was probably just two rooms.

Our parents were married in February 1915, and I was born in December. They had five boys and four girls: Floyd, Genevieve, Grace, Lavinia, Stephen, Mary Frances, Paul, Frank, and Leslie.

At home we never spoke Italian. My mother did not speak Italian, but I'm sure she understood a lot of it. If you were around where the older people were, they always spoke Italian.

When I was a child, Dad was always out working. He didn't have any property, but he worked for different people. I'll tell you about my father. He had more patience than any person I ever knew in my life. I would go with him when he had a milk route, back when the Model T was still here. In those days, they didn't have too many roads. He went from farm to farm to farm, all over this part of the country, and picked up milk. We would go make a run on the milk route and we would have as many as two flat tires. I've seen him take one inner tube, patch another inner tube, fix the flat tire, and never say, "Damn it."

Lavinia

Frank Verucchi told me that Dad would get stuck in the mud, have to unload all the milk cans, pull the truck out of the mud, load the cans again, and never even say, "Darn." He had all the patience in the world. Dad never hollered at us kids either. I don't think he ever spanked one of us. But we jumped like nobody's business if he ever said, "Did you hear your mother?" We didn't jump when we heard her; we jumped when we heard him say, "Did you hear her?" He knew how to discipline; he just didn't have to holler.

Floyd

Dad could do anything. He was a mechanic, he was a carpenter. He could solder milk cans the best. Anything he wanted to do, he could do. I think if my father had an education he would have been a heck of a smart man.

Lavinia

He was a man of few words. There was never a math problem he couldn't solve. Even when the kids came home with algebra homework, he took care of that just like he did the reading, writing, and arithmetic.

We were lucky. Dad always had a pickup. He would take apples from here to the market in Tulsa, Oklahoma, and he would bring back oranges. We generally had food that other families didn't have because of the trucking. I remember one time when I was eating an apple, Taffy [Oliver Pianalto] said, "You just ate around that apple and threw it away, just threw the core away. I could have eaten that whole thing, and you threw it away."

Floyd

I remember taking the screen off of the window, scraping the snow away, and sprinkling a little feed or seed to make a little trap. We would prop up the screen with a stick, and tied to the stick was a string. We would wait until all of the little snow birds came in there to eat, then we pulled the string so the screen would fall and trap them. Then we went out to pick up the snow birds, and would sit down and pick them and clean them.

Lavinia

Mother canned everything. She canned vegetable soup. When I stepped out of the school—we came home for lunch because the school wasn't very far from our house—I could smell the soup. That was my favorite thing.

Every day about 3:00 p.m., she would take three eggs and make a three-egg noodle. Mix it up, roll it out, and cut it. She made soup with the noodles, tomatoes, onions, and some kind of seasoning. She made that soup every night for Dad.

Floyd

There was a fellow by the name of Carl Stearns—we called him Uncle Carl—and he and my father were buddies. Uncle Carl would butcher a calf, then put it in his pickup and go around and sell the meat for about 10 cents per pound. Daddy or Mother would always buy a piece of meat. Either they bought it, or he gave it to them.

We used to have a milk cow. I can't remember where we kept that cow but we used to put a rope around her neck and stake her out in different places, move her around so she could eat. I think my dad got mad and sold the cow because nobody wanted to milk her. He was tired of milking it himself. He had plenty of other stuff to do.

When we lived on the old Sabatini place, I remember a little building out in back of the house, and when they butchered meat, they used to hang stuff in there. They would build a fire in there to cure that meat. It was a smokehouse. They didn't go to a store and buy stuff to cure the meat. I think they used hickory wood to make it smoke like that. When they butchered, they took a certain part of the fat, ground it up, seasoned it with salt and pepper, and packed it in stone jars. Mother would reach down in that stone jar for her seasoning.

I don't think that we had chores to do like if we were living on a farm. I think maybe when it was gardening time we helped with the garden a little bit. We did chop wood and carry wood to the house. It was very minor compared to what some people had to do. When you washed clothes, you built a fire under a kettle to heat the water. You had a tub, and you put the clothes in there. You had homemade soap like lye soap, and you washed on a wash board.

Lavinia

We would start washing on the west side of the house. We would stop and eat dinner [the noon meal], then we would move our tubs and everything to the east side of the house so we would be in the shade again. We washed all day long. There were nine of us kids, and by the time we got all of those overalls washed, hung up and dried, and took in, it was a big job and took all day. And ironing was worse.

Floyd

When they first brought telephones here, people got together and put the posts up and brought a single wire all the way from Springdale to Tontitown. People would hook on to that and you waited your turn to talk on the phone. Just one person at a time could use the phone. Everybody paid so much for upkeep.

I started school when I was about seven years old. I never finished the eighth grade. We had a parish school in Tontitown, and that is where I went. I don't remember a lot about school because I wasn't a scholar. I never really did well in school. Today it is a must. In those days I don't believe it was a must, because I came a long way with no education in my life.

We had nuns as teachers. They were the Sisters of Mercy. I remember there was a Sister deChantal [Devine]. I remember her because she hit me a few times. I believe she hated boys. She would send us home, because she would get mad and couldn't handle us anymore. When we got home, they would send us right back to school. I didn't live too far from school, and I made a lot of trips.

I remember one time Sister deChantal got after me for something and she was going to get me. In those days they used to whack you. She waited until we kneeled down to say the Angelus [a short practice of devotion] at noon. She was walking up and down with her book in her hand, saying the Angelus. I could see out of the corner of my eye that she was coming. She reached over the desk to hit me. The desk tops back then lifted up, and the top was up. As Sister deChantal reached across to hit me, I slammed the desk top down, and she fell down. She didn't hit me, but she sure sent me home.

We never had much to play with at school. You didn't have many baseballs; you didn't have any mitts, for dang sure. What we did play the most was shinny. [To play shinny, first you] go out in the timber and pick a limb that looked something like a hockey stick. We had two lines, and you'd get in the middle and start hitting a tin can towards your line. Whoever got the can over their line got a point. Boy, that tin can was beat up and it was flying around. It got pretty sharp by the end of the game. A lot of people got scars. Just boys would play.

I remember very well when the school burned [in 1927]. It was a two-story building with drain pipes coming all the way down. We were out at recess. Somebody stuffed grass up in that pipe and lit it with a match. It made like a chimney. I guess when we went back into school, the grass caught the wooden shingles on fire, and the building burned. They had gotten everybody out, but our sister, Grace, turned around and sneaked back in because she had gotten a new coat and she didn't want it to burn. She made it back out.

It seemed like it didn't take very long from the time the old school burned down until the new one was built. I remember that Joe Pianalto was sort of the coordinator of the project, and kept everything going. The men of Tontitown built the new school themselves. I suppose they had a blueprint because they did a heck of a nice job on it. They made all of the cement blocks.

I don't remember my First Communion but I do remember Confirmation. You had a class in school—in those days they taught religion in the school because it was a Catholic school. The bishop came up from Little Rock to attend our Confirmation. That was something that stuck in your mind pretty good.

In the old church [that was destroyed by a tornado in 1934], Bill Fiori and I fired the furnace in the wintertime to break the chill in the church. It was down in the basement. It wasn't cemented or anything, just a hole dug there. Every Sunday morning we would get up early, early, early and light that furnace. Somebody brought wood, and we used to cut up old tires to get the fire started and really going good.

I also remember when the new church was built after the tornado blew the old church down. I did a lot of work on the new church. I helped make cement blocks. They made the blocks in the school basement. We would carry them out, stack them in the open, and let them dry. They made blocks for maybe a couple of years before they started to build the church. I think my father oversaw the building of that church.

I remember having Christmas at the old Sabatini place. Aunts and uncles would come, Mother's people. We always went out and cut a big Christmas tree. We would string popcorn on a string and hang it on the tree. We lit candles and let them burn on that tree. I just look back on that now, and if that tree would have caught on fire, it would have just burned the house down, that's all. It never happened to us.

On Halloween, we would maybe get somebody's toilet [outhouse] and put it on an old wagon. I was between 14 and 18 years old when we used to do this. I'll tell you the best thing. Frank Perona had that store building on the [southwest corner of Highway 412 and Barrington Road]. He had a two-holer toilet out in the back of the store. One Halloween we were going to turn [Perona's toilet] over. We had a long rope. We got the rope around the toilet, and come to find out Mrs. Perona was in the toilet, so we didn't get to turn it over. Memo Morsani's toilet was always the first one we turned over.

The first grape festival I remember was held on the [northwest corner of Highway 412 and Barrington Road]. They laid these tarps—we called them wagon sheets—over scaffolds to make a shade. Under this they sold hamburgers and soda pop. In later years, they sold ice cream. I remember they had a guy who used to come, he had a wrestling contest. Some farmer would come in and wrestle this guy. That was the carnival or entertainment.

Lavinia

From the time I can remember, our house was right across the street from the carnival. They had a little wheel—they would put little toys all around it—and you'd spin the wheel and whatever it stopped on is what you won. It cost you a nickel or so. Then they had rats. You put your money down on a color, they let the rats out, and whichever color hole the rat ran down, that's who won. I think White River Red [a well-known local carnival game operator] is the one who had both of those. Later they had the swings; they were over in Pete and Mary Fiori's yard. The kind of swings that went way out. It's a wonder we didn't all get killed.

Floyd

When we were kids, we would go out at night around the country. We used to go 'possum hunting in the woods. We used to go to all the Holy Roller meetings. We used to skate on all the ponds when they would freeze over.

Bill Fiori's father had a horse and wagon. We used to get in that wagon—we would pack a few little things—and go down to the old Sabatini place where there was a pond. It was full of grass and water moccasins. We would clean up a place, park the wagon, and set up our camp things. We stayed there all night. At night we walked that pond and caught catfish because you could feel them with your feet. We never did catch any snakes, but they were there.

I think Prohibition was a big deal for Tontitown, because a lot of people sold wine and grapejack, which is distilled wine. A lot of people, if they could get the sugar, would put sugar in the wine before they distilled it, because the sugar would give it a higher concentration of alcohol. I'm not sure they always made alcohol out of grapes, because there weren't that many grapes. Maybe they used corn, or maybe some kind of grain.

When I was a kid, there was always a little still sitting on our kitchen stove. Maybe the still held 10 gallons. This still had a cover that came off. They filled it up with mash and put the cover on. Next they would get a paste made of flour and water and use rags to seal the lid on top. On top of the lid there was a tube that came out, rounded down, and went into a barrel of water. The water would condense [the alcohol steam inside the tube], and the condensation was the alcohol.

I think Carl Stearns was the guy who had the outlet [for selling the alcohol]. Carl would take it down to Fayetteville. He was, I wouldn't say prominent, but he was well known. He knew all the politicians in the country and I think they bought the alcohol. I can't say for sure.

I've seen [officers] come a couple of times. They came here one time—I could have been between 15 and 18 years old—and they raided Tontitown. But some way or another [the Tontitown wine and whiskey makers] knew [about the raid beforehand]. They did catch some people. We had a keg of whiskey down in the cellar. Grandfather Pierce, when he got wind [of the raid], dug a hole in the wood pile out back, put the keg down in the hole, and covered the wood back. They hauled [the confiscated] wine to Fayetteville and dumped it at the courthouse. They put the barrels in the gutter, knocked the plugs out of the barrels and just let it run down the street. There were a lot of guys at the other end of the street, sipping up stuff.

When Bill Fiori and I, Arthur Fiori, and Bill's brother, Charlie, were kids, there were these older fellows who would stay up at the corner in Tontitown and heist the college kids on Saturday and sometimes Sunday. The college kids would come up looking for a little wine or a little something. We found out where these [older] guys were hiding a quart here and a quart there to be sold. They would hide it out, and then we would get it, and save up three or four quarts. We'd go up to the corner, and the college students would come up and ask us where they could get [some wine]. We'd say, "Oh yeah, we can get you some." Then we would go dig up where we had put it and sell three or four quarts. For a quart of wine, I think we would probably get a dollar. That was a lot of money. The grapejack was more expensive. I never sold that, I just sold wine. One time we sold maybe four or five quarts of wine and that was a lot of money in those days, $4 or $5. We knew what to do with the money. We went to Springdale and we spent it all on Three Kings cigarettes. We got home and we didn't know what the hell to do with the cigarettes, so we hid them under a culvert.

I never experienced any anti-Catholic prejudice. Maybe from city to city they might have had a little friction. When we were kids we would go down to Elm Springs to the creek there and go swimming in the summertime. Those boys down there ran us off a few times.

Tontitown was always very political. These guys when they were running for office always came to Tontitown, because it seemed like Tontitown had a lot to do with politics. When I was 18 years old, my father gave me a dollar and I went down to pay my poll tax. He asked me how I was going to sign up. Well, at one time there were no Republicans in this country. There was just one guy that I knew that was a Republican, and that was Rinaldo Morsani. He always got to serve on the election board and made a couple of bucks. I thought, "Gee, if I sign up as a Republican, I might get on that election board and make a couple of bucks." So when my dad asked how I was going to sign up, I said, "Republican." He said, "If you sign up Republican, don't come back." I mean, they were Democrats from way back. I don't know why Tontitown was so important to the politicians.

Lavinia

Well, it was because there were enough people in Tontitown, and they all voted the same way, so Tontitown could swing a local election. They mostly all voted. They were good citizens. Very few, maybe only two votes would be Republican. That might have been Kate Neal or Rinaldo Morsani.

Floyd

The first truck our father owned was a Model T Ford. He would get someone to drive it to haul grapes or some produce to Springdale because that is where the market or the buyers were. One time, I think Cel Cortiana was driving a truckload of grapes to Springdale. When they crossed the railroad tracks in Springdale to get across to the place where they were buying grapes, a train hit the truck. I'm thinking Joe Taldo was with Cel. Joe jumped off the truck and ran all the way back to Tontitown. I remember that really good, because that was quite an excitement in Tontitown.

When I left school, I did a lot of things. I worked out on a farm, I picked cowpeas. We would get maybe half a cent per pound. We would work half of the summer and make maybe $10. Frank and Carrie Perona had a canning factory [on the southwest corner of the intersection of Highway 412 and Barrington Road]. The cannery was just seasonal, but I worked most of the year for them. I did everything in that cannery. I fired the boilers. I cooked the food in the retorts. I hauled all the way to Fort Smith and Oklahoma City. We would work six days a week, 10 hours a day, and at the end of the week we got a check for $6—a dollar a day.

When I would go to Fort Smith to pick up produce or to Oklahoma City to deliver canned goods, either Frank or Carrie Perona was with me. To go to Fort Smith was a big trip, because all the way down it was gravel, not blacktop, not pea gravel, but pretty good-sized rock. We would leave early in the morning to get down to Fort Smith. We would drive there and load spinach. They would hand a bushel basket of spinach up to you and you would dump the basket [into the truck], then walk back and forth on [the spinach] to pack it. Then we would haul it back to the cannery. We had a place at the cannery, it had a cement floor, and we would back the truck up and unload all that spinach with pitch forks. We would wet it down, because if spinach gets wet, it gets kind of mushy. They would can it the next day.

To can the spinach, first they washed it. Next they blanched it. We had only one size of can, I think they called it a two-pound can. They cooked the cans of spinach in retorts. A retort is a sealed, thick metal vessel. They would put the cans in round crates, and then put the crates down in the retort. You would get the pressure up, and the heat, and cook it. Then you take the crates out of the retort and cool the cans in a cement trough. That trough was probably 100 feet long. When the first crate got down to the end of the trough, they took it out and sat it on the floor. That was an all day thing. If they canned 100 cases a day, that was a big day.

I worked for the Peronas up until the time I moved to California in 1938. I went in the service in March 1941 and came out of the service in June 1945. I was in an anti-tank company in the infantry. I spent one year in basic training and the rest of the time in the South Pacific.

I met my wife, Laura, at a dance in San Juan, California. We got married in Reno, Nevada. Later we were married in the church in Gilroy, California. We had one son, James Floyd. I have four grandchildren, and three great-grandchildren.

Lavinia

Well, I guess when my husband, Jack [Zulpo], and I got big enough to walk and talk, that's how we met. He just lived around the corner from us in Tontitown.

The summer I was 13, Dad took me to Springdale and I got on the bus and went to Tulsa. Rita Taldo and my sister Genevieve, who had married Bennie Bean, lived there. Rita met me at the bus station. I spent the first summer with a Jewish family taking care of two children. I got $3 a week and had a half day off on Sunday. Every summer I went to work in Tulsa. This was before I married, during the war. I worked at the telephone company, then at Douglas Aircraft. While I worked for the phone company, we were transferred out to Anaheim, California. I worked there until I got tonsillitis. The doctor told me I needed to have my tonsils out, so I caught a bus and came back home and had my tonsils out. After the surgery I went back to Tulsa. That's when I worked at Douglas Aircraft. I was a riveter.

I started dating Jack after he came back from the service, and I had come back home from Tulsa. I guess we dated almost a year before we married. When I married Jack, we had a liquor store in Tontitown. Our first store burned 10 days before we married. We had our home in the back of the liquor store. We had everything in the home, ready to move in, and the liquor store was in operation. Jack was taking his sister Mabel to high school. He got up and went to the liquor store to light the stove before taking her to school. When he got back, the liquor store was burned. It didn't take long to burn after it started. Whiskey burns like gas.

We then moved into a little two-room house that Beato [B.] and Violet Ardemagni owned. Jack built a temporary liquor store, a little one-room store, and operated out of that until we rebuilt the store exactly like it was before it burned.

We had five children. Our first child was James Roger. He died at birth. Then we had Mary Ann, Joe, Mark, and Bill. I have eight granddaughters, and three great-grandchildren.

Floyd

I spent over 62 years in California. I came back to Tontitown because my mother was living with Lavinia, and I thought maybe if I stayed with them, I could be some help to take care of Mother, and to give Lavinia a little bit of free time. After Mother died, I went back to California but I didn't stay there too long.

Lavinia

Mother was nearly 105 years old when she died. When Floyd left after she died, I said, "Floyd, if you want to come back, just come back home." It wasn't quite two weeks and the phone rang. It was Floyd, and he said, "Guess where I am. I'm in Albuquerque, New Mexico, on my way back to Tontitown."

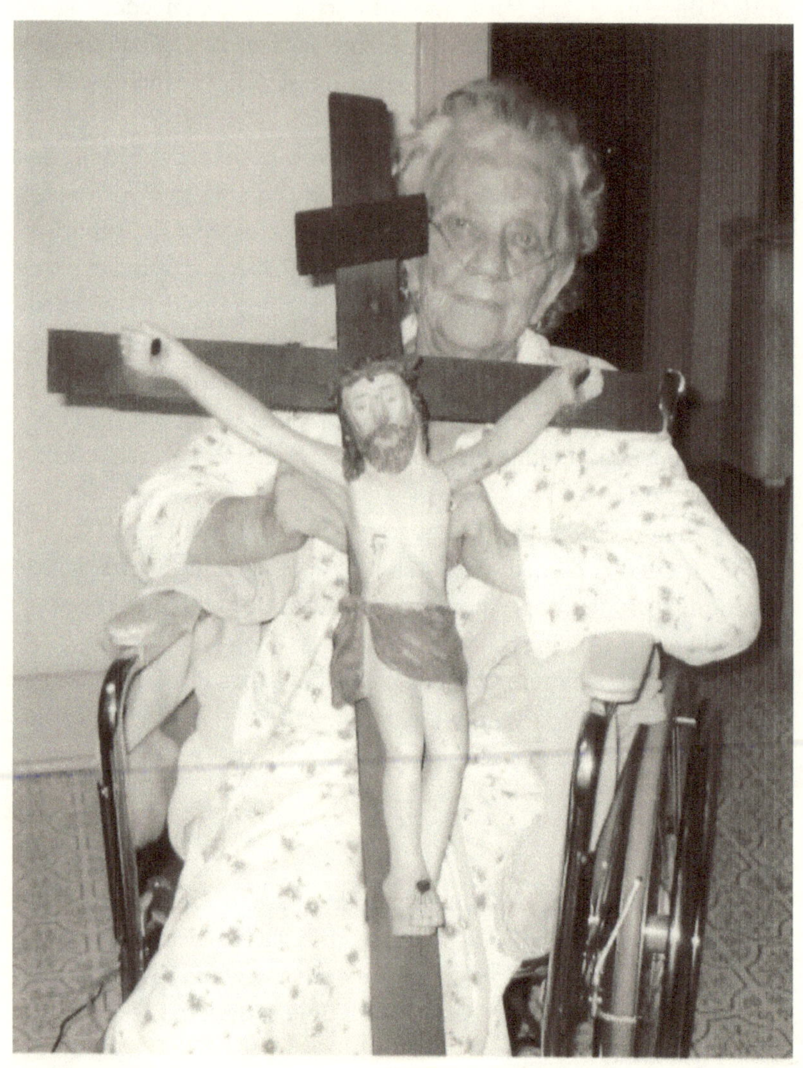

Eileen Cigainero Mantegani

EILEEN CIGAINERO MANTEGANI

Eileen Cigainero Mantegani was born in 1914 in Tontitown, Arkansas, to Giuseppe (Joe) and Iginia Pianalto Cigainero. She was 88 years old when she was interviewed in 2003.

My paternal grandfather was Giovanni Batista Cigainero. He came to America in 1883. He was a woodcarver. I remember him—he had a long white beard.

My paternal grandmother's maiden name was Metilde Tondolo. She also came to America in 1883. Their first home was in Paradise Ridge, Tennessee. They then moved to Texarkana, Arkansas, around 1893.

My maternal grandfather was Domenic Pianalto. He was a farmer. They came from Italy to Sunnyside, Arkansas. My grandmother's maiden name was Catherine Penzo. She died at Sunnyside in childbirth.

[Domenic and his four children were among the original settlers of Tontitown in 1898]. Domenic then returned to Italy and married Rosa Taldo. He then came back to America and the children he had left [in Tontitown].

My father was born in Italy in 1878. He didn't go to school. He was a child when his family came to America. He told me that when they were coming across the ocean, his hat blew off. He said, "Just leave it and let the birds build a nest in it."

My mother was born in 1894 in Italy. She had some schooling, taught by Miss Brady [Bernadette Brady, Tontitown's first schoolteacher]. At 12 or 13 years of age, my mother worked in Eureka Springs as a house-keeper and cared for kids and cooked for a family named Faulkner. She had to work to help support her younger brothers and sisters.

My mother's special skills were as a quilter, and she was also a midwife with her sister Linda [Erlinda Pianalto Haney] and Mrs. Virginia Morsani.

I was born in Texarkana, Arkansas. We moved to Tontitown when I was about nine months old. My father built our house and the barn and everything around it. He was a master carpenter. Papa could look at a window or door, cut it out without measuring it, and it would fit perfect. He was also a woodcarver. I watched him carve a little squirrel out of peach stone with a pocket knife.

There was five girls in our family: Catherine, myself, Alma, Madeline, and Lillian. We fought like a bunch of boys. Madeline had a temper. One time she threw a pair of scissors and hit Catherine in the eye. One time she pushed Lillian into the barbed wire fence. Once, Papa made a two-wheeled cart with a handle on it for us to play with. We blindfolded Catherine and put her in it. I don't know whose idea it was, whether it was Madeline's, or Alma's. But anyway, we were going and going, and got to the edge of the farm almost. There was a hill there, just about straight down. When we got there, we just turned the cart around and let it go. We could have killed her. Did we get a spanking! Mom was the disciplinarian in the family. Papa never did lay a hand on us. The only thing he ever said was, "Dad blame it! Can't you all mind?"

All five of us girls would follow each other up the lane to bring the cow home to milk. I chopped wood, and built fires and baked bread. Got dinner ready or supper ready for when the family would get home from picking grapes. We would have to go to pick up leaves to bed the cattle or we would get out and hoe in the garden, or clean up the yard, or work in the house washing and ironing. It took the whole day to do different jobs. We never did have much time to play at home. We did play marbles.

We did a lot of canning. That's all we lived on in the wintertime, was canned goods. We grew it all out in the garden. We always had cows and chickens, so we had plenty of milk and eggs. When you have bread, eggs, milk, a garden, and a cellar full of canned stuff, you don't really need to go hungry. A typical breakfast was coffee, milk, and bread. For supper we usually had leftovers. Papa would eat Post Toasties and milk for supper. We had rabbit and squirrel. Papa would hunt and kill

     EILEEN CIGAINERO MANTEGANI

only one at a time. He said more than that would go to waste, and you should leave one for tomorrow.

When my mother served spaghetti, she made it that day. She made one round and then she would roll it up and cut it, just like that. I'd say, "Boy, she'll cut her fingers off." But she never did hit her fingers; she had done it so long. We got the flour, sugar, and other staples at the store. We would go with the wagon and mules. The mules were named Ping, Bill, Jack, and Jew.

We had worlds of flowers. My mother would have us walking to church practically every Saturday with a big armful of flowers to put on the altar. She had beautiful gladiolas, dahlias, and just all kinds.

I had nuns as teachers. Two I remember are Sister Lucina and Sister deChantal [Devine]. At recess and at noon, Sister deChantal had four of us girls go to the church and work there. There was Clara Pellin, Mary Louise Pianalto, Agnes Lazzari, and me. There was one more girl, but I can't remember who she was. We would clean the candleholders and dust the altar. There was no play at recess for us. We didn't mind. I really enjoyed working up at the church. It was so peaceful.

For lunch I took bread and jelly. Agatha Morsani and her sisters would take bread and greens so sometimes we would trade sandwiches. My best friend in school was Helen Verucchi. She always took up for me.

When I was in the eighth grade, I had a goiter and had to go to Springfield, [Missouri] to have surgery. I never did finish school. I attended the school that burned [in 1927]. I can tell you what I heard [about how the fire started]. I don't know that it was true. Several of the boys, after eating lunch, stuffed paper up the drain pipe and set it on fire.

I really don't remember when we got electricity. I remember when the Manteganis got their radio. They had a Delco [battery] for their electricity. My father-in-law, Cesare Mantegani, had an old radio by his rocking chair. He would sit there and listen to the overseas radio.

My first memory of the grape festival is getting the ice cream at five cents a cone. It was there at the old [Smith] school [on the northwest corner of Highway 412 and Barrington Road]. There was a grape juice stand there, but I don't remember them having spaghetti.

At Christmastime, we had a Christmas tree and presents. Santa Claus came on Christmas morning. Christmas dinner was usually fried chicken and spaghetti. At Easter during Holy Week, we went to all the services. We had to walk, but we went to all of them—Holy Thursday, Good Friday, Holy Saturday. We would fast. We also dyed Easter eggs. We always had High Mass on Sunday. It was in Latin, we couldn't understand it, but it was pretty. I always did like the Latin Mass.

I met my husband, Gildo Mantegani, at school. He would come over and we would do homework together. We walked to dances at different homes on weekends. We got married in 1936. We were married in the basement of the school, because the church had been destroyed by a tornado [in 1934]. For our wedding dinner, my mother-in-law, Rosa Mantegani, did most of the cooking. We had risotto, and I think there was spaghetti, and salad. Afterward, we had a dance at the [Mantegani] Luncheonette. They had an open dance hall behind the Luncheonette— it was just a floor with a rail around it. They danced until way after midnight. But I was too tired to dance. I couldn't pick up my feet anymore.

My father-in-law, Cesare Mantegani, built the Luncheonette. They had a bocce court and a beer joint there, and a baseball field for years and years. I worked at the Luncheonette a little. Gildo's sisters and their husbands all worked there, so they had plenty of people.

When the Manteganis built their winery, Gildo had to run it. We sold a lot of wine. We took orders clear down to DeQueen, Arkansas. During the 1930s and 1940s, we would take wine and whiskey to Tulsa, Oklahoma, to some of the upper crust in society there.

When we were first married, we lived in a little one-room house next to the Luncheonette. Later we moved to the home I live in now, the Mantegani homeplace, so it would be easier for Gildo to take care of the vineyard. This house was built when Gildo was about 10 years old. The Manteganis made the blocks themselves. They had the forms, set them out to dry, and then when they were dry, they started the building.

Gildo and I had five children: J. C., Barbara, Gillie Ray, Zita, and Irvin. We have 18 grandchildren, and 30 great-grandchildren.

That picture of the Blessed Virgin and the Cross over there on the wall—that picture belonged to Father Bandini [the founder of Tontitown]. It was in the stairway in the old rectory. He told Miss Zelinda [Bastianelli, his housekeeper] that when he died, he wanted that picture to go to Joe Cigainero. So that's what Miss Zelinda did. She gave it to Papa. I love that picture.

    EILEEN CIGAINERO MANTEGANI

HELEN CRANE MORSANI

*Helen Crane Morsani was born in 1910 in Bristow,
Oklahoma, the daughter of Charles and Minnie Crane.
Her husband, Amerigo Morsani, was born in 1906
in Tontitown, Arkansas, to Emedio and Adele Papili
Morsani. Amerigo Morsani died in 1998.*

*Helen Morsani was 93 years old when she was inter-
viewed in 2003. Mrs. Morsani's daughter, Patricia
Harris, and nieces, Lillian Houghland and Earlene
Lewis, were present during the interview. Some of their
comments are included here.*

My husband was Amerigo Morsani. His parents were Emedio
Morsani and Adele Papili Morsani. In Italy, Emedio and his first wife
had two sons, Camillo and Memo. Emedio's wife died in childbirth.
Emedio, Camillo, and Memo then came to America, where Emedio
married Adele Papili [in Tontitown].

Adele was a child [in Italy] when her mother passed away. Her
father, Patricio Papili, then married a woman named Annunciata. They
had two children, Emily and Anthony. The family struggled financially,
so Adele was sent to live in a convent. When she was 15 years old, Adele
left the convent and came to America with her family.

Emedio was a farmer and a carpenter. He worked on the buildings
in Fayetteville a lot. I've heard Amerigo talk about taking his father in
the wagon to Fayetteville to work.

After the Papilis came to Tontitown, Adele worked at a hotel in
Monte Ne, just outside of Rogers. It was a resort community. There
was a family there that she worked for too.

I never heard Adele talk about how life in Tontitown when she

Helen Crane Morsani

first arrived there. I couldn't understand her, anyway. She never spoke English. She could understand it, but she never could speak it.

The Papili and Morsani families traveled on the same boat from Italy to America. [Both families were bound for Sunnyside.] Adele helped take care of Memo and Camillo Morsani on the boat coming over. And when Memo and Camillo were little, they stayed with the Papili family while their family was working.

 HELEN CRANE MORSANI

The Papilis and Morsanis were among those families who left Sunnyside [in 1898] to settle in Tontitown. [When they first arrived in Tontitown,] the Papilis lived in a barn along with the Morsanis. There were four or five families [living] in that barn while they built their houses. Adele Papili and Virginia Morsani took care of all the kids while the men were working.

The Papilis and Morsanis built their homes across the road from each other. They lived about a mile west of the intersection of Highway 412 and Barrington Road.

Clementina was the first child born to Emedio and Adele Papili Morsani. Amerigo was the second, followed by Anna, Candida, Elizabeth, and Agatha. Amerigo's name was chosen because he was their first male child born in America. That was important to them.

My family moved to Elm Springs, Arkansas, from Bristow, Oklahoma, when I was 10 years old. I met Amerigo when my friends and I came over to Tontitown. We went there to the dances which were held in the old school. Amerigo and I liked to dance together.

Before we were married, Amerigo had a racer that he stripped down to the bare necessities. There was just room for two in that car. We took it out on the main road. Anything was legal then. We had a lot of fun in that racer.

Amerigo and I were married in 1926. Six months later, we moved to Detroit, Michigan. Amerigo's cousin, Claude Morsani, lived there. Amerigo went to work as a carpenter. Our first three children, Helen Patricia, Leon Frank, and Bruce Paul, were born in Detroit.

We moved back to Arkansas in 1935. Then we moved to Oklahoma, where Amerigo had a job in Tulsa as an apprentice welder. In 1944, we had another child, Timothy Poe. In about 1945, we bought a farm in Talala, Oklahoma, where we raised cattle and wheat. Amerigo was working as a welder, and he would be gone for weeks at a time. The boys and I did the work [on the farm]. One year—it's hard for anybody to believe—I sowed 35 acres of wheat by myself. All the boys were gone. I just went out there and started the tractor and got busy.

I remember the cellar in the Morsani home. There were two levels, one in which they kept the wine, and one in which they kept the milk. I remember the salami and the onions and garlic hanging on the wall. The aroma was just wonderful.

Comments from Patricia, Lillian, and Earlene

Nonno and Nonna [Emedio and Adele Papili Morsani] had a great big stone oven in a building out back. It looked like just a mound of dirt with a door in it. The floor of the oven was about [Adele's] waist high. She was short. She made bread [in the oven]. They built a fire in the oven, and then they would brush it all out after the stones were hot. After Nonna baked the bread, she set it in the window to cool. And oh, we wanted a taste of that hot bread so bad. We would go and reach for it, and she would slap our hands, and chatter something in Italian. She was saying, "No, no, it's not good for you when it's hot. You wait until it's cool."

One time we were all at the Morsani house for Easter. They opened out this big table and put a board on it. They poured polenta all over this board. The chairs were seated around the table and they drew lines in the polenta with a knife in front of each chair. In the front of each place setting was a piece of chicken cooked in spaghetti sauce. We all ate off the same board—no plates. They gave us a spoon and we would just eat, eat, eat.

EARL MUSSINO

*Earl Mussino was born in 1926 in Gowen, Oklahoma,
to Domenic (Dick) and Allesandra (Alice) Maria Ceola
Mussino. He was 76 years old when he was interviewed
in 2002.*

My maternal grandfather was Santo Ceola. Before he died, he told
my grandmother, Maria, that he wanted her to marry his brother so
he could help with the kids. The brother was also called Santo.[1] They
lived in Sunnyside [before coming to Tontitown with the original group
of settlers in 1898]. The only thing I heard my grandmother say about
Sunnyside was all the mosquitoes they had there.

My grandmother [Maria] came from Italy with three children: Lucy,
Mary, and my mother, Allesandra. Fausta [another daughter] was born
in America. Grandmother then married the brother, Santo, and they
had eight children: Victor [Hi], Fred, Julia [Jay], Cecilia [Chill], Rinaldo
[Nel], Vicki and Genevieve. They also had Dick, who died. We always
referred to him as "poor Dick."

I was born in Gowen, Oklahoma. My dad was a coal miner there.
He was born in northern Italy. He came to America as an adult.

When we were living in Gowen, I remember my dad coming home
at night, black as the ace of spades, from going down into the mines. He
was all black, and he had a little carbide light on his cap. Most of the min-
ers there were Italians; at least the ones that visited my dad were Italian.

Dad made something called "chock" in Oklahoma. Chock is like
home brew, only with different malt. He never sold any of it. He used

---

1. Research by Jan McQuade Sturm shows that Maria Ceola's first husband was
Domenico Ceola. He died, and Maria later married Domenico's brother, Santo.
Jan McQuade Sturm, "The Original Settlers of Tontitown," *So Big, This Little Place*
(Tontitown Historical Museum, 2009), 149.

Earl Mussino

to give it to some of his buddies in the coal mine, but they caught him. Somebody turned him in, and they took him to the penitentiary at McAlister. I will never forget when Uncle Cel Cortiana took my mother, my brother, and me to see him. We got in there, and they opened this big hall door. They had a bugler, and he asked for "Domenic Mussino, up front," and here he came wearing prison clothes. He stayed in there three or four days. Uncle Cel got him out.

Dad continued making chock after he got out of jail. Then a neighbor, Mr. Frye, turned him in. They busted all his bottles, and the 12-gallon crock that he made it in. Then they went in the house with a stick and knocked all over the floor to see if he had a trap door in the floor [where he might be hiding the chock].

We moved to Tontitown when I was eight years old. My mother wanted to come back here; her family was all here. So my dad bought a 1926 Model T. We were coming over the mountains between here and Fort Smith, and the radiator started smoking along about Mount Gaylor. My dad said to my mother, "Alice, get out and put a rock under the tire." It wasn't hard to find a rock. There happened to be a little puddle of water nearby. Dad got a Prince Albert tobacco can, broke the lid off, dipped water from the puddle, poured the water into the radiator, and we made it to Tontitown.

The first memory I have of Tontitown was when we went to pick strawberries with Dad. We went down to Taldo's in a truck; I guess it was a Model A. It had a big bed on it, and we would all get on that bed, and go from our place to Taldo's place to pick strawberries. I would get one of those little boxes from my Dad and pick berries. When it was full, I would give it to him and he would put it in the big crate. The crate would hold 12 of those little boxes.

Our house had four rooms, a kitchen, a small dining room, and two bedrooms. It wasn't the best, but it wasn't the worst. I must have been 12 or 14 years old when electricity came through. Everything was better after electricity. When the telephone came out here, we were on a 12-party line. When you picked it up you could hear someone else talk, so it was hard to use sometimes. You know, it's human nature—when you pick it up [and hear someone talking], you aren't going to just throw the phone back down. There is no use lying about it.

My father spent most of his time in the Veterans Hospital in Fayetteville. They thought he had black lung from the coal mine, so he was in and out of the hospital a lot. He had a job with my uncle, Cel Cortiana. They had a big power line in Oklahoma and they were cleaning 50 feet on each side with nippers, blades, and hand tools. When my father got sick, Uncle Cel took me in his place. I was young, 13 years old, but I worked. I wasn't the main provider for the family; my dad drew a small disability check, about $40 a month, from the Army. My father was in World War I, but he never did talk much about it, and I never did ask him. He never did like war, I know that.

After we moved to Tontitown, Dad didn't make home brew much. He just made about 50 gallons of wine for our home use. There were several people in Tontitown in those days that made wine, beer, or whiskey, but I won't say their names. It was sort of a tradition. It was just sold to people coming by. They never did deliver it. It was very hard back then, and some people sold that stuff to feed their families.

My mother didn't work outside of the home. She just cooked—spaghetti, ravioli, homemade bread. She was a good cook. I really liked her cream pies. My mother made a lot of polenta. Polenta is cornmeal and water mixed up and cooked. She would make sauce, what we call umido, to go on top of the polenta. She would put in a pinch of this and a pinch of that. That is what makes it. What she put in it I don't know, but I know all the Italians had good umido.

During the Depression, we always had plenty to eat, because we killed rabbits and squirrels. We would kill a pig, and we always had big gardens. We had a couple of cows, mostly to make cheese and to have milk. We sold a little milk. Albano Maestri used to pick up the milk.

I went to school in Tontitown. I had Sister Adrian [McGrath] as a teacher. I really liked her, but she was pretty strict. During recess, I played marbles with my cousin, Gordon Cortiana. We would make a ring and put the marbles in there. He and I were pretty good so we would clean up the whole ring. We also played bocce, which is something like horseshoes. It has eight balls, and a little ball, and you try to get close to the little ball. Some of the big balls are red and some are black, and there are eight of them to a set, and you try to get your ball close to the little ball.

When I was in seventh grade, Gordon and I jumped out the school's cloak room window. Sister Agnes [La Bounty] was keeping us in after school because we had been a little naughty. We went to the cloak room and opened the window to jump out. It was a pretty high jump too. We got caught, and Sister Agnes had a little yellow stick, and she whacked me with that.

After that, I never went back to school. Gordon and I went to the wheat harvest in Kansas. We hitchhiked. I forget what part of Kansas we landed in, but we tried to find the first place that would give us a job. We met Gordon's twin brother, Gilbert, and Jimmy Fiori. We went into a restaurant to eat. None of us had any money. Gilbert, he was a booger. He said, "We will just put the bill under the bun and eat it with our hamburger." That's what we did, we ate the ticket. We couldn't taste the ticket because we were so hungry.

After the wheat harvest, I came back home. I helped my dad some and I worked for Mano Gasparotto a lot. He built a chicken house, and made me a deal to raise chickens for him. I never did make a dime. The gas was terribly high to heat the houses.

I worked with Uncle Cel on that one job clearing brush and briars out from under the big power lines in Oklahoma, and then I went to work in the winery for John Granata, and then I bought a new tractor and I worked in the vineyard. Then I bought a new pick-up. It was all gravel roads back then, and there weren't very many automobiles. I remember driving around out in the fields trying to learn how to drive. One day Mary Granata asked me to go pick up the Bastianelli sisters. That was the first time I was on the highway driving, but there were very few cars back then, so it didn't matter.

I remember when they were rebuilding the church that had been destroyed by the tornado [in 1934]. I didn't work on the church like some of the men around here did. I know they got all the gravel and stuff down here by the Osage and Illinois creeks.

During grape harvest time, my brother and I used to go out by the road and hold up a basket of grapes trying to sell them to make some money to go to the Concord Theater in Springdale. We especially liked the western shows. We used to have a show here in Tontitown during the grape festival. Cap Tiller [a man who owned a traveling picture show] would come and show western movies.

I can remember when we had turtle races during the grape festival, and I remember Virgil Fiori and Oliver Pianalto boxing. I don't remember any carnival. I remember the pie contest. Whoever could eat a whole pie the fastest would get a prize. My brother won. Boy, he had pie all over his hair. My cousin, Junior Pianalto, and I ran the pop stand for four or five years. Pepsi Cola or Coke is what we had. I think we sold them for a nickel. I can't remember them having hamburgers, but they did have candy and potato chips. Oh sure, they had spaghetti at the grape festival. We had dances. Virgil Verucchi was the bouncer. He was always throwing out the Elm Springs guys. They couldn't get along with the Tontitown boys.

When John Granata opened his winery, it was down in his cellar. If I remember right, he had about eight barrels. His two daughters, Alice and Dolly, and my brother, Joe, and I were working there. John wanted to make some blackberry wine, so we went to pick some blackberries. In the morning, before we went to pick the blackberries, my dad would get a sock and soak it in coal oil and put it next to our shoe with a rubber band around it to keep the chiggers from eating us up. That year I think we picked enough blackberries for John to make a barrel of wine.

John sold his wine locally. Then he added on to the winery. He got the big round vats and the crusher and he made apple wine and grape wine, but not very much blackberry wine. Then he added on again, and then he started delivering farther south. He sold a lot of wine.

He had quite a few workers during the time of the harvest. It seems like there was about eight or nine people working. When I used to filter the wine, it would go to the women to put the labels on. There were about four or five on the assembly line. He had a pretty big operation.

Bill Fiori and I had the job of fortifying the wine—mixing brandy into the big vats of wine to raise the alcohol content. The brandy was 120 proof. The revenue man was there as we poured the brandy in the vat. The revenue man would put the tester in there and see what the percentage of alcohol was. Bill said, "You watch the revenue man, so we can sneak some of this brandy." Gilbert Cortiana got a three-gallon bucket, and he stuck it under there and got a bucket of brandy. The revenue man didn't see that, I'll tell you for sure. We were having a lot of dances in the school basement and other places, so we took our brandy to the dances.

I guess I worked at the Granata Winery for two or three years. When I was 16, I went to work setting ceramic tile in Pryor, Oklahoma. Bill Fiori had a two-seated Chevrolet and some of us would drive to Pryor to work. We would go to Pryor on Monday and come back on Saturday. It was open range then, and one morning it was foggy and we hit a cow on the way, because we couldn't see.

I worked in Pryor until I was 18, when I got my greetings from Uncle Sam during World War II. Two days after I was 18, I had to go to Little Rock to get my examination. That was in 1944. I spent 12 weeks in basic training in Texas. On a bus coming back, I looked out and saw [a sign that said] Fayetteville. I though, Oh boy, I will be in Fayetteville [close to Tontitown] for a while, but when I looked again it was Fayetteville, North Carolina. I was very disappointed. Then they shipped me right

     EARL MUSSINO

to the *George Washington,* the boat to take me to France. It took 12 days on that big boat. It was just putt, putt, putt.

I was in the infantry. I was on the front the whole time I was in the service, except for one time when I got a three-day pass. I was free to go wherever I wanted, and I goofed up. I had gotten a letter from my dad, and he wanted me to go see his brother in Italy, because I was on the border of Italy. But I had a good friend who wanted to go to Paris. I was young, just 18, and so I chose to go to Paris with my friend. I regretted it all my life.

During combat, you have the first scout, second scout, and then your company. They made me first scout. When we first relieved the 45th Division, we got off the truck in a big open field. You could hear the mortar shells. I was out front, I was the decoy, the one to get shot first and let the rest know to hit the ground. When I got in the timber, I could smell something rotten. I looked to my left and there were two dead Germans. I looked to my right and there was one. The first scout was not a good thing to be.

I was in the Battle of the Bulge. I will never forget that. It was in wintertime, in January. There was snow, a lot of snow. The United States sent over a lot of real good, heavy, white clothes with fur to keep you warm. In the Battle of the Bulge, the Germans had surrounded us and they got our clothes before we could get them on. We could see them wearing our clothes. That Battle of the Bulge was pretty bad, but all over there it was pretty bad. The Battle of the Bulge was our last stand. The Germans put up a battle.

We helped take [liberate] several villages. When you go into a village, it's like a desert. You see no one. Then after you take the village, in a couple of days, they start coming out of the cellars and back from the fields. When the Germans surrendered, my buddies and I took a lot of prisoners with a white handkerchief.

I have a lot of memories about the war—pretty scary, a lot of them. One time my buddy and I were in a fire storm, and we were taking turns guarding. There was a big tree about 200 or 300 yards away, and that tree walked. Now, don't tell me that a tree won't walk. The next morning, we put a peg there where that tree was, and it still walked. I bet we put 500 bullets in that tree. Anytime anybody tells me a tree won't walk, I know better. It will walk.

One of my best buddies was a Frenchman. He was kneeling down, and I was kneeling down and firing. I told him, "Let's go," and I gave him a nudge and he fell over dead. I had a canteen on my hip and it was hurting me, so I put it in my backpack. In a little bit, I felt something I thought it was blood, and when I got up, it was water. They had hit my canteen, and water was coming out of it.

While I was in the service, I really kept in touch with my mother. She used to write letters to me, and Bill Fiori wrote me letters. One time I got a package from my wife. We were not yet married, but she sent me a box of cookies. They were all crumbs when they got to me, but they were good.

I stayed in the Army about 10 months after the war was over. I didn't have enough points. You see, back then they went by points. You had some points if you were married, more points if you had children, and so forth. Well I didn't have any points, so I stayed a little longer than some of the other guys.

When I discharged in 1946, I came back home to Tontitown. I got off the bus in Springdale, and a cop came to me and asked me where I lived. I told him Tontitown, and he said, "Is anyone coming after you?" I told him no. He said, "I'll drive you home." I said, "Thanks a million, but I want to walk it." He said, "You got a pretty heavy pack there." I said, "I know, but I want to walk." I was proud to be home, so I wanted to walk.

It was about 5:30 a.m. when I passed the old Mantegani Luncheonette where Bill and Fern Fiori lived and ran the café. Bill just happened to look out the window and saw me. He ran out to the road in his shorts. Right there in the road, he grabbed me around the neck and we hugged each other. Boy, that was great. Fern fixed me a breakfast of bacon, ham, toast, and eggs. I mean to tell you, it was something. It was really a wonderful feeling. It's something that I will never forget.

My wife's name is Beatrice Taldo Mussino. She grew up in Tontitown. I have known her almost all my life. We started dating after I got home from the service. I used to go down to her house in the evening to peek in the window to see if I could see her. Sometimes her uncle, Dick Taldo, would come outside and catch me. I'd say, "Dick, you got a match?" I had to tell him something to throw him off. I don't know how many matches I got from him.

I had a horse. Beatrice and I would go riding on horseback, no

     EARL MUSSINO

saddle. Her mother let Beatrice go with me because I was Italian and a Catholic. If I had been an outsider, she wouldn't have let Beatrice go. We started going to dances with our friends in Tontitown, then started going steady, and finally I asked her to marry me. We got married in 1948. We had a big wedding, lots of people, lots of food—chicken, spaghetti, salad, and homemade bread—and lots of dancing.

My mother-in-law, Dora Taldo, and her friends prepared our wedding dinner. They were in the school basement cleaning chickens for the dinner when Mano Gasparotto came down there. He had just bought a chicken picker machine [to clean chickens]. He told the women that he would take care of that; they didn't have to boil the water to pick the chickens. Mano said to me, "Go get those chickens and take them up to my place. We'll use the chicken picker machine." I got about 10 big chickens and took them to Mano, but he didn't know how to use the machine. He started the machine, and the leg went that way, the wing went that way, the breast went that way. He tore those chickens to pieces. The women were kind of teed off. I tell you, Mano was something else.

When I came back from the Army I went to work raising chickens for Mano. I was drawing my $100 a month from the government. I wasn't making any money raising chickens, and Mano wanted to build the Venesian Inn restaurant, so Bill Fiori, Eugene Pianalto, and I helped him build it. He also built a little service station and a motel. We worked there quite a bit. When Beatrice and I got married, we lived in one of Mano's cabins for a time, and she worked in Springdale, at Rowland's Clothing Store. Then Mano wanted her to be a waitress in the evening. We didn't have any money, so she would work there in the evenings to try to make a little money. She came home one evening with a fifty-dollar bill. Someone from McIlroy Bank in Fayetteville gave it to her for a tip. She told them it was too much, but he made her take it. A fifty-dollar tip was really something back then.

My brother, Joe, and I borrowed some money and built a chicken house so we could raise chickens for Charlie George. Then we got four cows from Charlie. I'll never forget, we went out in the field with Charlie George in his Cadillac to pick out the cows that we wanted.

We lost $800 on our first batch of chickens and Joe said, "I'm going to Tulsa to work in tile." I said, "Well, we are going to have to tell Mr.

George something." So I went to Luther George [Charlie's son], and told him we would pay him $5 a month or whatever we could. He thanked me for coming in to tell him. Then Beatrice said she wanted to raise a batch of chickens. I didn't want her to, but she did. She made $800 and cleared our debt. After that we got out of chickens and cattle.

I told Joe that if he ever needed a helper in tile that I wanted to be his helper, and he finally got me in as his helper. We really didn't have any money to pay rent in Tulsa. Joe and his wife, Goldie, lived in an apartment, and Joe said, "We will go get an army cot and you can stay in my kitchen until things get better." So I did. When it got a little better, Beatrice came and we rented an apartment in Tulsa.

I was Joe's helper for about a year. We wanted to go in business for ourselves. The rep from Pomona Tile in Arkansas City, Kansas came out to talk to us. We told him we wanted to go in business. He said, "What about money?" Well, we didn't have any, so we told him we would go up there and pick up the tile for every job and pay him as we got the tile. He said, "We can give you $500 credit." There was not much tile work going on [in Northwest Arkansas] except for the bankers and the Georges, who used a lot of tile. But we went on, and we started getting pretty good business around the area. We started out as Tontitown Tile. Then we dissolved and Joe kept the Tontitown Tile while I went under M and M Tile.

Today, I work 12 or 14 people in the shop. It used to be that I bought my own trucks and hired workers by the hour. At one time, I had six or seven trucks. Then it went to sub-contracting, so now I sub out eight or ten carpet layers and three or four tile layers, and I don't have anybody by the hour except those in the shop. My inventory is always right here [in my pocket]. I write my inventory on a sheet of paper. This is my computer.

We are a family operation. Got my four kids in there—Gary, Ann, Bill, and Wayne. Got three of my grandchildren in there. I'm not on the payroll, but I guess I am always the first one there and the last to leave. I think as far as being a success in business, if you work hard and treat people right, you can make a success of it anywhere.

In 50 or 100 years, what would I like for my great-great-great-grandchildren to know about my life? That I did alright, and that I was a pretty good grandpa and a pretty good father.

SISTER EUGENIA (CLARA) PELLIN

*Sister Eugenia (Clara) Pellin was born in 1916 in
Tontitown, Arkansas, to Edward and Rose Marie Rosa
Pellin. She was 88 years old when she was interviewed
in 2004.*

My paternal grandparents never left Italy. My maternal grandparents, Zenobio and Johanna Rosa, and their two children, John and
Rose, came to America about 1895. They lived in Sunnyside until 1898,
when they moved to Tontitown [with the original group of settlers].
My mother, Rose, was only two years old when the family immigrated
to Sunnyside, but she remembered when they had to fill sandbags to
control the flooding [of the Mississippi River] there.

My father told me that when he was a child in Italy, his family lived
at the foot of the Alps. He took part in grazing their cattle on the slopes
of the Alps. He came to America when he was a teenager. He worked
as a coal miner those first years. He taught himself to read the English
language from walls papered with newspapers.

The children in our family are Albert, Florence, Clare—I changed
my name to Clare because that's what I was called—Virginia, Marion,
Richard, and then Mary Louise and Julia, the two babies who did not
live. One lived to be eight months and the second lived to be five months.

We lived on a farm just northwest of Tontitown. We children had
to gather eggs, feed chickens, carry well water, and carry wood for
cooking and heating. Breakfast was mostly fried eggs, French toast or
biscuits, oatmeal, Cream of Wheat, and hot chocolate. Mother did a lot
of canning—tomatoes, green beans, beets, peaches. Butchering time in
the winter provided ribs, liver, ground meat, salami, and sausage links.
Three or four families combined their milk and took turns pressing and
molding curds into rolls of cheese.

Sister Eugenia (Clara) Pellin

When I was in about the eighth grade we were baptized Catholic. Both our parents were baptized Catholic, but they did not marry in the church, and they didn't practice the religion. So neither were we baptized, and a lot of people harbored hard feelings because they thought [our parents] should have us baptized. We always had the feeling, though, that we didn't quite belong to that community. We didn't belong to the Elm Springs community, where the first three of us children started school. We went to school in Elm Springs a couple of years before we transferred to Tontitown. We didn't feel we belonged to that community, nor to the Tontitown community. I guess that was the drawing card for us to become Catholics. One of the nuns prevailed upon my dad to let us be baptized. So we were baptized, all six children. That was in about 1932.

I remember several of the nuns who taught at Tontitown: Sister Frances, Sister Declan [Conway], Sister Brendan, Sister Peter, Sister deChantal [Devine], Sister Carmelita [McCaffrey], and Sister Josephine [Delaney]. When the school burned [in 1927], I remember Sister Declan carrying a statue under each arm as she came out the burning building. She had to turn from side to side to get through the door, and in doing so, she decapitated both statues.

When I was in about the eighth grade, I started thinking about becoming a nun. The same nun who encouraged my father to let us children be baptized had been talking to me about vocations. Sister said, "You have to listen to God." She made the remark that sometimes a vocation comes to you that somebody else has rejected, did not listen to, did not follow up on. That must have made some impression on me because shortly after, I felt like I had the obligation. It sort of stayed with me. It sort of plagued me.

I completed the ninth grade at Tontitown, and then went tenth through twelfth grades at St. Anne's Academy in Fort Smith. When I went to St. Anne's, I had to do it on my own. I did not share with any-body that I was plagued with this idea that maybe God is calling me. I just sort of followed my nose and got the idea to write to St. Anne's Academy. I wrote about wanting to go to high school. I did the letter myself. I did not have any help about wanting to go. I had no means of going. No means of doing anything. No money. No anything. You cannot believe the poverty, and what we did without.

I went on the bus by myself to St. Anne's. I was going with the idea of doing something like Helen Sbanotto was doing. She was living with a family in Fort Smith, helping to take care of a little girl who went to Immaculate Conception School, which was right across the street from St. Anne's, where Helen attended school. I was expecting to do some-thing like that. But instead, they offered for me to live at the boarding school. It was like a scholarship, because I was that needy.

My parents knew I was going to go to high school at St. Anne's, but they didn't know what was in the back of my mind. It was hardly there, but I could not get rid of it. I sort of went by that and followed through. When I graduated, I did not go home that summer. Seems like I worked for a family named Burk, who lived on Eighteenth Street [in Fort Smith]. Because I was a convert, I was advised to wait before entering the convent.

About October, my sister and two brothers, my uncle, my mom, and a neighbor, George Sutton, came by. They were moving to California. My father had been in California a couple of years. He had written me after I graduated and asked me to try and convince the family to move to California. Evidently he prevailed upon them. He realized that he would have to move out there, because things were so bad [in Arkansas] during the Depression.

Anyway, they went on to California. They thought I could go along with them. Well, I just couldn't, right then. But then I thought about it. Next year I would be going to the convent, and I wouldn't have a chance to visit with them. So about the end of November, I transferred to California. I thought I would be able to get a job. I didn't right away, but then later I got some work in Ocean Park. They were living in Gilroy.

I stayed in California until the following September. I don't know how the sisters in Fort Smith got in touch with me; maybe I had written them, I don't remember. Anyway, they wrote to tell me that I had been accepted to enter the next candidacy class which started on September 8. So, early in September, using money I had earned over the summer working in a canning factory, I drove from California. At the same time, my sister Florence, who had been living in Muskogee, Oklahoma, was on her way to Tontitown before she went to California to join the family. I told her to wait for me in Tontitown.

Soon after I arrived in Tontitown, I got a telephone call telling me that if I didn't get on the train that night, and get to Webster Grove, Missouri, by the following morning, I would miss the candidacy class and would have to wait another six months or a year. So that's what I did. Florence didn't know what to think. She was so sad, it was as if she heard I had cancer or something like that, and she wouldn't see me again.

There was a class of 18 of us at Webster Grove. Candidacy lasted six months. We were called postulants. During that time, we wore a kind of veiling and a skirt and blouse with a sort of cape. It was a tacky thing. After six months, we were received and had the veil and the coif.

It's comparable to a wedding ceremony. They used to have quite a ceremony for that, and make it as if you were a bride of Christ. You could just dress in a bridal gown. Thank gosh that changed.

Once we received the veil, we wore the habit, which was the pleated habit with the belt. It was black. Only the nurses wore white habits. I wore the habit for another year, that is, the canonical year. The Church required that you spend that year without studying, that is, no college or anything like that, and grow in the ministry. Strictly pay attention to your spiritual life, and study the vows that you were going to be going into.

After that, there's the second year novice. You have another whole year until August 15 or 16, and then there is first profession. That's when you get the black veil and black habit. From there, that's when you go out into the ministry. You can be assigned to the ministry, which I was. I was thinking of nursing, but I was assigned to teaching. You didn't get to pick your profession back then. We have much more to say now.

At certain times during the process, you had an interview with a representative of the Church, a priest, to determine if you were doing this of your free will.

Three years later, you received your ring. The rosary was a part of the habit already, given when we were novices, right after postulancy. It was the cincher, which is the belt and rosary and white cross. It ended not in a crucifix with a corpus on it, but with a cross with a white band on it.

At the postulancy, when we received the habit, Mother Fidelia said, "And what is your name going to be next week?" I thought of "Eugenia." I knew a Eugenia Hamilton in school at St. Anne's. I kind of liked the name Eugenia. I didn't want to get Polycarp or something like that. So Mother Fidelia said, "And why Eugenia?" If they thought you had an attachment to the name, or a reason that was foremost, you probably wouldn't get it. I said, "I just don't want Polycarp, or something like that." That was enough for Mother Fidelia.

We went to summer school for years because that's how we completed our professional preparation. At that time, teachers weren't even required to have a BA. I completed a bachelor's degree and a master's degree in education at the University of the Incarnate Word in San Antonio, Texas. Later, I completed a master's degree in library science. I lived at Mount St. Mary's in Little Rock and commuted to North Little

Rock. After that, I was in Fort Smith for almost two years. Then came final profession, and I went to Slovak a year, Mena a year, and then to St. Elizabeth's, eight miles south of Morrilton. It was a public school. From there I went to Baxter, Missouri, for a year, then back to Fort Smith at Immaculate Conception, then to St. Patrick's School in North Little Rock. I was there four years.

I went into hospital accounting at the hospital in Brinkley, Arkansas. After that, I went to Tontitown to teach. By then it was a public school. I was there three years, 1956 through 1959. Public school was not really that much different from parochial school, as far as teaching. We had to observe a few things, like not putting up a crucifix and things like that on the wall.

I stopped my years of teaching and ministry in 1989, with my sabbatical that I went on for three months. I was in Little Rock through 1999. While I was living at the convent, they had no librarian or archivist, so I offered to fill in. Now I'm retired and living at Mercy Crest [a Sisters of Mercy retirement home in Barling, Arkansas], where I maintain the library and have various volunteer jobs. I was much more retired in Little Rock than I am here at Mercy Crest.

RICHARD PELLIN

*Richard Pellin was born in 1924 in Tontitown, Arkansas,
to Edward and Rose Marie Rosa Pellin. He was 80 years
old when he submitted a written interview in 2004.*

My father talked about working in a railroad roundhouse at one
time. He also worked at a rock quarry some. He had been on his own
since a very young age, eight or nine. My mother was a fine seamstress.

I was born on a farm in Tontitown, where we lived until I was 12.
We then moved to Gilroy, California. My brothers and sisters are Albert,
Florence, Sister Eugenia (Clara), Virginia, Marion, myself, Mary Louise
(died at eight months), and Julia (died at five months). I don't remember much about my siblings. Seems like they were away from home a
lot. Albert was in the CCC and later worked in terrazzo in Oklahoma,
I think. Florence went to Muskogee to work, Clara to Fort Smith to
school, and Virginia to Fayetteville to work. Marion and I were too
young to go anywhere.

Before and after school, my chores were to feed chickens, pigs, and
stock, gather eggs, bring in firewood, and carry water to the house for
cooking and washing. Older kids usually milked cows and did heavy
lifting.

A typical breakfast was fried eggs with bacon when we had it, coffee
with milk and sugar, homemade bread, and butter. Foods I remember
include salami, cheese, fresh pork and veal, potatoes, tomatoes, peas,
corn, cabbage, lettuce, peanuts, grapes, strawberries, chickens, eggs,
pasta, beans, milk, and butter. My mother canned tomatoes, string
beans, and grapes. She made strawberry and blackberry jelly. She took
milk to Dick Franco's and she and Teresa Franco pooled their milk to
make cheese. We got our meat from butchering farm animals—pigs,

Evelyn and Richard Pellin

calves, and chickens. We went to Springdale with a wagon and team of mules and bought several sacks of flour, 100 pounds of sugar, and a smaller sack of salt.

My teachers in Tontitown were nuns. I remember Sister Declan [Conway], Sister deChantal [Devine], Sister Barbara [Mattingly]—they were not necessarily my teachers, just names I remember.

I walked to school. Sometimes when it rained, Dick Franco would pick up his children with a wagon and team of mules and I would get a ride also. For lunch at school, I probably took homemade sausage, homemade cheese, grape jelly, and homemade bread.

The businesses in town that I remember were Perona grocery and post office on the southwest corner of [Highway 412 and Barrington Road]; Maestri grocery, about one block west of Perona's; and Baudino's drug and general store, about one block south of Perona's. Perona's cannery was southwest of there.

When we were kids, for fun we made stilts and used them a lot. We played in the barn, sliding down stacked hay, which was a no-no. We hunted birds with a homemade slingshot.

I don't remember much about our family Christmas traditions. We hung our stockings on Christmas Eve. Christmas morning, we went to Mass. We usually had chicken for Christmas dinner.

At Easter, we fasted for Lent. I don't remember Holy Week. I don't remember coloring Easter eggs either. For Easter dinner, we ate lamb, if we had one. If not, we had chicken again.

I can't remember pulling any Halloween pranks, but I heard of older boys turning over outhouses, or swapping teams of mules from one barn to another. I also heard of disassembling someone's buggy and reassembling it on his barn roof.

As best I remember, the grape festivals were held [on the northwest corner of Highway 412 and Barrington Road] across the road from the grocery store and post office. We got to have an ice cream cone and maybe Cracker Jacks.

We moved to California in 1936. Dad made a down payment on a new Ford sedan which we drove to California. It was Mother, Virginia, Marion, Uncle John, and I. Plus we had to have a driver because Virginia was just learning how to drive. I think the driver's name was George Sutton.

My first job away from home was delivering papers in Gilroy, California. The pay was $5 per month for delivering and collecting at the first of the month.

I served in the Navy during World War II. I was drafted. I tried to enlist, but I was over 18 and at that time, you could not enlist after your 18th birthday.

I met my wife at a Saturday night dance in San Juan Bautista, California. We dated twice a week. We went to Saturday night dances, maybe a show on Sunday or just for a ride in the country. We were married in 1944 in California. I was still in the Navy at that time. For the first few months after our marriage, my wife lived with her parents and I went back to Virginia, where I was stationed, and then to Florida, where she later joined me.

After I got out of the Navy, I worked for Ladd Hardware on a pump crew for seven years, and then to I went to work at Pacific Gas and Electric. I worked there for 32 years.

We have four children: Larry, Michael, Beverly, and Annette. We have ten grandchildren, and three great-grandchildren.

My hobbies are hunting and fishing. I did some leather carving for a couple of years, making some purses, wallets, belts, and a couple of pistol holders.

ANDREW PENZO

Andrew Penzo was born in 1930 in St. Louis, Missouri, to Angelo and Flora Bariola Penzo. He was 72 years old when he was interviewed in 2003.

My paternal grandparents were Dominic and Catherine Tisato Penzo. They and their son, John, arrived with the original Tontitown settlers in 1898. The rest of their children were Joe, Angelo, who was my dad, Angelina, Ed, and Pete.

Grandfather Penzo was a coal miner and a farmer. He worked as a miner in Coal Hill, Arkansas. He was a big man at one time, but in later years he was stooped over quite a bit from hard work. He was a strong individual. He had high principles and morals, was a good community worker, and a church-going man.

My maternal grandparents were Dominic and Theresa Roso Bariola. Grandfather came to America in 1909. Grandmother came as a child with her father, Giuseppe Roso, and three other children in 1898 with the original Tontitown settlers.

Grandfather Bariola worked in the Oklahoma coal mines. My mother, Flora, was born in Craig, Oklahoma. Her siblings were Leno, Alice, Rosie, Guy, Henry, Josephine, and Thelma.

My dad completed the third grade in school. He told me it was really rough back then. They depended on hunting wild game and what they could grow in the garden. No store-bought anything. Tough times, but they seemed to always have plenty to eat. According to him, they had a happy childhood. They played stickball, baseball, and bocce with all the neighborhood kids.

Mom and Dad lived in the same neighborhood. They played together all their lives. When they married, they lived with Grandfather

Andrew Penzo

Bariola for a while. It wasn't very long until they moved to St. Louis. That's where I was born. Dad worked in the rock quarries there. I was around two years old when we moved to Tontitown. My siblings are Luellen, Claudine, and Celester. We were like most kids, we fought a lot. Luellen was a scrapper.

Dad was very good at math. You could tell him that you had a piece of lumber one inch thick, twelve feet long, and six inches wide, and he could tell you the square feet, just like that. He was a pretty good carpenter, but he was better at growing stuff. He was a better farmer than anything. He pruned a lot of vineyards and orchards.

I don't know what grade Mother completed in school. It couldn't have been much. Her family moved here from Oklahoma when she was 10 years old. Mother didn't like to talk about her childhood. She lost her father very young. It was really rough. She was never a child. She was the oldest of eight children. When she was 12 years old, she carried her younger sister across the field two times a day to a wet nurse, because her mother had pneumonia. When she was 15, Mother went to Miami, Oklahoma, to work as a maid. She had to work and send money home to keep from having four of her brothers and sisters put in foster homes because they didn't have any money. She worked there five years, then she came back and married my father.

Mother was a number one seamstress, and one of the best cooks in the country. Believe it or not, she was probably as good a farmer as my dad was. She knew everything about all the crops, when to plant, when to harvest, you name it. She was excellent with us kids. She sewed all our clothes.

Some of the foods I remember are polenta, of course, and quail, squirrel, rabbit, and chicken. We grew lettuce, tomatoes, green beans, peppers, and cucumbers in the garden. Mama made pasta from scratch; we ate that sometimes three times a day. We did a lot of canning also. We never did have beef; we only had salami and sausage. We all raised hogs to butcher. The only meat was fowl, rabbit, squirrel, and what have you. We only had one cow. Every calf that was born was sold for cash. We didn't butcher any beef. When our laying hens got too old to lay, you didn't eat them, you took them to the store and you bartered. They gave you so much a pound for them. I remember walking up the road to Claude Morsani's store, carrying two old hens. Mom had a list of priorities, what she needed the most, like baking powder, sugar, coffee. They gave me so much per pound for the chicken. Whatever those chickens brought, whether it was $1.80 or whatever, we started at the top of Mom's list and went until we ran out of money.

My mother made cheese at the Bariola house. Several families got together and donated the milk, and then they would split the cheese. Joe

Bariola was actually the cheese master. When we were kids, we would all gather around and watch him. He had this huge copper kettle on a swivel. Joe would put the milk in the kettle, and they built a big fire under it. You know how when milk gets hot, it begins to curdle. Joe would stir it, and it would look like cottage cheese on top—they called that puina. All us kids used to reach in there and get us some to eat. He kept telling us to quit. Naturally, like most kids, we didn't quit. So he got us gathered around and sat us down close to him. He spoke only Italian, he couldn't speak a word of English, but we could understand every word he said. He said, "Do you know in Italy what we did to kids that stole the cottage cheese off the top of the milk?" Everybody said, "Nah, nah, nah." He said "We built a big fire under a kettle. We didn't put milk in there; we put the kids in there. When your feet got hot enough you jumped out of there and you did not steal any more cheese!" He scared us to death. Of course, he laughed. He thought it was funny. It did put an end to it. He was a clown.

The chores we had to do depended on the season. Daily we had to help milk, carry in wood, chop and split wood, and feed the chickens. In the summertime it was picking, pruning, and tying the vineyards. Every night after school we would work in the fields. We plowed, planted, or picked behind a team of horses. There wasn't much playing. We didn't go to the neighbors to play. We worked.

I attended school in Tontitown, then graduated twelfth grade from Springdale High School. I remember a few of the nuns we had as teachers in Tontitown. Sister Genevieve [Chafe] is the one that stands out. She's the one that used the ruler real well. Sister Bernadine [Lake]. I was crazy about Sister Bernaldo [Kaelin] and Sister Madonna [Hall].

My best friends in school were Andrew and Palmer Franco, and Cecil and Mike Ardemagni. At recess and lunchtime we played baseball or football. We learned how to dance, how to jitterbug, in the school basement. There was a jukebox. During the lunch hour when it was raining or cold, I didn't eat lunch so I could learn how to dance. When I did eat lunch, it was a jelly sandwich, soaked clear through, or a baked sweet potato. That was it.

Here is a funny story I remember from school days. We had to stand in line to come in from recess or lunch. We all had to be quiet and file up the steps. Every day or week someone different got to hold

ANDREW PENZO

the door open. This one particular day, Helen Pianalto was holding the door. I remember that when I came up the steps and turned to go in, she stuck her tongue out at me, and I stuck mine out back at her. Sister Genevieve saw me and didn't see Helen! I stayed in from recess every day all week for that. I got five or six licks on the knuckles, and five or six licks on the open palm, twice. I didn't stick any more tongues out at girls.

When I made my First Holy Communion, we were having Mass in the school basement. Our church had been destroyed by a tornado [in 1934]. I remember Mother telling us that a statue of the Blessed Virgin Mary was damaged during the tornado, but not to the extent that it could be disposed of. Some of the men were asked to get rid of it, and they wouldn't do it. In other words, they wouldn't finish destroying it. They had that much respect. I remember them building the new church. All the men donated their time and labor. I know my dad helped. I remember Jim Finn falling off the top and nearly killing himself.

Our family Christmas tradition was for Santa to come on Christmas Eve, before Midnight Mass. There was always one present per child if they could afford it. We walked to Midnight Mass. We had chicken and dressing for Christmas dinner. It was always a nice meal. We always went to Mass on Easter Sunday. The Easter Bunny came sometimes. We always had Easter bread.

The first grape festivals I remember were held where the old Tontitown Mercantile is now [on the northwest corner of Highway 412 and Barrington Road]. I thought they were great. Soda pop for a nickel, a hamburger for 10 cents. You could get your picture taken for a nickel. It was a big wide world. It was a chance to meet everybody. They had dances there in the old [Smith] school building there on the corner. As best I can remember, it was not a grape festival as such. It was a thanksgiving, a feast, a picnic is what it was. My dad called it a picnic.

I remember Frank Baudino's store, and John Mollar, who ran it. There was Claude Morsani's store—Albano Maestri owned the store before Claude bought it. Beato [B.] and Richard Ardemagni operated a grocery store in the lower level of Frank Perona's building. The Perona family lived upstairs. The Franco canning factory—Mom worked at that canning factory, they all worked there as young girls. Mr. Strabala had a blacksmith shop a little farther west from Claude Morsani's store.

My first job away from the farm was when I was still in high school. I worked for Dick Lester's father, blacktopping roads in the summertime. He had an asphalt company. I was paid 50 cents an hour. That was great back then. After high school, I went to the University [of Arkansas], and then I went to Colorado to school. Next I went to Korea. I was in the Navy. I joined to keep from getting drafted, let's put it that way. I was stationed in Washington, Florida, California, and then all over the Far East—Formosa, Japan, the coast of Korea.

I met my wife, Peggy Jo Pendergraft, in high school. She asked me for the first date. Frank Maestri was fortunate enough to have an older brother, Steve, who had a convertible. Frank and I borrowed it all the time and we double-dated. That was our only way of transportation. We went to movies, ballgames, and dances.

Peggy and I were married in 1955. I was still in the Navy. We lived in Florida for three or four months. Honeymooned on the beach every day. That was a tough life. After my discharge, I worked for Curtis Hornor Tire Company in Springdale for a while. Then we moved to Wichita, Kansas, where I worked in the tile business with Gilbert and Gordon Cortiana and that bunch. Some of Andy Franco's brothers were there too. Then I came back to Arkansas and worked in Fort Smith for a year or so at Arkansas Tile and Terrazzo. I started at Jones Truck Lines in Springdale in 1958. That's where I ended up, for 33 years. Good working conditions and good pay.

Peggy and I have four children: Phillip, Andrea, Toni, and Michael. We have ten grandchildren. As far as hobbies, I enjoyed hunting. I love sports of every kind. Gardening has always been a hobby. I used to play tons of golf. I like to play cards and travel.

One of the greatest experiences of my life was a trip that Henry Piazza and I took to Valli del Pasubio, Italy in 2000. My main purpose in going was to find my kinfolks. The mountains are full of Penzos over there. I met a woman named Clelia Cicchellero. She was a Penzo before she married. She was 76 years old, and when we figured out that our grandfathers were brothers, she just burst into tears. She told me that my grandfather, Dominic Penzo, left there in 1896 and that her brother corresponded with him until World War II. That was something I didn't know. When Italy declared war on the United States, they couldn't write to each other. They didn't hear another word until I went over there.

　ANDREW PENZO

Once we figured out we were related, the first thing Clelia asked me was, "What happened to Dominic?" I told her about Tontitown, and that he was buried there. She was just so relieved to know that he wasn't persecuted or anything. She didn't have any idea.

It was kind of embarrassing to me because they thought that I should be able to speak Italian fluently. They couldn't speak a word of English, so I would tell the older ones, "Now listen, I can understand everything you say to me if you will speak the old dialect, and don't speak too fast." So they toned it down, and I could communicate. After the third day, it was just like growing up here in Tontitown, when our parents spoke to each other in Italian. Words came back to me that I hadn't heard in 50-odd years. Before you knew it, we were just speaking fluently back and forth.

They still had the old processions from the church to the cemetery. You walk into the cemetery and every name that you have in Tontitown and names that you've heard all your life are in there. It's the most beautiful cemetery you ever saw.

Peggy and I were sitting outside there on a bench and I saw this guy standing there talking to another guy. I told Peggy, "That man is a Roso, I promise you." I could tell because he stood the same way Albino Roso stood, so erect with his chin up. So I walked up to him and said, "Are you a Roso?" He said, "Si, Roso." He told me that back in the days when our folks left there, they were so oppressed. They had nothing. He said they cut every tree up to the tree line in the mountains, and sold the wood. The cattle had grazed every bit of grass. There was nothing left.

The people there were so friendly. They wanted to know everything about America. How is it over here? What did the immigrants do when they got here? What was their work? How did they live? How were they treated? One of them, Augustino Taldo, said, "Italians are very good workers." I said, "That's right. People [in America] recognized that right off, and they wanted [Italian] labor." They had so much pride in heritage. So much pride in family.

Sister Xavier (Josephine) Perona

SISTER XAVIER (JOSEPHINE) PERONA

*Sister Xavier (Josephine) Perona was born in 1921 in
Tontitown, Arkansas, to Frank and Carrie Piazza
Perona. She was 81 years old when she was interviewed
in 2002.*

My mother was born in Italy in 1888. When she was born, Mother
only had one lung, and she was not able to stand up. Apparently one
leg was real short and there was something wrong with her hip bone.
Her mother took her to all the doctors, and they just said, "Take her
home, make her comfortable. She's going to die. There is no use in you
spending any more money on her." When Mother was seven years old,
Grandma Piazza heard of miracles that were being performed in a village several miles from her. Grandma carried my mother on a pillow, and
walked—it was almost a day's walk—to Santuario Basilica in Vicenza,
Italy. I don't know what she gave as an offering, but it wasn't very much.
She prayed and prayed and prayed. Before they left, Grandma stood
Mother up. Mother could stand up, and Grandma helped her with a
couple of steps. Of course, she was weak because she had never stood
up before. My mother got well. She had x-rays and they found that she
had both lungs, and her bones were perfect. She did have a miracle at
this place.

My maternal grandparents, James and Angela Piazza, brought their
family to America in 1895. Mother was seven years old. They came over
on a boat with a bunch of immigrants. They were at sea for one month,
because they got lost, and the boat almost turned over. They had a hard
time. The storm knocked Mother down and she hurt her leg again.
They went to New York. It took several weeks before Father Bandini,
who was taking care of them, took them to Sunnyside by way of New

Orleans. They were in Sunnyside for a year or so. They were having swamp fever there, malaria. Mother's family was one of the few families that did not lose anyone at Sunnyside. People were dying, so they left. Father Bandini took them to Tontitown [in 1898]. Father Bandini was their guardian. He took care of them.

My father was born in Italy in 1881. He came to America in 1904. My parents met in Eureka Springs, Arkansas. Mother was working there for a Judge Hemingway. She was Mrs. Hemingway's maid. Mrs. Hemingway tutored her. Mother was very bright, especially in mathematics. She had a business mind. I don't know how Dad landed in Eureka Springs. He worked as a yard man there. He did not know English. Mother taught him English. That's the way they met.

My parents were married in Tontitown in 1908, and first lived on a small farm south of town. Their children were James, who only lived one day, Johnny, who was 17 when he died from a brain tumor, Angelina, Louis, Josephine, and Frank Junior.

I don't remember it, but I know my parents had a little canning factory south of Tontitown. It was down a hill. Daddy operated that canning factory for two or three years, and then he built one [on the southwest corner of Highway 412 and Barrington Road]. He built a house for us there too. It had two floors. On the bottom floor, we had a grocery store. Mother and Dad operated that for a while, and then they rented it out.

My parents both worked awfully hard. When they built the canning factory in Tontitown, they were down there day and night. Mother did the weighing and the buying, and she did the paying. They contracted the tomatoes out. Dad would furnish the seeds, and the farmers would grow the tomatoes for him and then bring them in to the canning factory. Mother was back and forth because it was walking distance [to our house]. During the busy season, Dad would often sleep at the factory. My fond memory of Dad is how he would whistle as he walked from the factory to our house. I can still hear his whistle.

I don't know how many people worked at the factory. It was a large building, and it was full [of workers]. The hired hands worked with the boilers. The ones who came to peel tomatoes or stem beans were paid by the bucket. They just came when they could. It was seasonal work, canning green beans, tomatoes, spinach, and grape juice. Lewis Haney was Dad's right hand man at the canning factory. I don't think Mom and Dad could have gotten along without his help. He was a great person, loyal and kind.

My brothers also worked at the factory. They made a lot of trips to Van Buren and Alma to pick up spinach and green beans. Uncle Pete Perona would come every summer to help in the canning factory, and just be with the family. He was not married. He would stay six or seven months sometimes. He was a great morale builder, kept us happy and laughing.

We sold the canned goods to two brokers. Kraft was one of them. A lot of times we'd put our own label on them, which was Perona Canning Company or Tontitown Canning Company. Sometime they would want to use their own labels, so they would ship their labels to us and we would label our product with their label. Instead of shipping as "Produce Packed By" it was "Produce Packed For." My parents retired from the canning factory in 1941. My brother Louis then took over the factory, and closed it in 1946.

Mother had a green thumb. She was known for her beautiful flowers on her back porch, and in the dining room. She raised beautiful geraniums and many varieties of potted plants that she especially grew to be used in church. That was her joy, to have the altars decorated with her flowers.

She was a wonderful cook. Lemon pies, sugar cookies, and spaghetti were her specialties. Mom never forgot the nuns; she kept them supplied with canned goods, pies, and cookies. I can still see that large dishpan in the kitchen, full of sugar cookies. Mom often would have the priests over for an evening meal. We always had wine in the house but that was not one of our priorities, unless we had polenta.

Mom had no training, but she was a good nurse. They would call her when someone was in labor and ready to have a baby. She would pick up her package of supplies that she had sterilized in the oven—a sheet, a cord, stuff like that. She always had two of them ready. When they called and said, "Come on, Mrs. Perona," she'd take a package of supplies and go deliver the baby.

John Mollar's general store was a huge brick building. You could find everything in there. You just asked Mr. Mollar for what you needed, and he would jig out someplace and find it. I mean that store was full.

You could barely walk through the middle. I made a lot of trips to his store just to see Mr. Mollar and get a piece of candy. He was a brilliant man, a musician, a very holy man. He taught piano lessons. I took lessons for a couple of months.

Cap Tiller came once a month to the old [Smith] schoolhouse to show picture shows. He would stay a couple of days. That was great.

I attended St. Joseph's School in Tontitown. We were taught by the Sisters of Mercy. Sister Barbara [Mattingly] was there and Sister Genevieve [Chafe]. I was real close to them. Alma Cigainero lived with them. She and I were buddies. We studied together.

In September 1936, I left Tontitown to become a nun. I was about 15. Father Francis Xavier Dollarton was the priest assigned here when I entered the convent. He was a great, holy priest. In fact, I took my name, Xavier, after him. Father was a family friend and guided me to the Benedictines in Fort Smith. All I knew were the Sisters of Mercy nuns, because they were our teachers in Tontitown. I just figured if you're going to be a nun, you'll be a Mercy nun. But Father Dollarton said, "Oh no, Jo, I'm going to take you to Fort Smith to see the Benedictines at St. Scholastica Convent. That's where you belong." He took me to Fort Smith and introduced me to the superior. We went back three or four times until I did enter. Father Dollarton told me, "Live close to home, and you can be seen."

I was in the tenth grade when I went to the convent. I was so homesick; I just thought I would die. Apparently I cried all the time. It was sort of a standing joke at the convent. Every time they would see me coming in from different missions, they wanted to know "if the river was still overflowing."

Richard Roso, what a booger he was. He always teased me quite a bit. The first year I came home, we were having coffee together. Before I went to the convent, I always used cream and sugar. So Richard said, "Do you take any cream and sugar?" I said no. He said, "You mean they're so stingy down there they don't even let you use cream and sugar?"

We were not restricted during the first year at the convent—we could have visitors. The second year is what we called our canonical year, and we were only allowed three visits a year. We could write three letters a year. Our studying was all church history and Benedictine history and religion. We did not go to school in any other subjects. We also had work to do. I worked outside, gathering rocks, doing the garden, farm work. That was from eight in the morning—after prayers—until lunchtime, and then right after lunch until suppertime. After supper, I helped with dishes in the kitchen.

The first year we wore a black dress with a little veil. At the end of that year, on June 24, we received our black habit and our coif—a headdress and white veil. That was for two years. Six years after we entered, we took our vows of poverty, chastity, and obedience, and received a ring that indicated we were wed to God.

After I became a nun, I stayed at St. Scholastica for three years. I was sent on a mission to Dermott, a small southeast Arkansas community where 90 percent of the people were black. There were no Catholics there. The church had blown down several years earlier. The closest church was about 10 or 15 miles. The WPA had built a hospital there, which we took over. I did not have any nurses training at that time. There were five of us: one sister for the operating room, one sister for dietetics, one sister as supervisor, and then another couple of us. I was down there two and a half years, waiting to go into nurses training. Then I went to Boonville, Missouri, where I completed my registered nurse degree at St. Joseph Hospital. I retired in 1992 and took a sabbatical to Spokane, Washington, then returned to St. Scholastica Monastery as infirmary nurse for six years. I've been a nurse for 58 years.

Beginning in 1965, nuns were allowed to wear street dress rather than habits. I really loved my habit. I still have my veil. In every hospital I worked in, even the Veterans Hospital, I always asked if they preferred that I wear my veil, or go without. They said, "Just do whatever you want," so I did wear my veil, and of course my pins. I was known as Sister Perona, and they did respect me. I still have my black veil, and when I go to funerals I still wear my habit.

Mother was an invalid for 12 years before she died. She couldn't go up and down the steps. Daddy had an elevator installed in their home in 1954; before that, she would go up and down the stairs on her hands and knees. She wasn't able to go to church. Our home was across the street from the church, so Mother would sit in her wheelchair in the living room and they would open the door and window of the church so she could see the altar. She could see Father saying Mass. Mother died in 1965, and Dad died in 1973.

Tontitown is amazing in that it has kept cohesiveness, a sense of community. I think it is the Italian in them! We have a sense of pride of Tontitown. Even though the population hasn't grown a whole lot, it is just a good little old town.

　　　SISTER XAVIER (JOSEPHINE) PERONA

CLAUDINE PENZO PIANALTO

Claudine Penzo Pianalto was born in 1934 in Tontitown, Arkansas, to Angelo and Flora Bariola Penzo. She was 69 years old when she submitted a written interview in 2003.

My paternal grandparents were Domenico and Caterina Tisato Penzo. They came to America in 1896 with the original group of immigrants from the south Arkansas plantation of Sunnyside who founded Tontitown in 1898. The children of Domenico and Caterina were Angeline, John, Joe, Ed, Pete, and my father, Angelo.

My maternal grandparents were Dominic and Theresa Roso Bariola. Grandfather came to America in 1907 as an adult. Grandmother was a child when she and her father, Giuseppe Roso, came from Sunnyside to Tontitown in 1898. Her mother Lucia died in Sunnyside. My Bariola grandparents' first home in Tontitown was on the corner of [present-day] Sbanotto Road and Ardemagni Road. They also lived in Krebs, Oklahoma. The children of Dominic and Theresa were Lino, Alice, Henry, Guy, Josephine, Rosie, Thelma, and my mother, Flora.

My parents, Angelo and Flora Bariola Penzo, grew up in the same neighborhood in Tontitown. After they married, their first home was on [present-day] Ardemagni Road. My parents had four children: Andrew, Luellen, me, and Celester, nicknamed Husk.

I completed ninth grade in Tontitown, then tenth through twelfth grades in Springdale. In Tontitown, our teachers were nuns. I remember Sister Georgine [Conway], Sister Ricarda [McGuire], Sister Bernadine [Lake], and Sister Bernaldo [Kaelin].

The first church I attended was in the school basement, where they

Claudine Penzo Pianalto

were having Mass while a new church was being built [to replace the church destroyed by a tornado in 1934].

I met my husband, Leo Pianalto Jr., at a parish dance. We were married in 1967. Our first home was on Pianalto Road, where I still live today. We have one daughter, Jennifer Ann.

EGEDIO PIANALTO

Egedio "Gile" Pianalto was born in 1919 in Tontitown, Arkansas, to Joseph and Annie Cigainero Pianalto. He was 83 years old when he was interviewed in 2002.

My paternal grandparents were Pietro and Teresa Pianalto. They were in Sunnyside before they came to Tontitown [in 1898]. My dad was eight years old when they came over. They came here to get a better life, I guess. That is why most of them came. They had three boys when they came: Joe, Geno, and Alphonso. One son, Egedio, died on the way.

My grandfather was a hard worker, and the strongest man I ever knew. He was a blacksmith and a carpenter. He made all his own tools. He could build anything. He built his own house with logs and mortar. He hewed and notched the logs. He did a wonderful job; the house was there a long time. I read an article about my grandfather that said he worked [on construction of some of the buildings] at the University of Arkansas. He walked from Tontitown there every day and back.

My parents met in Texarkana, Arkansas. My mother's family lived in Texarkana, and my dad worked in a wagon shop there. They must have known each other pretty well, because after Dad came back to Tontitown, he called my mother and told her if she wanted to get married, to come on up here, and she came. They had seven children: Matilda, Mary, Josephine, Gile, Pete, Louis, and Philip.

Dad was a farmer, and we had chores to do before and after school, like feeding the cattle or horses, milking the cows, slopping the hogs. In the summer we worked in the fields.

My mother used to go down to a little spring to wash clothes. She carried the clothes there and back. She sewed her own clothes. She was a pretty good cook. Breakfast might be caffè latte. That was coffee,

Esther and Egedio Pianalto

cream or milk, and sugar, with homemade bread in it. Sometimes we would have a slice of salami or a piece of cheese. We ate a lot of pasta. We had vegetables, and homemade cheese and salami. If the hog was too fat to make salami, Dad would go to Springdale and buy some beef to put in it. We sometimes kept milk or butter cool by putting it down in the well. Let it down on a rope, not into the water, but far enough down the well to keep it cool.

 EGEDIO PIANALTO

Mother loved flowers, and she loved to visit. She used to go by wagon to see Aunt Iginia [Pianalto Cigainero]. She also loved to fish. She used to go to my pond to fish. One time she caught a fish, and it got away. Mother went in the pond after that fish.

My dad loved music, and he loved dances. We used to have dances at our house. The Pianalto boys—Leo's boys, they are third cousins to me—played music. Dad loved having people around. Different houses had dances. I remember going to a dance down as far as Lewis Haney's, north of Elm Springs. I also remember going to Katy Taldo's house for dances.

After the church was destroyed by a tornado in 1934, Dad helped to build the new church. He helped with the management of [the construction project], to kind of get things lined out. We had a dump truck. I hauled gravel and worked with the cement.

I completed the eighth grade in Tontitown. I was in school when the building burned [in 1927]. I don't know how the fire started, but it started on the outside of the school, in the right corner. After that, we went to school in [the old Smith schoolhouse, on the northwest corner of Highway 412 and Barrington Road]. It had a stage in it, and a big open room. There was an open place on the right side, if you are standing in front of it. We went to school there maybe two or three years, until a new school was built.

I remember one of the nuns who taught us, Sister deChantal [Devine]. She was fair, but she was really strict, and she got her way just about every time. My best friends in school were Artilio Bariola and Francis Finn. Lenor Brunetti was another one of my buddies. At recess and noon we played shinny with a tin can. For lunch I took a salami sandwich or a jelly sandwich.

One funny thing I remember about school was how my brother, Louis, could just look at some of the boys and make them laugh. It didn't matter if the nun was there or not, they were all laughing, and Louis was sober as a judge.

We walked to school a lot, but for a long time we had a horse and buggy. We would take the horse to Frank Baudino's. He had a shed, and we would put her in there during the day. After school, we would go hook her up to the buggy and come home. Going with a horse and buggy was a lot of fun. One time we hooked the horse to the buggy to go to school, and the horse knew so much about what to do, that before we got in the buggy, we looked out, and she was gone. Silvio Pianalto stopped her down the road. The horse knew where she was going, so she left without us.

I don't think we made too much out of Christmas when I was a kid. I do remember one toy we got, a red wagon. My sister, Mary, was pulling me in the wagon and I let my hand go out, and I got hold of the woodstove. Boy, it left a scar that's still there.

Christmas dinner was turkey or sometimes ham. One time, Dad went down on the creek and got a goose. Uncle John [Cigianero], one of Mama's brothers, always had goose for Christmas. He came up here from Texarkana all the time.

I remember when the grape festivals were held where the old Ardemagni store sits now [on the northwest corner of Highway 412 and Barrington Road]. They had a hamburger stand. I don't think they had spaghetti dinners like they do now. They played games, had races. Local people played music.

I only worked at one job away from the farm before I got drafted, and that was at Granata's Winery. Making wine, bottling, and I even hauled wine for a while.

When I was drafted into the Army, I reported to Little Rock. In no time at all we went by train to California for training. Then one night we loaded up, went to a ship, and went to Australia. We were on the water 22 days. We stayed around Australia, then went to New Guinea and stayed there in the jungle for 16 months. That was not fun at all. There had been combat there, but all we had was snipers. Next we went to Manila, in the Philippines. We were not there very long before it was all over with, and I came home. I was in the service three years, nine months, and a few days. I made $21 a month in the Army.

I had just started in the Army when my sister, Mary, gave my address to Esther [Marendo], who lived in Pennsylvania. Mary was married to Esther's uncle, [Chuck Fucci]. Esther and I wrote to each other for almost four years before I got out of the service. When I got out, I went to Pennsylvania to see Esther. My brother Pete was with me. We drove in an old Chevrolet. Not too long after that, Esther came to Tontitown to see me. Her brother came with her, and they stayed two days. We got engaged in Noel, Missouri, before she went back home. There was a group of people along that night—Jack and Beanie [Lavinia] Zulpo, Bill and Fern Fiori, a whole bunch of us. We got married right after that.

We lived in Tontitown for a while, and then we moved to Pennsylvania. Esther was pregnant, and she got homesick, so we went back to Pennsylvania. Our son Joe was born there. I went to work in the silk mill while we were up there. We hooked twine on the cones and let it run. I didn't like it. It really made your hands sore. We didn't stay in Pennsylvania too long. We moved back to Tontitown and had another son, John. Today, we have four grandchildren.

The only career I really ever wanted was farming. I never had much time for hobbies. I started playing bocce when Gildo [Mantegani] had a bocce court at the old Luncheonette, across the highway from the Venesian Inn. I didn't play there too much, but I remember the men who did, because I was there a lot. I played over at Hi [Victor] Ceola's house. He built two bocce courts there, and on Sunday we would go over and play. Everybody worked during the week, so we mostly played on Sunday. In the winter we played cards on Sunday. We played pitch, most of the time. It was fun.

Elsie Mae Fiori Pianalto

ELSIE MAE FIORI PIANALTO

Elsie Mae Fiori Pianalto was born in 1931 in Tontitown, Arkansas, to Peter B. and Mary Cortiana Fiori. She was 74 years old when she was interviewed in 2005.

My paternal grandfather, Domenico Fiori, came to America with his two young sons, Antonio and my father, Peter B., in 1896. I think Dad was about seven years old when they came. They first went to Sunnyside, and then in 1898, they came to Tontitown with the original group of settlers.

My maternal grandfather, Eustacchio Cortiana, was also with the original group from Sunnyside. He was a widower with six children: Domenico or Dick, Virginia, Giuseppe or Joe, my mother Maria or Mary, Celeste or Cel, and Luigia or Louise. Mom was four or five years old when she came to America.

Mom completed the third grade in school. As a young girl, she worked for a family in Fayetteville. She lived with them, and did house chores, cooked, washed, took care of kids. She never talked about old times to me much.

My parents had seven children: Bill, Charlie, Clara, Dorothy, twins Virgil and Virginia, and me. I was 10 years younger than the twins. I was born at home. Dr. Cooper from Elm Springs delivered me. None of my brothers or sisters even knew Mom was pregnant. When the kids came home from school for dinner [lunch] one day, Dad told them to go in the bedroom to see what Mama had. They were so excited; they didn't even eat their dinner. They ran back to school to bring all the kids over to see me.

My brother Virgil was drafted into the Army in World War II. He was killed in the war, in Anzio, Italy, in 1944. He was 22 years old. He is buried in Italy. I was at school when Mom and Dad got the news of Virgil's death. A man from the Army came to our house and told my folks that Virgil had been killed. Somebody came to school to get me.

Dad was a jack of all trades, a handyman. But he was bothered with asthma, so he had a hard time breathing. I remember him sitting on the front porch and giving himself a shot in the arm so he could breathe. It was very scary to me.

Mom's feet and legs were very bad. She always walked on her tip-toes, especially on her left foot. She was always in pain, but it never slowed her down. She was on her feet constantly and never complained.

Mom did a lot canning. The only thing I did not like to can was peas. We had to pick the peas, then we used the hand-cranked wringer washing machine to shell them. We had to make a tent around it with a sheet or something so the peas wouldn't pop out all over the place. We still had lots of peas on the floor.

When we canned ketchup, Dad would put a big copper pot on the fire and throw the tomatoes in there to cook. We let them get soft, and then we had a funnel-like thing we used to would use to squeeze the juice out. We would can the tomato juice first, then can the rest for use as ketchup.

To make jelly, we put cooked grapes in a pillowcase and tied that to a broom handle placed across the backs of two kitchen chairs. We would catch the juice dripping out of the pillowcase in a pan, and make jelly out of that.

When we butchered hogs, they made sausage and put it in casings. The sausage was hung in the cellar until it had a lot of *muffa*, or mold, on it. They would grind up salt pork. Mom packed that into large crocks and kept it covered in the basement. She used salt pork to make grease when she made her spaghetti sauce.

Mom baked wild blackbirds. She called them "chi-chi birds." Dad rigged up a window screen, still in the frame. He tied a long string on one side of the frame. He ran the string inside the window on the back porch. The frame was propped up towards the back porch. Dad would put some birdseed or chops [chopped grain] from the chickens underneath this frame. When birds would go under it to eat, he pulled the string. The screen fell flat and trapped the birds. Dad would then go pick the birds up and kill them. We would get them ready to cook by picking

      ELSIE MAE FIORI PIANALTO

off the feathers and taking their heads off. Mom would cook them in the oven. I don't know the ingredients she used. I know she put lots of sage in them. It was good.

When I was growing up, we didn't have a vehicle. If we needed groceries from Springdale, Dad would hitchhike into Springdale, or if somebody was going he would ride, usually in the back of a truck. Sometime he would ask someone to bring groceries to our house.

I was 17 when my father was killed by a hit-and-run driver on February 14, 1948. He was walking on Highway 68 [present-day Highway 412]. It happened right in front of Pete Tessaro's house. Dad, his brother, Tony, and Pete Tessaro were walking home after playing cards at Hugo Pozza's house. I had just gotten home from a date with Gabe [Pianalto]. I was talking to Mom when we found out Dad had been hit by a car. Mom and I put on our coats and walked to [where the accident happened]. Dad was still lying there when we arrived. We never found out who hit him.

I attended school in Tontitown through the ninth grade, and then graduated from Springdale High School. I had nuns for teachers through the eighth grade. I remember Sister Georgine [Conway]. Sister Quintilla [Halter] was the disciplinarian. Sister Bernadine [Lake] taught me to crochet. They were all very good teachers.

Some of my best friends in grade school were Ida Mae Taldo, Mabel Zulpo, Connie Franco, and Lillian and Pauline Pianalto. We were all in the same grade. At recess we played hopscotch, jacks, and tag. I never took my lunch. I walked about two blocks and went home for lunch.

We used to go to the convent and wash dishes for the nuns. It took us a long time to do the dishes because we would go upstairs and dress in their habits. We always wondered if the sisters had hair, because we never could see any.

We liked going to John Mollar's store because he would give us candy. You would go in the store and you wouldn't see him, but he was always in there playing the piano. Mom sent me to Mr. Mollar's store one time to get rigatoni. She always called them stove pipes because that's what they looked like. So I went down to the store and said, "My mom wants some stove pipes." Mr. Mollar said, "Oh my good child, I don't have any. The only stove pipe I have is on the stove." I finally told him what I meant, and he got me some rigatoni.

At Easter, we colored eggs and had an Easter egg hunt. Mom made fugassa. She would work it up and let it rise. She would get up during the night to punch the dough down [to keep it from flowing out over the pan]. Next morning she made it into loaves. She would clip the center of the loaf with her scissors to make a design. She also made each of us kids a small fugassa. She took a piece of dough and rolled it by hand into a long piece about 12 inches long. She wrapped this around a boiled egg and then baked it in a pie pan. On Holy Saturday we took our special loaves to Holy Saturday service, and Father would bless them.

The earlier grape festivals were held in the [Smith] school building [on the northwest corner of present-day Highway 412 and Barrington Road]. They had booths. They had spaghetti dinners in the school basement. Cap Tiller, who owned a traveling picture show, would show movies in a big tent or in the school. We paid 25 cents to see the movie. They had a Ferris wheel, but not as big as they have today. They put up a big swing in our yard, close to the pecan tree.

I met my husband, Gabriel Pianalto, through his sister Lillian. She and I were good friends. Gabe and I would only go out on Saturday evening and maybe Sunday evening, but not during the week. We didn't spend much money. We just spent time together, maybe go get a hamburger and see a movie once in awhile. He worked at the Pianalto Brothers Garage nearby, so I would see him almost every day.

We got married in 1951. We had our wedding breakfast at the home of my brother and sister-in-law, Bill and Fern Haney Fiori. Next we went to Fayetteville to Green's Studio to have our picture taken, and then we had the reception at Mom and Dad Pianalto's [Gabe's parents, Leo and Lucy Ceola Pianalto]. We had a dance that night in the school basement. Gabe and I stayed there until everybody was gone. We helped Father [L. H.] Schaefer close the door and lock up. Father told us, "You two aren't supposed to be here, go home." We didn't go anywhere [for a honeymoon], just to our house, which Gabe, Francis, Lawrence, Junior, and Dad Pianalto had built. The lumber they used was from the old [Smith] school building.

Our children are Brenda, Virgil, Patrick, Doris, Bernard, Silvia, and James. We have six grandchildren.

Gabe worked his entire life as a mechanic. He never did retire. He

     ELSIE MAE FIORI PIANALTO

passed away in 1997. Now, I start my day with Mass. I go to church every morning. I enjoy my family. They are very good to me, and I love them all very much. I have to go to McDonald's every morning; Gabe and I used to do that. Then I just piddle around the house, crochet, sew, work crossword puzzles, or just sit there. Whatever I want to do. I try to help out at church as much as I can. I have a good life.

Francis Pianalto

FRANCIS PIANALTO

Francis Pianalto was born in 1924 in Tontitown, Arkansas, to Leo and Lucy Ceola Pianalto. He was 78 years old when he was interviewed in 2003.

My paternal grandfather was Domenico Pianalto. He was born in Italy, and died in Tontitown. In Italy, Grandfather was a teacher at night, and in the daytime he worked other jobs. My paternal grandmother was Catherine Penzo Pianalto. She was born in Italy. She died in Sunnyside, along with twins.

Grandfather Domenico and his four children, Leo Giuseppe, who was my father, Erlinda Marie or Linda, Iginia Carolina, and Giocinto Pio or George, migrated from Sunnyside to Tontitown with the original settlers in 1898. Their first home was a log cabin near the [southeast] corner of Highway 412 and Barrington Road. Grandfather went back to Italy and talked to a priest and told him he had lost his wife in Sunnyside and had to have another wife to help raise the children. The priest told him about a little lady who lived down the road named Rosa Taldo. Grandfather met her and married her and took her back to Tontitown to help raise the kids.

The children of Domenico and Rosa Taldo Pianalto were Caterina Dionisia, Dionisio Mariano or Dave, Giuseppe Iginio Sisto or Joe, Ignazio Cesare, Carolina Maria or Lena, Ignazio Francisco or Frank, Pia Maria Lugia, and Maria Lugia Assunta or Mary Louise. Ignazio Cesare and Pia Maria Logia died as infants.

My maternal grandparents were Domenico and Mary Zulpo Ceola. I know Grandfather was in the Italian Army because I saw pictures of him at Nonna Ceola's house. They had a farm, they raised a small vineyard, strawberries, and tomatoes, just like everyone else. Their children were Fausta, Alice, Mary, and my mother, Lucy. After Nonno Ceola died, Nonna married his brother. Their children were Victor or Hi, Domenic or Dick, Fred, Julia, Rinaldo or Nel, Cecilia or Chill, and Genevieve.

My dad, Leo Pianalto, was seven years old when he came to America. In Italy, Dad helped his father with chores. They grew grapes; Dad had to climb a tree to pick grapes. He took care of the cows; he milked them by hand. They shared the milk with the three families that lived in their little log cabins in the Alps. He helped shoe the horses. In the summertime, he took the cows to the green pastures where there was tall grass on top of the mountain. In wintertime there was snow on the mountain, so he would take the cattle down toward the home. They cut trees, and had to build scaffolds high enough up the trunk so you could get the saw to go through the trunk. The base of the tree was too large for the saw to go through it.

Mama and Daddy were both working in Fayetteville at the time they met. Mama worked for a Mrs. Marinoni. Daddy worked at the Ozark Grocery Company. I guess Mama was so beautiful that when Daddy just saw her for the first time, he said, "I think I will get my horse and buggy and take you home." They had a happy life together.

Daddy and Mama had 13 children: Eugene, Lawrence Sereno, Olivia Lillian, Gabriel Dominic, Oliver Vincent, Francis Clarence, Leo Alfred or Junior, Olivia Catherine, Leonard Floyd, Lillian Marie, Edward Wilford, Juanita Mary, and Raymond Vincent. Olivia [Lillian] died at the age of five of diphtheria.

Mama had a job of washing diapers and clothes, and there was never a dull moment with her. She was a working lady, and a beautiful person. She had a Singer sewing machine, and she kept it singing a lot, mending our overalls and shirts and little holes in the knees of our pants. She was busy all the time.

Nonna Ceola would to walk to our house and help Mama wash, and every time a baby was born, she would come and help out with the kids. When Junior and I would see Nonna coming, we would run to meet her because she would always stop at Claude Morsani's store and buy a little sack of stick candy, sugar cane candy. She always spoke to us in Italian and we couldn't understand much. She usually walked through the field, but sometimes she would catch a ride with Albano Maestri. He hauled milk, and she would ride with him in the milk truck.

A tragedy happened at Nonna's house. A little boy named Fred passed away in the living room. He was just a little toddler. They were getting ready to [butcher] a bunch of chickens. They were boiling the water to scald the chickens. This little toddler, Fred, was running across the floor and stumbled into the hot water. Nonna said his last words were, "Mama, change me." It was a sad story.

Nonna Ceola made home brew for all of us. Everybody would go down to Nonna Ceola's—she had a regular road there that was well-worn. Even us boys would go down and buy a bottle of beer once in a while. It was 10 cents a quart. The beer was kept in the basement where it was cool. If the beer was shaken on the way up from the cellar, when they pulled the cap off, the beer would hit the ceiling. So we had a water bucket to catch some of it. We would pour it in our glass and it would foam. We would have a big laugh over that.

Dad finished the eighth grade, and then went to business college for one year. Dad could do anything. He was good at singing and playing the harmonica. He taught me how to play the harmonica when I was just a little boy. I sang in the choir with Dad when I was just six or seven years old. The choir loft used to vibrate when Memo Morsani and the boys sang.

We worked four acres of ground north of our barn. We planted two or three acres of corn, tomatoes, potatoes, peaches, grapes, and apples. We pruned grapes and put in new posts. In the winter, we mainly worked cutting timber to use for fences and vineyards.

Our chores were to milk the cows, check traps to make sure that they were set to catch rabbits, and cut wood and carry it in. We had a heater that used coal or wood. We had to cut a certain length of wood for the cookstove, and a certain length for the heating stove. We would have to go get the cows and they were always at the farthest end of the farm, which was 60 acres. We would get on an old mule and ride bareback to get the cows.

When I was a boy, I had steel traps. I would set them and catch animals like 'possums, or a small skunk which we called a civet cat. I would sell them for 15 cents a hide. That was a lot of money in those days. I used box traps to catch rabbits. On my way to school I would take a dressed rabbit to Miss Mary and Miss Zelinda Bastianelli. They gave me 10 cents for a dressed rabbit. It was good money, because wages back then was 10 cents an hour.

One time Uncle Victor Ceola, Uncle Fred Ceola, Uncle Nel Ceola, Daddy, Gabriel, Lawrence, and Oliver decided to go rabbit hunting. The snow was knee deep. They went out with their guns. They said there were so many rabbits they couldn't shoot them. The snow was so deep the rabbits would jump up and they couldn't go anywhere. They just got clubs and killed them. They carried 73 rabbits out of the field. Junior and I had the job of helping to clean, skin, and dress the rabbits. Mama washed, cut up, boiled, and canned about 73 quarts of rabbits. We had rabbits galore to eat through the year.

Mama did a lot of canning—peaches, apples, rabbits. We had our own apple orchard, and our own grapes. We made a lot of jellies. I think Dad made cheese sometimes. The older it got the better tasting it was. It was really good when it had a little green in it.

We would butcher a hog and a calf at Christmas time and would have salami, ham, and bacon. We had bread and coffee for breakfast every morning. Mom would get a big pan and put a few tablespoons of coffee in with some milk and boil it. We would sometimes add a little wine or homemade whiskey to black coffee. That was very good.

We used to make wine and we had a nice little still for making whiskey. Junior and I had the extra jobs of making whiskey and raising chickens. We had two incubators out in the garage. We kept the still full of wine. We would go out and check it, and when it was ready, we would pour it into a quart jar or a gallon jug. We always had our job cut out for us. We had people that would come in from Fort Smith to buy a gallon of whiskey every once in awhile. We sold it for $10 a gallon. It was a little extra way of making a living.

Eugene made our first radio. He bought a little kit and put a crystal in one place and a coiled wire in another place and a little pin going down on this crystal. He had earphones hooked up to it. It didn't have batteries. He had a special room that Daddy built for him and Lawrence, because we got crowded in the old house. Eugene put that little radio on a bench and we all took turns going in and putting the earphones on and listening to music. Eugene later became an electrician.

     FRANCIS PIANALTO

Here is a story about Junior. One time we were throwing rocks. A vehicle was coming down the road, and Junior said, "I'm going to knock out the windshield when he gets up here." I told him he better not. But he did and broke the windshield of Albano Maestri's milk truck. Mr. Maestri just got out of the truck, came over to Junior and said, "Junior, I have a broken windshield because you threw rocks at it." I wasn't supposed to tell on Junior. Junior, I am sorry.

Oliver was very good at playing marbles. We'd play, and he would say, "We are playing for keeps." I said, "I want to play for fun," but he didn't listen. He would draw a circle and put 10 marbles in the middle of the circle. He would knock all my marbles out. I would start crying, and I'd go to Mama and say, "Oliver got all my marbles and it made me sad." Then Oliver had to give them back to me.

Sometimes Mama would want to give us a spanking for something. We could run real fast. Junior and I would do something wrong and we would both get a whipping. Dad was good with a razor strap, all three straps hooked to one. We would get twice the whipping if we ran away. If we would just stand there and take it, we would get a sting. It was better to just take it. We did try to escape sometimes. Sometimes the older brothers would chase us. They would catch us and get a rope and tie us up to a tree. We had lots of fun playing outside.

My first job other than picking tomatoes, beans, strawberries, and grapes on the farm was working in the Perona canning factory in Tontitown. Junior and I would go sometimes and pick spinach, grown right there in Tontitown. We would tip beans for 10 hours a day, and make a dollar a day. We would give 90 cents to Daddy and we would keep 10 cents for the grape festival. Then we would save our 10 cents, because Nonna would buy us an ice cream at the festival.

I completed ninth grade in the school that is still there today. We had nuns as teachers. I can't remember the names of all of them. The one I do remember is Sister Genevieve [Chafe] because I still have the marks on my hands [from being hit with a ruler for punishment]. I wasn't a good kid, but I was probably like all the rest of them. I liked to get into mischief—fights, wrestling, playing rough, and sometimes saying something I shouldn't. It seems like there was three or four Musketeers in every school class—Fredie Taldo, Stephen Maestri, Louis Pianalto, and myself. Joseph and Earl Mussino were there too, but they weren't as bad as I was. I missed recess a lot because I had to write lines. Sister Genevieve said, "Write this 100 times." I said, "Yes, Sister." I would take two pencils and hold them and write, "I must not do this." I used two pencils so it would go faster.

We usually walked to school. Occasionally Nazzareno Ranalli or Cousin Silvio Pianalto or Bennie Piazza would come by in their cars and pick us up. We rode our bikes sometimes. I bought a bicycle from Lawrence one time. He had made a carrier in the front and rear, and it had a crossbar. We put two little kids on the crossbar—Olivia on the front, and Leonard on the back. Junior and I put both feet on the pedals. Our feet were small. We all rode that bike together. Sometimes, someone would have to get off and push.

Our favorite sandwich to take for lunch was peanut butter and jelly. Mama fixed our sandwiches, and Eugene carried lunch for six of us kids in a gallon syrup bucket. Sometimes we would take cocoa and sugar and mix together and make a spread for our bread. At times I would go down to Mr. Mollar's store and get a nickel's worth of cookies and drink a soft drink.

We played ball at recess and noon. We would make our bats and balls. We had a board or a hickory stick trimmed down for a bat. We did not have mitts; we would catch bare-handed.

My cousin, Louis Pianalto, used to call me names. I was a scrawny little boy. One time Louis bopped me on the ear so hard that I hit the ground. He said, "I can whip you boxing; now I want to know if I can whip you wrestling. On the way home after school, we are going to stop at the pond at Earl Mussino's and we are going to wrestle." So we started wrestling. We rolled down in the pond. I would end up on top of him, so we tried again. Back to the top of the pond, roll down, and I would end up on top of him again. Louis said, "Well, I know I can whip you in boxing, and you can whip me in wrestling." He was a very kind person, and he sure was good at boxing. One time he told me he wanted to give me a ride home in his Model T. There was a steep hill with water at the bottom of the hill. Louis gave it the gas at the top of the hill. We flew down there and hit the water, and we just laughed.

The three stores where we would shop were Claude Morsani's, Richard Ardemagni's, and Frank Baudino's. John Mollar, Mr. Baudino's brother-in-law, ran the Baudino store. Mr. Strabala had a blacksmith shop located about where Mama Z's restaurant is today. We would stop on our way home from school and put our hands over the muffler of the engine that was running that turned the wheels. I think the Bausingers ran the little garage and service station that was by the Venesian Inn. Eugene, Gabriel, and Lawrence built Pianalto Brothers Garage after getting out of the service. I started working there in 1949. Jake Jaro had a café next to Claude Morsani's store. Jack Zulpo had a liquor store next to the café. The Peronas had a canning factory on the south end of the block where the old hotel used to be. There was a dance hall behind the little café [Mantegani's Luncheonette] across from the Venesian Inn. There was a baseball field next to the Luncheonette. There were three different ballparks in Tontitown: one on Barrington Road across from the Baudino store, one in the school yard, and the one beside the Luncheonette.

When I was about 14, Oliver, Gabriel, and Lawrence got on their bicycles and went up to Highfill and saw an old truck that would run. It was a 1926 Chevrolet station wagon that was used to haul passengers home from the train depot. The engine would run but the truck wouldn't move. My brothers told the truck owner, "We would give you $25 for it, but we only have $15, so we will also give you a calf worth $10." The owner said okay. They came home and got their wagon and team to pull the truck home. Dad said, "Where are you all going?" They said, "We are going to pick up a truck. We have to take the calf up there too, because we sold it." "You mean you got a truck that won't run and you sold my calf for $10?" That is the way we started to be mechanics. We took that thing apart and put it together. When they first put it together they put it in reverse and it started going forward. They put it in low gear and it went backwards. They said, "There is something wrong," and they took it apart again and got it all straightened out.

Daddy bought Cousin Gino's 1934 Chevrolet truck. We drove it to church and to town. I helped Dad keep it up. I enjoyed going to the ballgames, or picking up a bunch of kids wanting to go to the creek. We had lot of fun. I would take my guitar down there and play and sing.

My first automobile was a 1931 Dodge. Lawrence bought it in Kansas during the wheat harvest for $250. When he was called off to the service in 1940 or 1941, he put it up on blocks. He came home one day with a Mercury 1950 and said, "I'll sell you boys that car for $50 if you want it." Junior and I each gave him $25 for our first car. It was a dandy.

For Christmas, we always hung up the biggest socks we could find. We hung them on a nail in the wall around the stove. I believed in Santa Claus, and I always put in a big order from the Sears Roebuck catalog. One Christmas I said, "Junior, come here." I pulled a box of toys out from under the bed and said, "We are going to get this for Christmas. There isn't no Santa Claus."

At Easter, we would go outside and look for weeds to put in water, and then drop our hard boiled eggs in to dye them green. We made little tracks like a rabbit leading to the Easter basket, and put the Easter eggs in there.

The early grape festivals were held around the old [Smith] schoolhouse. We had soda pop from a barrel that had a spigot at the bottom. It was a nickel. Ice cream was a nickel. Hamburgers were a dime. I sold hamburgers and pop in a stand on the west side of the old schoolhouse. Cap Tiller showed movies. There were games, horseshoes, wrestling, sack races, tents with singing. Daddy got out there and sang one time, and once there was a brass band.

Before the [Smith] schoolhouse was destroyed, there was a place on the east side of the building where they used to sell grapes. The farmers would bring their grapes and stack them there for buyers to pick up and haul to Springdale.

[After I finished school] Junior and I built six little chicken houses and two big houses to raise chickens and get out of debt. We were in debt four or five years. We went to the wheat harvest in Kansas to work for Uncle George and Aunt Clara Barenberg Pianalto four or five years. I also worked at the canning factory.

During World War II, I was in the Navy two years, one month, and 16 days. I trained in California and then shipped out to Hawaii. From Hawaii we went to the island of Saipan. We invaded from the west side of Saipan. Our ship took soldiers to the shore. Then we would go back for ammunition and food supplies, whatever the soldiers needed. It was a terrible battle.

I came back home after I got out of the Navy. One night Eugene, Curley [Virgil] Sabatini, and I were going to a dance at an old skating rink on Rainbow Curve in Bentonville. Leon McAuliffe's band from Tulsa was playing. I saw a real pretty girl there. Her name was Lena Gaiche. I asked her to dance. She danced so good and so smooth and looked so sweet. From then on, we started going together. We were married in 1951.

We lived with Daddy and Mama while we were building our house. Daddy and Junior helped me build it. Before we built, I had to find water. I asked Dad where I should I dig, and he said down at the end. I witched the well and marked it with a cross. With a pick, we dug a well 70 feet deep and hit water.

After Lena and I married, I worked at the Pianalto Brothers Garage in Tontitown for 23 years, and then worked at Willis Shaw Trucking for 21 years, until I retired in 1993. Our children are Joyce Marie, Floyd Allen, Rose Mary, Stephen Francis, Christine, Vernon Joseph, Sandra Louise, Vincent Raymond, and Thomas Randal. We have 25 grandchildren.

As hobbies, I enjoyed trapping, hunting, skating, and playing the French harp, guitar, and harmonica. I liked to sing. We had house parties at Uncle Fred's, Uncle Joe's, different places. We had polenta smears, and they would call us up and say, "Bring your instruments and let's have a dance."

There are a lot of memories I can't let go of. I do a lot of dreaming. When I was in the hospital one time, I dreamed I saw Jesus, Mary, and Joseph. They weren't 12 feet away from me. I thought I was dead, because they were coming after me with their arms stretched out, facing me, with a heavenly blue sky, and it was so beautiful. I have never seen anything more beautiful than Jesus, Mary, and Joseph reaching out to me and saying, "Let's go." I said, "There is so much to be done here yet," and they disappeared. Then I woke up. There was a reason for that. God wasn't through with me yet.

Lena Gaiche Pianalto

LENA GAICHE PIANALTO

Lena Gaiche Pianalto was born in 1932 near Highfill, Arkansas, to Domenico and Luigia (Louise) Cortiana Gaiche. She was 73 years old when she was interviewed in 2005.

My maternal grandfather, Eustacchio Cortiana, came to America with six children: Domenico or Dick, Virginia, Giuseppe or Joe, Maria or Mary, Celeste or Cel, and Luigia or Louise, who was my mother. Eustacchio's wife, Lucia Strobe, had died in Italy. Eustacchio and his six children came from Sunnyside to Tontitown in 1898 with the original immigrants.

I think my mother completed the third grade. Seems like I remember her saying that as a young girl, she worked for families with children.

My father was 24 when he came to America. From what I have heard, he worked in the coal mines in Dow, Oklahoma. He was a farmer here in Arkansas.

My parents married in 1910. Their first home was about one mile north of Tontitown. They had five children: Elizabeth, Edith, James, Pete, and me. I was the youngest child. I was 13 years younger than my youngest brother, so [for most of my childhood] I was the only child at home. I didn't have much interaction with my brothers and sisters.

By the time I was born, my parents owned an 80-acre farm near Highfill [northwest of Tontitown]. They raised cattle, chickens, tomatoes, strawberries, and grapes. We canned vegetables and fruits from our farm. We had to carry water from a spring down at the bottom of a hill, until Dad put a ram in the spring and pumped the water up the hill. Later, he had a well drilled close to the house.

My dad butchered a hog every year. He would cut it up and make sausage, lard, bacon, and ham, enough to carry us through the winter. He would put the meat in the cellar. He made a fire and made it smoke, so we would have smoked bacon and ham.

We would kill a rooster or hen once in a while when they got too old. We caught them in the chicken house when they were still roosting. That was easier than chasing them all over the yard. I remember my mother wringing their necks. Then she would scald it—put hot water over it to make the feathers easier to pull out.

We had plenty of milk for us to use and drink, and for Mother to make cheese. We sold milk in five- and ten-gallon cans. Dad had a separator to separate the cream from the whey. We sold the cream and fed the whey to the hogs. We also made butter from the cream.

We bought our staples in Gentry or Springdale, or in Tontitown, at Claude Morsani's store or Ardemagni's store. We drove to Bentonville to pay our taxes.

I went to school at Rocky Comfort. I would have breakfast, go milk the cows, and then go to school. It was about a mile and a half walk to school. If it was raining or snowing, I didn't go. I took peanut butter and jelly sandwiches and egg sandwiches for lunch most of the time.

I stayed in Tontitown with Aunt Mary Fiori for a period of time, a week or maybe two weeks, so I could go to school in Tontitown and take my instructions to make my First Holy Communion.

I graduated eighth grade from Rocky Comfort when I was 15, I think. Then I worked on the farm until I got married.

I met my husband, Francis Pianalto, at a dance hall on Rainbow Curve in Bentonville. We started dating every Wednesday. We would go to a movie, or he would just come over and my mother and I would fix dinner. We would just stay there and visit. We didn't go out very much. We dated for a year before we were married in 1951. I was 19 years old. My sister Liz, who was 20 years older than me, helped me make my wedding dress.

After we were married, we lived with Francis's parents, Leo and Lucy Pianalto, for a few months until our house was finished. Francis, his brother Junior, and their father built our house. His brother Eugene did the wiring. This is the house we are still living in today.

Francis was a mechanic at Pianalto Brothers Garage. Eugene built the garage originally, along with his brothers, Gabe and Lawrence.

Francis helped them, and he later bought out Eugene's part. Francis also worked 25 years at Willis Shaw Trucking.

We have nine children: Joyce Marie, Floyd Allen, Rose Mary, Stephen Francis, Christine, Vernon Joseph, Sandra Louise, Vincent Raymond, and Thomas Randal. We have 25 grandchildren; 24 are living. We have four great-grandchildren.

I used to do a lot of canning—peaches, beans, tomatoes—and my children helped me peel apples and peaches, and tip beans. We bought apples and peaches by the bushel. We raised our own beans. We canned tomatoes, and made tomato juice and tomato puree.

I always had a washing machine. My first washing machine was down in the basement. You washed the clothes in the washing machine, then put them through the wringer. You had to rinse them in two different tubs. The two tubs were on a stand. We rinsed them, put them through the wringer, and then rinsed again. I didn't have a clothes dryer for many years. In fact, I still don't use my dryer much because it is not vented to the outside, and I don't like for that much moisture to go under the house. So, we hang our clothes [outside on a clothesline] most of the time.

When our children were old enough, they helped in the garden. We had two cows to milk. The oldest son would help milk the cows. We had some hogs to feed. In fact, they all helped. Their uncles, Junior and Edward Pianalto, had vineyards, so during a certain time of the year the kids would go out and break off the sprouts—the suckers, they were called—that would come up on the vines. When grape time came, I would go out with the kids and we would pick grapes together. When our son Floyd was about 15, he drove a truck for an egg company. Thomas, when he was big enough, worked for Bobby Pianalto, helping him with the chickens and the hogs, whatever he needed him to do on the farm. When our girls were about 13, they got jobs babysitting, ironing, or working at the Venesian Inn. All my girls worked at the Venesian Inn. Thank God there was something for them to do, that the Good Lord provided the way. When our youngest child was about 12 years old, I went to work at the Venesian Inn myself. I worked part-time there for 17 years.

Helene and Louis Pianalto

LOUIS PIANALTO

Louis Pianalto was born in 1924 in Tontitown, Arkansas, to Joe and Annie Cigainero Pianalto. He died in 1975. Mr. Pianalto's wife, Helene Fucci Pianalto Newman, and their daughter, Kathy Pianalto Miller, submitted a written biography of Louis Pianalto in 2003.

The paternal grandparents of Louis Pianalto were Peter and Teresa Marigo Pianalto. They and their three sons, Joe, Geno, and Alphonso, arrived in Tontitown [from Sunnyside] with the original immigrants in 1898. Peter Pianalto was a blacksmith. He was a massive man with huge shoulders, very strong. He would lift logs for his home by himself. He had bad eyesight as he grew older and had to use a cane.

The maternal grandparents of Louis Pianalto were Giovanni and Metilde Tondolo Cigainero. They came to America in the late 1800s.

Joe and Annie Cigainero Pianalto met when Joe was working in Texarkana, Arkansas, where Annie's family lived. After they married, they lived in Tontitown. Their children were Matilda, Mary, Josephine, Gile, Pete, Louis, and Philip. The children were all hard workers. They helped with the farming, milked cows, and plowed strawberries. Louis was so little when he was plowing that his ears barely hit the handle of the plow. The kids always had to plant seed on the Fourth of July, while everyone else got to go swimming. One time they threw away the seed and went swimming instead.

Joe Pianalto was a farmer and carpenter. He also made great wine. One time the revenue man came to Tontitown and went to open the spigot on each barrel to get rid of the wine. Uncle Gus [Cigainero] went behind the man and turned them back off. They only lost a gallon of wine that day.

Annie loved to fish and take care of her flowers. She quilted all the time. She canned tomatoes, turnip greens, peaches, and apples. She made cheese. The family ate lots of salami, cheese, squirrel, rabbit, and garden vegetables. They raised hogs and butchered them for pork. They raised chickens, but bought their beef. They bought staples such as flour and sugar from Mr. Mollar's store.

Louis Pianalto completed the eighth grade in school. He always liked to make people laugh. One time Richard Ardemagni was going to tell Louis's dad that Louis was smoking at recess. Louis went to get a gun to take care of Richard!

The businesses in Tontitown during Louis's childhood included Ardemagni's store, Morsani's store, John Mollar's store, Perona's feed store, and the old hotel.

Louis's family always had a big dinner on Christmas and Easter. They fasted during Lent but didn't dye Easter eggs.

Louis's first job away from home was working in California with Oliver Pianalto. Then Louis got drafted. He went into the Navy, and was on a submarine. He was stationed in Connecticut.

Louis met his wife, Helene Fucci, when he went to Meadville, Pennsylvania, to meet his brother and sister-in-law, Gile and Esther Pianalto. Louis and Helene began writing to each other, were married in 1948, and moved to Tontitown.

Louis was a farmer and a tile setter. He set tile in the winter and farmed in the summer. He belonged to the Rodeo of the Ozarks trail ride. He loved to dance and help other people.

Louis and Helene had four children: Michael, Robert, Kathleen and Sammy. Another child, Gile Dino, died as an infant. The family also has five grandchildren, and three great-grandchildren.

PETE PIANALTO

*Pete Pianalto was born in 1921 in Tontitown, Arkansas,
to Joe and Annie Cigainero Pianalto. Pete was 81 years
old when he submitted this written interview in 2003.*

My paternal grandparents were Pietro and Teresa Marigo Pianalto. They came to Tontitown with the original immigrants in 1898. They came with three children, Joe, Geno and Alphonso. My grandfather was a blacksmith and bricklayer.

My maternal grandparents were Giovanni and Matilda Tondolo Cigainero. They came to America in the late 1800s. Their first home was in Tennessee. They had the following children: Vince, Louis, Mitch, Flore, Gus, John, Joe, Kate, and Annie, my mom.

Dad met Mom when he went to Texarkana [Arkansas] to work. Their children are Matilda, Mary, Josephine, Egedio, Pete, Louis, and Philip.

Dad was a farmer and worked in the mines. Mom did not work outside the home. She did a lot of quilting and gardening. We ate a lot of vegetables, spaghetti, and sausage. Mom canned everything. She made cheese. We raised our own meat. We purchased our flour, sugar, and other staples in Tontitown.

Before and after school we milked cows. We ate breakfast after we did the chores. For breakfast, we usually had coffee and bread.

I completed the eighth grade in Tontitown. We were taught by nuns. I usually took a sausage and jelly sandwich for lunch. At noon and recess we played ball and marbles. Once in a while I would sneak out of school to smoke.

At Christmas, we always went to Midnight Mass. We usually had chicken for Christmas dinner.

Pete Pianalto

Our family tradition at Easter was to fast during Lent, attend church services during Holy Week, and dye Easter eggs.

The early grape festivals were held at the old [Smith] schoolhouse [on the northwest corner of Highway 412 and Barrington Road]. I remember when Dad ran the sack race at the festival.

My first job away from home was at an aircraft factory in California. Then I was drafted, and went into the Air Force. I was stationed in Texas, Indiana, North Carolina, and England.

I have known my wife, Lucy Franco, since we were in school together. When we started dating, we would go out once a week, usually dancing. We married in 1948. Our children are Deloris, twins Donnie and Ronnie, and Roger. We have five grandchildren.

I have been a farmer all my life. My hobbies are playing bocce and attending ballgames.

Albert Piazza

ALBERT PIAZZA

*Albert Piazza was born in 1927 in Tontitown, Arkansas,
to Domenico (Dick) and Blanche Taldo Piazza. He was
75 years old when he was interviewed in 2002.*

My maternal grandparents, James and Clementine Costa Taldo, had three kids with them when they came to America: Blanche, who was my mother, Emilia, and Joseph [Joe Jack]. They later had Edward, Argie, Irma, Olivia, Rita, and Margaret.

Grandmother Taldo was an ordinary woman. She was good at cooking and sewing. You had to be back then. I don't remember too much because I was about nine years old when she died.

Grandfather Taldo was a farmer. During the winter months he used to go to Oklahoma to work in the mines. A lot of the men did that.

My paternal grandparents were James and Angela Piazza. Their children were Angelo, Joe, Jimmy, Bennie, Dick, who was my dad, Mary, Josephine, Carrie, and Teresa. Grandfather Piazza was a short man. He was tough, a hard worker.

My father was born in Italy. About his childhood here in Tontitown, he told me they did a lot of hunting and trapping. They lived on a lot of rabbits and quails in the first years. He went to school like they did in those days, just a few days a year. I don't know what grade he completed.

My mother was also born in Italy. When she was a teenager, she worked in Fort Smith as a housekeeper. She had a rough life as a child. Her dad was strict. She did go to school a little bit.

My brothers and sisters are George, Hubert, Henry, and Nora. I'm the oldest. I was born right here in this house and have lived here all my life. This is the first and only home my parents ever had.

Our chores as kids were to milk the cows, feed the chickens, and work in the grapes. In the summer, they also worked in the tomatoes and beans. We raised hogs and had to feed them.

We were never hungry. Our breakfast was mostly coffee, milk, and bread. We butchered hogs and made sausage. There were fruits and vegetables, all home grown stuff. Mother canned peaches, tomatoes. She did a lot of canning. She made cheese. We kept milk and butter here in the house and in a hand-dug well down there in the holler. We had flour to make the bread and spaghetti. Everybody had spaghetti.

I completed the sixth grade here in Tontitown. School and me didn't work too much. The teachers were nuns. I remember Sister Madonna [Hall]. I remember the mean one, Sister Genevieve [Chafe]. There was Sister Bernadine [Lake], who was short and kind of chubby. There was a young one, but I don't remember her name. For lunch I mostly took peanut butter and jelly, and salami. At recess we just played outside.

I remember a canning factory, a store, a winery, and a filling station as the businesses in town. Mary Maestri's [restaurant] was here then. She started serving dinners a long, long time ago.

After a tornado blew the church down [in 1934], we went to church in the school basement for a long time. My dad helped with the construction of the new church. He made blocks and stacked them up at the school, and then they started construction. The men of the town built the church. That's where my dad fell and hurt his leg.

At Christmastime we didn't have to go to school. Santa Claus came Christmas Eve or Christmas morning. Sometimes he came during Midnight Mass. We didn't do much special.

During Lent, there was no meat on Friday, for sure. During the week, you were supposed to only eat two small meals and one full meal per day. We had to work, so we didn't fast all that much, but we did some. We never did eat meat when we weren't supposed to. On Ash Wednesday for sure we didn't eat meat.

The grape festivals used to be held in the afternoon, because at night there wasn't any electricity. My dad and brother went up there and bought some ice cream and walked around and came home. It was at the old [Smith] schoolhouse, where Richard Ardemagni's store was built later [on the northwest corner of Highway 412 and Barrington Road].

 ALBERT PIAZZA

I remember just a few swings, and the guys who used to come out and have a movie theater under a tent. One time there were wrestlers.

I never worked away from the farm, except for a few days at the canning factory. I wasn't in the service. I never had time for hobbies. We had 17 acres of vineyard. We had 180 acres altogether. After the war started in the 1940s, I started in raising chickens. Chickens fired the country up.

I think it's a better world now than when I was young. We have all the conveniences today. We didn't used to have nothing. Times were tough back then. It's not a more religious world, but better in some ways.

David Piazza

DAVID PIAZZA

*David Piazza was born in 1924 in Tontitown, Arkansas,
to Ben and Edith Tomiello Piazza. He was 78 years old
when he was interviewed in 2002.*

My paternal grandparents, James and Angela Piazza, came from
Italy [to Sunnyside]. They came to Tontitown with the original settlers
in 1898. I don't know anything about them.

My maternal grandparents were Silvio and Mariana Tomiello. I
remember when Grandfather Silvio lived in California with Uncle Virgil,
and my grandmother lived in Chicago with some of the children. Frank
Verucchi lived in Chicago too. Every winter when Frank would come
down to Tontitown for a visit, my grandmother, Mariana, would come
with him. Us kids would go outside and catch bluebirds, sparrows, and
woodpeckers. We'd bring them in the house to our grandmother and
she would clean and cook them for us.

My brothers and sisters are Ernest, Virgil, Phillip, Lawrence, Joe,
and two girls, Lucy and Rita. Our house wasn't very big. There were
three bedrooms. The girls slept in one, the boys in the other, and the
old folks had their own room. We had a big enough table for all of us
to sit around.

Dad was a farmer. He raised grapes, tomatoes, beans, strawberries,
every vegetable you can name. We sold our produce to Brogdon and
Hazel Produce [brokers in Springdale]. We also raised chickens, hogs,
and cattle. Mom worked out in the field with Dad. She'd go out and pick
corn, beans, tomatoes, and strawberries, go to the shed and pack them,
then come in and do her housework.

We butchered hogs, and always had pork, ham, bacon, salami, and
sausage. Mom would make the sausage into patties and fry them, layer
them in a big crock, pour grease over the sausage in the crock, and put

the crock in the cellar. When we wanted sausage, we just took out what we needed.

Sometimes Mom would go out and catch a chicken, pick the feathers off of it, and cook it. We didn't always have chicken, sometimes we'd have meatballs, and we ate a lot of wild rabbits. We used to kill the heck out of them rabbits. We caught them in the wintertime in the snow. You'd walk around in snow up to your knees. The snow was so deep the rabbits couldn't get up and run, so we just knocked them in the head with a club. Lot of times Mom cooked them in ketchup or umido.

We also had box traps set to catch rabbits. We'd get up early and run [check] our traps up through the woods. We took the rabbits out of the traps, knocked them in the head, and threw them in a tow sack to deliver them. We took them to [Frank] Perona, Cel Cortiana, and Mary and Zelinda Bastianelli. They paid us a dime a rabbit. We'd take that dime and go down to Mr. Mollar's store.

Us kids began doing chores as soon as we could carry a bucket. We carried buckets full of turnips to feed the cows. We got up before the sun came up. We would milk the cows, go see about our rabbit traps, then come back home and walk all the way to Tontitown to school. That night we did the same thing—walk home, bring in wood, feed and milk the cows, feed the hogs. There was no running around. Back then, there was no questions asked. Our parents told you what they wanted you to do, and you did it or got your tail kicked. There was no putting it off till tomorrow. They didn't have to keep telling us over and over. Our parents were not rough with us, I don't mean that. They were strict, and we respected them.

We plowed with a mule, walking right behind him, barefoot. Usually mules are stubborn, but boy, not that one. I plowed many an acre of strawberries and tomatoes, walking barefoot behind that old mule. We always went barefoot. We had just one pair of shoes. We worked in the fields barefoot, you dad gum right we did. We plowed corn, beans, everything, barefoot. Picked tomatoes barefoot. I could jump through a briar patch and not even get a scratch.

After school and on Saturdays, we helped Dad in his grape vineyards. He would cut off [prune] the vines he wanted removed, and leave them hanging on the wires. Then us kids came along behind and jerked the cut vines off the wire and threw them into the middle of the

　　　DAVID PIAZZA

rows. That's how I caught on to how he was pruning, how many buds to leave on the vines. Then we took a team of horses, hooked on the harrow, and pulled the vines to the end of the row. We'd pile them up and when they had dried a little bit, we burned them.

To make grape cuttings, we'd drag a bunch to the house and work on that in the winter. You cut pieces about 12 inches long, leaving two or three eyes or buds on each. You cut straight across the bottom, and slanted across the top. You put several in a bundle about six inches around and tied them with a string, top and bottom. Dig a hole, put them in the hole upside down, and cover them till spring. Then in the spring we'd dig them up and plant them in rows. We didn't do this every year, but when we needed to plant more. Vineyards last a pretty long time.

When I had my own vineyards, I did it a little different. I hooked my tractor to the brush hog and would run up and down the rows and cut the vines into smaller pieces. But I learned the basics of how to do it from my dad.

We sold milk commercially. We put the milk in a 10-gallon can and then put the can in the spring to keep cold. Each morning we carried it down to the road and the milkman would come by and pick it up. Hugo Pozza was the milkman, then another guy, I think it was a Bariola. I don't know where they hauled the milk to.

We cut wood and hauled it. Dad would cut a rick of wood, put it in the wagon, and haul it up to Ardemagni's store. Dad didn't get any money, he [traded the wood for] groceries like sugar and flour instead. I think it was Pacifico Pianalto or old man [Felix] Ardemagni who had the store at that time. We also hauled wood to old man [John] Granata. We hauled it to everyone. When the kids were out of school at Christmastime, we all helped cut and stack wood, then Dad would haul it in his wagon.

Dad made his own wine. One time we had a barrel of wine blow up. Dad was making wine in the cellar. He had drained the wine from the pomace [skins and other solids] and was putting it in barrels. Instead of leaving the spout open, he just closed it. That damn thing got mad and blew the end plumb out of the barrel.

One time my brother Ernie and I got into real trouble. Dad had us cleaning out the pulp from the barrels, then we rinsed them out. As we worked, we were sipping right along. We got through and started out of the cellar, and neither one of us knew which way we was going! We got a pretty good whipping. We never did that again.

Dad used to make home brew too, but I don't know how you do it. He had a big old crock, and he put water in it, then something else, I think it was malt, that he used to get it down at Ardemagni's store. Then it turned to beer. He got a little hose and ran the beer into jugs when it was ready. It doesn't take as long as wine.

Mama made cheese at home. She put a tub of milk on the stove, put her stuff in it, cooked it till it clabbered, poured it into a mold, and let it drain and age. Boy, I tell you what, that was good cheese. That's what we had to eat—cheese, homemade sausage, and homemade bread. We ate the heck out of that stuff. And oh boy, did she ever make butter. She would put cream in a half-gallon jug and shake the heck out of it, back and forth, until it turned into butter. Boy, was that good. We kept our milk and butter in the spring to keep it cool. Dad had it fixed to where the cows or animals couldn't get to it. When we needed milk or butter we just went to the spring to get it.

We ate a lot of soup. It had a little of everything—tomatoes, carrots, potatoes, maybe a chunk of meat. For dinner, Mom always made a big pan of spaghetti with homemade sausage and homemade bread. She made her noodles each time we were going to have spaghetti. She'd mix it up, roll it out with a rolling pin, then roll it up and cut it with a big knife. She would shake it loosely and spread it out on a table to dry. She didn't make thin spaghetti, she made wider noodles.

Mom used a lot of tomatoes to make her polenta and umido. She used butter and onions, and as far as meat, we ate what we had— sometimes squirrel, sometimes rabbit, chicken, or not too often, beef. Our biggest thing was pork.

Besides rabbits, we killed wild birds for food too. We'd skin and clean the birds and give them to Mom. She'd have a big bowl of birds, and with that she'd make a big pot of stew or umido, and a big pot of polenta. She'd put the big bowl of polenta in the middle of the table, along with a big pot of birds, rabbit, squirrel, chicken, whatever we had, and it was good. We had a gallon jug of wine sitting on the floor, and we drank a glass of wine with every meal, even us kids. I'll tell you what, we never had a cold, never had a snotty nose or nothing. We were healthy.

We carried water from the two springs on our farm. We dipped the water out of the spring with a bucket. The cows drank from the spring, so we didn't have to carry water to them. We carried water for the chickens and for our use in the house. We did our laundry outside: heated the water, dumped it in tubs, used a washboard, and then rinsed the clothes.

The springs were where we took a bath, and by golly, that was cold water. You know how we warmed the water? We had 50-gallon barrels out there, and we filled them half full of water and let the sun warm the water. When evening come, we all took a bath right there in a tub. Sometime we would walk down to the creek and take a dip in the afternoon. In the winter, we had to warm the water in a pot on the stove and put it in a No. 3 wash tub.

We never had a store-bought shirt. Mama sewed. She made all the dresses for the girls out of feed sacks. When we bought feed for the cows she would try to get two or three sacks of the same design to have enough to make something out of it.

We walked to and from school. Once in awhile we hitched a ride with the milkman, Hugo Pozza. Mom and Dad had an old Model T. When they'd go someplace they would go in the car. Us kids, we had to walk. We'd take a biscuit or bread and jelly, maybe an egg sandwich or sausage for lunch. We were taught by nuns. They were good to us, but they were strict.

When I started school I couldn't even write my name because my parents did not know or speak English. That's what made it so hard for me. When we sat down to the table at home until the time we went to bed, there wasn't an English word said from either one of them. See, I started school and learned a little bit of English, then Ernie started and he learned a little bit, then Lucy started and she learned a little bit. As we went along, our English got stronger and better. I quit school after fifth grade because I was needed to help Dad with the farming. I was 12 or 13 years old.

When electricity came through, it was the best thing we ever had. We could see what the hell we were doing. Up to that time, we had a kerosene lamp in each room. When we studied, we had to get right up under the lamp to see. That's the reason we always ate an early supper and late breakfast—that way, we didn't have to have light. The only way we could see to tie our shoes was to open the door on the woodstove. That's the truth.

We never did know too much about what went on in Tontitown, [because we lived out in the country]. We just lived in our area and played with the kids in our neighborhood: Albert, Rosalie, and Florence Pianalto, and Joe Ranalli. We'd go to Albert's house—the Pianaltos lived across the creek—and play horseshoes and baseball until it got dark, then we would come on home. On Sundays we'd go fishing down on Brush Creek. We'd walk through the fields clear down to Javello's [who lived on Brush Creek]. We used worm and crawdads for bait.

When we got a little older, we got us a bicycle. On Sunday afternoon we'd ride all the way from our house to Springdale to the Concord Theater. It was all gravel roads, a good 10 miles or more each way. It cost a quarter to get into the show.

I helped make the cement blocks for the church [built to replace the church that was destroyed by a tornado in 1934]. I helped my dad and Silvio Pianalto make the blocks down in the school basement. They'd mix up cement in a wheelbarrow, put it into a mold, and let it dry. I would then pick up the blocks and take them by wheelbarrow to the building site and unload them. Albano Maestri was the boss. All the men of the parish worked certain days, and they brought their children who were big enough to help. It was all done by hand. Old man [Joe] Lazzari built all the backdrop wood behind the main altar and the side altars. He would put a board on sawhorses, and he would run a blow torch back and forth over the board and stain it different shades. Boy, it was beautiful.

I helped load and unload a lot of the rocks that are under the church. We had a big stack of rocks on our farm because we had to pick rocks out of the field to plant strawberries. When they got ready to build the church, Louis Perona drove his old truck out there and a bunch of us boys loaded the rocks into the truck. Then we drove back to the church, unloaded the rocks, and the men would put the rocks in place. They were going to put a cement floor in the church, and then they changed their mind. Under the floor of that church, there isn't enough room for two rabbits, it's so full of rocks.

Ardemagni's had a store on the southwest corner of Highway 412

     DAVID PIAZZA

and Barrington Road. It was a two-story brick building. Ardemagni had a grocery store on the first floor, and Frank and Carrie Perona lived on top of it. Carrie was my dad's sister. The Peronas had a canning factory. Me and Dad went down one time with a big load of tomatoes. They were beautiful tomatoes. I guess they had more than they could use at that time, because Carrie said, "We are going to have to dock you on these tomatoes. They are a little too green." My dad said, "You won't have to dock me very many times because I won't be back." We went home, opened the gate, and let the cows have the tomatoes. No kidding.

We used to go down to Mr. Mollar's store to buy a pencil. He would give us a piece of candy. We'd go for a penny pencil and get a piece of candy. We thought that was something. That store was all cluttered up. You couldn't find nothing anywhere. You could pull a string here and turn on a light bulb there. Oh my God, he had cats everywhere. You opened the door and the cats knocked you down.

The grape festivals were held where Ardemagni's Tontitown Mercantile building is today [on the northwest corner of Highway 412 and Barrington Road]. There used to be an old schoolhouse on that corner [Smith schoolhouse]. The ice cream stand and Coke stand were on the west side of the school. You could buy an ice cream for a nickel. We used to go down there with a quarter and come home with a nickel. They had an old Ferris wheel. We didn't go very many times because we didn't have much money.

The first job I had away from the farm was for old man [Cesare] Mantegani. He had a winery. I helped bottle wine, carry boxes, label wine, load trucks, a little bit of everything. Then I went to work for John Granata's Winery. He had six or so women working there bottling, labeling. They hauled their wine down the mountain to the Fort Smith area.

All that winery work was before I was drafted. I was only gone a month and 13 days. I went into the service and they found out my back had been broken and they sent me home. Then I got a job at John Late Chevrolet in Springdale. Albert Pianalto was working there at the time, and he told me if I wanted a job, he could get me on, and I could ride to work with him. I didn't have transportation for myself. I rode with him for a long, long time. Then I bought me an old car.

I met my wife, Minnie Evans, when my sister Lucy was working at the Fayetteville City Hospital. Minnie worked at the hospital too. Albert Pianalto was going with a girl, Ocie, who also worked at the hospital. Ocie and Minnie were both from over around Hindsville in Madison County. One night we were all going over to take Ocie home. On the way we lost the darn car battery. The damn thing fell out of the car. We walked back down the road in the dark and found the battery, put it back in the car, and took Ocie home. That was the darnedest time. We laughed and laughed. Albert and Ocie later married each other.

I'm not sure how long Minnie and I dated before we got married. I know it was two years or longer, because I got so damn tired of driving around them stumps to get over there to Madison County, we just got married. We have two children, Louetta Sue and David Duane.

What was the hardest part of my life? I didn't have any hard part. I was just pulling right along with the rest of them.

     DAVID PIAZZA

JOSEPHINE PIAZZA

*Josephine Piazza was born in 1927 in Tontitown,
Arkansas, to Angelo and Angela Penzo Piazza. She was
75 years old when she was interviewed in 2002.*

My paternal grandparents were Giacomo [James] and Angela
Piazza. They came to Tontitown [in 1898 with the original settlers] from
Sunnyside. Their children were Mary, Teresa, Carrie, Joe, Angelo, who
was my father, Domenic, James, Josephine, and Bennie.

I don't remember anything about my Piazza grandparents. They
died before I was born. I've been told that my grandmother was red-
headed. They use to call her Rosa. That is Italian for "red." Also that
she used to prune and tie grapes. On the sixth day of April, it was real
cold. She went out and tied grapes and she got pneumonia and died.
Our people had a really hard time.

My maternal grandparents were Domenico and Catherine Penzo.
They also came to Tontitown through Sunnyside. I know this because
my mother told me they had a little girl that got that fever and died in
Sunnyside. Her name was Angela too. She was older than my mother.
Because of the malaria, Father Bandini took the families up here [to
settle Tontitown]. Domenico and Catherine came with one son, John.
Their other children, who were all born in Tontitown, were Joe, Ed,
Pete, Andrew, and Angela, who was my mother. As a child, my mother
worked in the field picking berries and grapes. She was a good picker.
She was fast.

Grandmother Penzo was sick for 30 years. I don't know what was
wrong with her. She was in bed and Grandfather took care of her. He
died six months before she did.

When my parents married, my father was in his 30s, and Mother

Josephine Piazza

was 18. They were 16 years apart in age. When my mother was just a little girl, and my dad was big, he saw my mother running around in the yard. He told her mother, "Keep care of that little girl, because I'm going to marry her one of these days." And by golly, he did.

Mother was a widow at age 21. Daddy and Mother each died at the age of 37. I was six months old when Daddy died, and I was 15 years old when Mother died. All I know about Daddy's death is that he and his brother Joe went to the woods to sharpen posts and they took him home in the truck dead. A belt on a piece of machinery broke and the belt struck Daddy and killed him. He got killed down in that timber on Ardemagni Road, across from where Uncle Andrew and Flora Penzo lived.

After my daddy's death, Mother was left with two babies. I was six months old, and my sister Catherine was two and a half years old. Mother had a hard time. I don't know how she did it. She continued to live in the Piazza home place. Uncle Joe was the only one still living in the house. She had a couple of cows to milk. I don't know just when, but later she married Daddy's brother, Uncle Jim Piazza.

When my sister, Catherine, first started to school, she didn't know how to talk English. Italian was all [my parents] knew. English, they didn't know nothing. We learned Italian before we learned English. Later on, my mother knew how to talk English.

I went to school through about the seventh grade. Sister Adrian [McGrath] was the one that taught me about all the time. She was kind of rough, but she made us learn. For three or four years we went to school in the same room, and Sister Adrian was always my teacher. The next year I was going to get to move to another room, and I'll be darned if Sister Adrian didn't move too. So I didn't get away from her. I never did get in trouble. I got a C minus; I never did get a D or an F.

At recess some kids used to play ball, stuff like that, but I never did. I just sat around. At noon we walked home for lunch. We had an hour, so we had time to walk home and back.

One of my best friends in school was Theresa West. She came from Hindsville [in Madison County]. Her mother died when she was young. I guess Leon Zulpo was my boyfriend. They used to tease me about Leon all the time. We were in the same grade.

We walked to school and to church. It was all dirt roads. When it rained, it was nothing but mud. When Catherine made her First Holy Communion, she had to hold up her dress to walk up to the church because the road was so muddy.

I remember the church that blew away in a storm [in 1934]. After that, we had to go to church in the school basement while the men of the community built a new church. They took turns, and worked a day at a time. Uncle Jimmy didn't go too much, but they all took their turns.

We walked up to Tontitown to get groceries. Of course, we had our own eggs and our own milk. We planted a garden. We didn't buy no canned beans, stuff like that. Well, we didn't have money to buy too much stuff. Claude Morsani had a store, and oh yes, Mr. Mollar's store. They say that once somebody was buying a pound of hamburger meat, and as Mr. Mollar was weighing the meat on the scale, one of his cats was on the other side eating the meat as Mr. Mollar was trying to package it. He was a good old man. He used to give us candy whenever we went up there.

We always had plenty to eat. Lettuce and stuff out of the garden. We had lots of soup. Chicken and spaghetti, for sure. We'd have to run around half the day to catch a chicken to kill it. We'd chase until it got tired of running.

We would butcher hogs. Uncle Dick Franco used to make sausage. I remember Pete Pianalto's daddy came down and made sausage. You need a damp cellar to keep sausage because you hang it up and it has to get mold on it from the moisture. That sausage was good though.

Mother made cheese in a little old building [on the northeast corner of Highway 412 and Tessaro Lane]. People used to bring their milk there, and then they made cheese every few days. We had a cistern where we kept milk and butter cool. We put them in a bucket and wheeled the bucket down close to the water. It was cold down there.

We did a lot of canning. We used to can 400 quarts of ketchup every year, for four people: Mother, Jimmy, Catherine, and myself. We picked the tomatoes, and washed them and cleaned out the stem part. Then we put them in a pot and cooked them down, outside in the big pot, if you had a lot to cook, otherwise, we cooked them in the house. We let them cool off, and then we would set a big screen on top of a big pot and pour the cooked tomatoes into the screen. We rubbed the tomatoes through the screen with the palms of our hands. Then we cooked that pulp until it was thick, or until we got tired, I guess. We'd add a little salt, maybe a little pepper, and carry it in the house. We scalded our jars in a pot of water, filled the jars with ketchup, and sealed them up. We used ketchup for everything—spaghetti, soup, umido, chicken.

We heated the water for laundry outside on a wood fire We had a real big copper kettle, the same one we used to make ketchup and other things. Just fill it up and heat the water, then fill a tub out of the kettle

    JOSEPHINE PIAZZA

and rub like hell on a rubbing board. We made our own lye soap and used that. We had two tubs: one we used to soap and wash the clothes, the other we used to rinse them. We didn't have a wringer. We had to wring them by hand and then hang them on a clothesline.

For bathing, we would carry the water in, heat it, and put it in a washtub. We bathed in the washtub. We didn't take a bath every other minute like we do now. We probably bathed on Saturday night. Of course, we always washed up. We had a porch there with a table on it, and we washed up there. We didn't have indoor bathrooms. We had to go outside to the *chaso* [bathroom].

For light, we used coal oil lamps. When electricity first came [to Tontitown], Mother didn't want it. They wanted to plant the electric poles in our field, and she didn't want them to do that. They had to go around, and it made them mad. After Mother died, and we grew up a little more, my God, we had to have electricity. They let us have it. It's a wonder they did.

We didn't have much free time when we were growing up. On Sundays we used to walk to Uncle Dick Franco's, Andrew and Flora Penzo's, or sometimes Uncle Dick Piazza's. At home we used to play dominoes and pitch. Catherine and I never went nowhere to play [with other children]. My God, they wouldn't let us get out of the house.

At Christmas, we went to Midnight Mass. Dinner was like any other day. Oh, we probably made a pie once in a while. At Easter, we tried to fast during Lent, just like we do now. Don't eat meat on certain days. We probably cooked some eggs. If Mother made fugassa, I don't remember it. Catherine and I never did.

The first grape festivals I remember were held where the Ardemagni store is now [northwest corner of Highway 412 and Barrington Road]. At first the women cooked the spaghetti at home and carried it up there. Then they started going from house to house, collecting food for the festival dinners. I'd give two chickens, you'd give two chickens. The women would kill the chickens, scald them, peel them, and cook them for the festival. I started working at the festival when the dinners were still held in the school basement. I washed dishes at first. Emma Verucchi, Mary Tessaro, Theresa Zulpo, and Dora Taldo made spaghetti.

I don't remember one day when Mother was well after I was born. One time she had appendicitis, and she was three weeks in the hospital.

Catherine and I were just little girls. [Joseph and Elizabeth Strabala] had a blacksmith shop right across the street from our house, so Mother got Mrs. Strabala to stay with us. She would cook a little dinner for us and then call Mr. Strabala from the shop and he would come eat with us. We ate so doggone many beets. I said to myself, "I will never eat another beet." But you know what? This year Ernie [Piazza] gave me a quart he canned last year, and boy, were they good.

Mother also had female trouble. She was going to have surgery but she didn't want to go to Fayetteville [to City Hospital] because women working there knew her. So she went to the Prairie Grove hospital. The doctor didn't know too much about what was wrong with her. She bled to death in the hospital [in 1942].

Uncle Jimmy—remember, Mother married him after Dad died— was with us for 18 years after Mother died. At the time she died, we had one chicken house. We milked cows and planted a few beans some-times. Later, we started working in the fields for other people. We tied a lot of grapes, that's for sure. We tied grapes and raised chickens for Sam Kelly, just south of here. After Catherine and I were living by ourselves, we raised chickens for Richard and Olivia Roso.

Catherine and I would work in the fields all day, then come in and cook supper. We'd cook spaghetti. We would make a pretty good-sized batch of sauce and freeze it. We took the sauce out in the morning to thaw, so when we finished [working with] the chickens at night, we didn't have to do everything from scratch for supper.

When Catherine was about 36 years old, she bought a truck. She had to get Sam Kelly to show her how to drive. Uncle Jim wouldn't show her, because he didn't want us to go nowhere, you see. I never drove it much. I drove it to Henry Piazza's one time and I told Henry, "That's it for me, I'm scared." I did drive down in the field a few times.

Uncle Jimmy remarried in 1961. They moved to Sam Kelly's place, and then later moved to Bentonville. He died of cancer in 1965.

It was hard for Catherine and I after our mother died, but we got along pretty good. I used to do the washing. Catherine did the ironing. She patched our clothes. She ran the sweeper and dusted. I would sweep and mop. I'd go out and feed the damn hogs, feed the damn chickens. Catherine cooked, and I cooked a little bit, but not very much. We did the best we could, and we made it. We always stayed together.

     JOSEPHINE PIAZZA

J. H. POZZA

*John Hugo "J. H." Pozza was born in 1932 in Tontitown,
Arkansas, to Hugo Dominic and Lucia Ardemagni Pozza.
He was 70 years old when he was interviewed in 2002.*

My paternal grandparents, John and Enrica Pianalto Pozza, were
married in Italy and arrived in Tontitown with the original settlers from
Sunnyside in 1898. They had five children: Virgil, Concetta, Tom, Hugo,
who was my father, and Lena.

My grandfather Pozza was a businessman. He opened the first general merchandise store in Tontitown. He died of cancer at an early age,
so I never knew him. Grandmother Pozza lived with us after he passed
away. She was a good cook, and a good homemaker, as all Italian people
are. She was born on April Fools' Day. When we were little kids, we
would try to fool her, and she would say, "You try to foolie me!"

My maternal grandparents, Felice [Felix] and Enrica Pianalto
Ardemagni, were also among the original Tontitown settlers. Their children were Gene, Beato, Mike, Richard, and Lucia, who was my mother.

My grandfather Felix had big vineyards, and a very good winery, a
bonded winery. My cousin Michael Ardemagni and I used to help bottle
the wine. We ran the hose from the barrel down to the bottle, and we
would take the out of the bottle and put it in our mouth. Nonno Felix
never did catch us.

During Prohibition, they would come around and check to see if
you had wine or anything. If you did, they would break the barrels and
throw them out in the ditch. Well, they did that to my grandfather, and
the wine was flowing down the ditch. My father said he and one of the
Fiori boys—I forgot which one—got down on their hands and knees and
drank the wine out of the ditch.

J. H. Pozza and Annabelle Pozza Miller

Nonno Felix used to tell a poem to us kids. He would recite it in the Cremonese dialect, from Cremona, Italy, where he was from. When Nonno would speak in his Cremonese dialect, Nonna Enrica would say, "Quit cussing!" The name of the poem is "La Vacchetta," which means "The Little Cow." It goes like this: Once I had a little cow, she gave a pail of milk. I put it in the cabinet, and a fly came and drank it all up.

My grandmother Ardemagni was in bed 10 years before she died. She was paralyzed. Nonna was a large woman. I think a stroke is what paralyzed her.

My dad completed eighth grade in school. Nobody went to high school in those days. Dad was a carpenter, and a grape farmer. He worked at the CCC Camp at Devil's Den, near West Fork, for a long time. He used to walk from Tontitown to Devil's Den. Sometime he would get a ride.

I guess Mother completed eighth grade. She wanted to go on in school, but her father wouldn't let her. In those days girls didn't go on in school. They stayed home, got married, and had babies. Mother did not work out in her younger days because she was needed at home. Mother was mild-mannered, and a very talented person. She was a good cook, and was musically inclined. She was the organist at our church for many years after John Mollar died.

There are three children in our family: Annabelle, myself, and Felix. I was born at home. Dr. Cooper from Elm Springs delivered me. He was a dedicated country doctor. His wife accompanied him. She made out the birth certificates, and she made mine wrong. I was born January 18, but she put down January 17, so I had a little trouble later on.

Dad was an avid outdoorsman. He loved to hunt and fish. Uncle Tom Caldarera and Uncle Arch Cameron would come to hunt some weekends. They hunted rabbit and quail, then Nonna Enrica Pozza would put them all in the oven to cook, and she would make polenta.

One time Dad wanted to take me hunting in the woods behind our house. He took me by the hand and we started walking down to the woods. I started crying and said, "I don't want to go hunting." I went back to the house and went into the kitchen with my mother and helped her cook. I wasn't very macho.

We had chores to do each day. Feed the pigs, slop the hogs, feed the chickens. During the summer we would pick strawberries, grapes, and beans. I also worked at the Venesian Inn when I was a little older.

We had a cellar full of canned goods. Mother canned everything. Most of our meat came from butchering a hog. We ate a lot of polenta, salami, and salsiccia, or sausages. Breakfast was usually just caffè latte—milk and coffee.

I attended school in Tontitown through the eighth grade. I carried my lunchbox to school, and had sandwiches, I guess. Lots of salami, *fatta in casa*, which means homemade. Riley Tessaro was a good friend of mine. I remember Sister Bernaldo [Kaelin]. She liked to hit with a stick. Sister Bernadine [Lake], she was a good old soul. I liked to draw so Sister Bernadine would corner me at Christmas, Thanksgiving and other holidays to draw scenes on the blackboard with colored chalk.

My sister, Annabelle, tells a funny story about school. Some of the boys were going down to the outside toilet to smoke. Sister Genevieve

[Chafe] went down after them. Later the boys put a big sign outside the toilet that said, "No Women Allowed."

I went to Springdale High School my freshman year. My sophomore year I transferred to Morris School for Boys in Searcy, Arkansas. It was a religious school founded by the Franciscan Brothers. I returned to Springdale for my junior and senior years.

Joe and Lizzie Strabala had a blacksmith shop just east of our house. Leo Pianalto's kids and all of us walked home from school together and passed right by the blacksmith shop. He had a big machine out front with a pipe that would spew out this smoke. One day when it was snowing, we stuck snow up that pipe! He caught us, and we start running. He had a bad temper, that Mr. Strabala. Mrs. Strabala, she was nice. We used to go over there to get cookies all the time. She was really a good person. He was too. Hard-working. He could make a wagon wheel from scratch.

I remember Mr. Mollar's store. He would always give us candy. They say he used to put on his white suit and walk through the graveyard at midnight. He rang the church bell every day at 6:00 a.m., at noon for the Angelus, and then again at 6:00 p.m.

We attended Midnight Mass at Christmas. Santa Claus came on Christmas morning. Aunt Tabby Pianalto would bring us lots of toys and things—leftovers from the people she worked for in Tulsa.

I remember one Halloween when someone got an outdoor toilet and put it right in front of Ardemagni's store. The toilet had a sign on it that said, "Open for Business."

The first grape festivals that I remember were held where the Tontitown Mercantile building is [the northwest corner of Highway 412 and Barrington Road]. I remember ice cream cones for a nickel, the Ferris wheel, and Cap Tiller, who showed movies in a tent.

I worked in the library while attending the University of Arkansas, where I majored in Spanish and minored in art. Then I went to Middlebury College in Vermont, and earned a master's degree in Italian. I also attended one year at University of Florence, Italy.

After I finished with college, my first job was teaching English in the Dominican Republic. I taught elementary school children, both Dominican and American. I taught in Honduras for two years, the same thing. After Honduras, I got a Fulbright Scholarship for two years in

Florence, Italy. I taught English there for five years. I also taught in Lucca, which was close to Florence. Then I taught Italian for two years in Maplewood, New Jersey. After that, I taught art to American Army brats in Germany for seven years. Then I went to Iran for awhile. I didn't like that.

I don't think the world is a better place today than when I was young. Life was much simpler then. We had more fun when we were young, because we were young.

Children of Joseph and Erma Ranalli. From left: Anthony, Agatha Ranalli Penzo, Norbert, Albina Ranalli Dalla Rosa, Christopher, and Paul.

JOSEPH AND ERMA BUSATO RANALLI

*Joseph Ranalli was born in 1921 in Tontitown, Arkansas,
to Nazzareno and Catherine Fachesato Taldo Ranalli. He
died in 1974.*

*Erma Busato Ranalli was born in 1919 in Little Italy,
Arkansas, to Antonio and Maria Busato. She died in
1961.*

*Six children of Joseph and Erma Ranalli participated
in a Ranalli family interview in 2003. Those present
were Anthony Ranalli, Agatha Ranalli Penzo, Norbert
Ranalli, Albina Ranalli Dalla Rosa, Paul Ranalli (twin
of Pauline, who is deceased), and Christopher Ranalli.*

Our paternal grandfather was Nazzareno Ranalli. He immigrated
to America from Italy in 1907. He was not married at the time.

Our paternal grandmother was Catherine Fachesato Taldo. She
arrived in Tontitown in 1905 with her first husband, Massimo Taldo, and
one son, Bartolo or Bert. The Taldo children born in Tontitown were
Marcella, Tilford, Placida or Pearl, Bill, and Eugene. Massimo died, and
his wife Catherine married our grandfather, Nazzareno Ranalli, in 1919.
They had a son, our father, Joseph Phillip Ranalli. They had another
baby that was either stillborn or didn't live very long.

Our maternal grandmother, Maria Busato, was from Little Italy,
Arkansas, down near Little Rock. She came [to America from Italy]
through Ellis Island to Chicago, then down to Little Italy. Her first husband, Anthony Busato, died. Then she married Frank Zulpo. Because
she was red-headed, they called her Rosa. Later in life, she wanted to
be called Bianca.

Nonno Nazzareno Ranalli was a farmer. He raised horses, cattle, grapes, strawberries, and tomatoes. He worked for Granata's Winery, pruning grape vines. He also pruned grape vines and worked for other local vineyards. Nonno was a small man, with black hair and a large mustache. He was very kind and soft-spoken. He walked everywhere and always wore overalls. Nonno lived a very frugal life. Old timers say that Nonno cooked in a rusty old iron skillet.

Nonno would walk across the field to come to our house. One time he came running through the pasture just as fast as he could. Some of the cows had died. They had gotten into the sweet sudangrass [which is poisonous to cattle] and there was a bunch of them already dead.

We were picking grapes with Nonno one time and a wasp stung him. He was smoking a pipe with Prince Albert tobacco. He pulled the stem out and dabbed the nicotine on the wasp sting.

When Nonno became ill, he stayed with us before he went into a nursing home. We had a bed in the living room and he stayed there for quite a while. He had hardening of the arteries. We used to take him wine when he lived in the nursing home.

Our dad, Joe Ranalli, completed sixth grade in Tontitown. He liked school. Dad talked about Sister Wilhelmina [Dower], one of the nuns he had as a teacher. One time something happened at school and Dad jumped out the west window and ran home. He couldn't speak any English when he started school. He said Chino Finn was the interpreter for him.

Dad walked to school, and carried a lard bucket packed with home-made bread and garlic for lunch. He set up box traps along the way to school to catch rabbits. On the way to school, he checked his traps. He sold rabbits to the Bastianelli sisters for a nickel a piece.

Dad told a story about one of the Cortiana twins, Gilbert or Gordon, wanting to go to the bathroom and the nuns wouldn't let him go. He needed to go real bad, so he just pulled the trash can up by the desk [and relieved himself].

After school, Dad would go to the post office to see if there was any mail. When Ex-Lax first came out, they sent samples in the mail. Dad thought that was pretty good stuff, and he ate it all. Before he got home, he said was carrying his pants.

Dad's family worked a lot, so they always had plenty to eat. For breakfast, they usually had caffè latte, which was coffee, milk, and bread.

They put wine in their coffee too. They butchered, and had rabbits and squirrels for meat.

Our mother, Erma Christine Busato, was from Little Italy, Arkansas. She completed eighth grade and then went to a business school in Little Rock. Growing up they had grapes, a few cattle and chickens, just general farming. Her mother had a café in North Little Rock for a long time.

Our parents met when Dad was visiting in Little Italy. They got married in San Diego, California, where Dad was stationed in the Navy during World War II. Dad and Jake Jaro joined the Navy together. They went to join the Marines, but it was during lunch hour and the Marine recruiter was gone, so they just walked across the hall and joined the Navy. They were cooks in the Navy.

After Dad got out of the service, he and Mom came back to Tontitown. They moved into the old homeplace, and built Nonno Nazzareno a little house to live in.

Dad did a lot of butchering and carpentering. He helped build Gildo Mantegani's chicken houses. He and Joe Mussino went to Oklahoma to build chicken houses. He farmed for himself and also worked at Granata's Winery about 35 years.

Mom sewed just about all of our clothes. She made a lot of bread. She grew a garden each year. She canned everything—wild plums, tomatoes, grapes. When she made grape jelly, we could smell it on the way home. She would send Anthony out to pick blackberries. One time, he didn't come home for a long time because he ate all of the berries. He always came home with a black mouth but no blackberries. She canned rabbit meat by pressure cooking it. She would put the cooked rabbit in umido.

Dad would send us out in the spring with a colander to pick radicchio, a dandelion green. You have to pick them before they bloom or they are very bitter. We ate a lot of those with bacon pieces and bacon grease. That was our salad. We also picked poke salad, and we would go to the creek to get watercress and cat tongue.

Nonna Maria Busato Zulpo moved to Tontitown from Little Italy in 1959. She moved here to be close to us because we were all the family she had left. Nonna outlived two husbands and five kids. She had only been here a couple of years when Mom died in 1961, due to complications during childbirth. Us kids ranged in age from Anthony, who was fourteen, to Chris, who was only two years old.

After Mom died, Chris would stay with Nonna one day, then with Nisia Tomiello one day, then with Aunt Pearl [Taldo Ceola] one day. They rotated taking care of him. We'd get up in the morning and milk the cows, and then Norbert or Anthony would drop Chris off. Chris knew the difference between who he stayed with. When he stayed with Aunt Pearl, she made him toe the line. She was tough on him. When he stayed with Nonna, he got by with anything.

One time after Mom died, somebody came by and told Dad that maybe he needed to divide us up. Dad got so mad. He told the man no, and he ran that man off. There are not many men who would have done what Dad did. He kept us together.

Dad drove a truck for Granata's Winery. Anthony would get up at 1:00 a.m. and take Dad up to Granata's to get on the truck. Then Anthony would come back home, go to bed, and get up at 5:30 a.m., when he and Norbert would go milk the cows, and take Chris to his babysitter. Anthony usually drove us to catch the school bus each morning. We would leave the car at M and M Tile and catch the school bus there. After school, we would get off the bus and get in the car, go get Chris, and go home to do our chores. Agatha shucked and shelled corn. The boys did the milking. Albina and Agatha had to gather eggs.

We always had plenty to eat. Most of the time for breakfast we had caffè latte or toast with homemade grape jelly. After school we fixed supper. We usually had a big skillet of fried potatoes. Dad was a good cook, and Agatha had learned to can from helping Mom. We canned a lot in the summertime. We had a lot of strawberries and tomatoes.

The Tontitown businesses we remember are Mr. Mollar's store, Morsani's store, and Ardemagni's store. Richard Ardemagni used to let us put everything on credit, and then Dad would pay at the end of the month when he got his milk check.

Dad and Nel Ceola used to make grapejack, which is a distilled wine. They used to make it in the barn, or anywhere they could get away with it. One time an FFA teacher from Springdale High School wanted to come home with Chris to look at the hog Chris was raising. Dad and Nel were making stuff down in the barn, so they had to cut Chris off real quick.

Dad used to bottle beer in the cellar, and if he bottled it too early, sometimes the bottles would explode. One night Dad got a phone call from Uncle Hi [Victor] Ceola wanting him to go over there because his beer was blowing up. Dad got his hard hat, raincoat, and a pair of goggles and went to Uncle Hi's house. They opened up bottles so they wouldn't blow up in their face. They would catch it in a big dish pan. Uncle Hi was really shook up.

If Dad thought he had bottled the beer too green, he would take an old milk bucket down in the cellar and a tow sack to cover it up so if the bottle blew up, it wouldn't blind you. If you put it in the refrigerator, after it got cold it was alright, it wouldn't do that.

One time Nonna Zulpo was staying with us during the night, and one bottle would blow up, then another. Sometimes one would blow up and hit another, which caused a chain reaction. She jumped up and thought someone was shooting.

We used to butcher beef and pork. Dad made lots of salami. One winter we butchered 26 or 28 hogs for other people. We'd butcher one on Friday morning, then Saturday and Sunday we would make salami out of it. Dad would get us up in the early morning. He had a .22 rifle and some bullets, a dishpan, knife, and knife sharpener. Then, ka-boom. They shot the hogs first, mostly to stun them, and then they would cut their throat. They would hang them up and skin them out. They were scalded and scraped too. The old folks would take out a vineyard and keep the old posts, then use them to build a big fire. They heated water in a big kettle, then poured the boiling water over the hog and scraped the hair off. Sometimes they put ashes in boiling water to scrape them easier. They didn't waste anything. We used everything but the squeal.

We all helped Dad make grape cuttings. We would eat supper and do our chores and clean up, then everyone went to the basement to make cuttings. You clip runners of new growth off the grape vines and then cut the bottom and the top two or three nodes on each run-ner—that's where you get the grape vine's hardwood. Next you bundle them up, put them in the ground upside down to heel them in, then dig them up the next spring and set them out in a nursery row. When Chris was too little to make cuttings by himself, he would sit down and peel the bark off the cuttings. He loved to peel the bark. When he stayed at Aunt Pearl's, he would go up in the vineyard with Uncle Hi and just peel the vines. We peeled the bark off because it would keep the scale [an insect pest] out.

We had an old used black-and-white TV. We would be sitting there watching it and when someone would walk across the floor, the picture would scramble up on it. We would go over there and hit it to get it going again. We got tired of doing that, so Dad made a deal with us that if we helped him make enough grape cuttings to sell, we would get a new color TV. That's the way we got a lot of our things. We had to work for them.

Through the summer we would haul hay for people. In the evenings after school we would pick corn, shuck it, and shell it. We had five acres of bell peppers one time down at Johnny Javello's farm. Anthony and Norbert would catch the mule and drag the double shovel all the way from our place to Javello's. Pete Penzo would join us down there and he would work the middles out while Norbert and Anthony would pull them out. We sold the peppers to Shaver's Produce in Springdale.

We raised pigs and corn. We would go out on the tractor with the trailer behind it and everybody would throw corn in from the sides onto the trailer. Then we would take it to the corn crib. Other times we would take a load of corn in the pickup to the Johnson Feed Mill. Old man Johnson would add all ingredients to it [for livestock feed] and bag it back up and throw it back into the truck for us. Johnson Mill was a long ways off back then. We thought we were going to the big city. When we did things like that, it was a big deal.

We had a rooster that hated Albina. When she gathered eggs in the evening, he would spur her or chase her around the barn. She started taking a baseball bat, broom, or a stick with her, and that rooster didn't bother anybody else.

Albina was always getting hurt. She fell out of the jeep one time coming home from school. She was sitting on Agatha's lap with her back against the jeep door. The jeep went around a corner lickity-split, the door swung open, and Albina fell out and dragged her head along the rocks. One time she was jumping on the bed in the back room, and all of a sudden she was out the window. It was a real high window, and the fall knocked her out.

The nuns Chris had as grade school teachers were strict. He remembers Sister Winifred [Favre], Sister Alice [Janesko], and Sister Adrian

[McGrath]. Sister Vivian [McNally] helped him a lot. His first grade teacher was Sister Jovita [Zarnoski]. Sister Carlos [Musquiz] was a young nun who played the guitar, and was a favorite of the students.

Our dad died suddenly in 1974. He had a heart attack while working in the garden. There were still four of us living at home—Norbert, Albina, Paul, and Chris. Agatha, Anthony, and Pauline were married. We just carried on, still a family. A guy came by one time after Mom and Dad passed away and checked on us to see if we were doing okay on our own. We told him we didn't need any help.

After we lost our mother, we all had to pitch in together and do our jobs. We just did it. It made us stronger people. You can't go back. You take responsibility for your life and go on. A good family makes it through.

Margaret Taldo Roso

MARGARET TALDO ROSO

Margaret Taldo Roso was born in 1920 in Tontitown, Arkansas, to Giacomo (James) and Clementine Costa Taldo. She was 83 years old when she was interviewed in 2003.

In about 1903, my parents came to America with three children: Emilia, Joseph or Joe Jack, and Blanche. After they settled here, they had Edward, who died when he was a young man, Argie, Irma, Olivia, Rita, and me. My dad worked in the mines in Oklahoma.

My mother said the first thing she did when she and Dad got married back in Italy was to go up into the attic where they kept the corn, to see if they had enough food to make it through the winter.

I don't remember too much about my older brothers and sisters. Jack picked up and left one time and was gone for quite some time. Edward went to Chicago and worked for a while. He came back, I guess about 1930, and he was driving a '29 Model A. Then he worked on the farm at home. They used to raise a lot of strawberries.

Mom baked a lot of homemade bread in the outdoor oven. We ate pasta and soup. We canned green beans outside in a tub with a fire built under it. We'd put tiles in the bottom of the tub so the jars wouldn't break. We cooked tomatoes in an open kettle, then cooked them on the stove and put them in jars.

We butchered hogs. We had sausage in the wintertime and the summertime too. We had chicken. We never did butcher beef. Someone used to come around peddling beef, and we would buy some of that. We didn't have a way of keeping it [refrigerated], so we didn't buy much. Sometimes we would hang meat in a container down in the well to keep it cool.

We had milk cows. As far as milk and butter, we just kept it and ate it as fast as we made it. We used to sell milk, so we just kept enough to make a little bit of cream to make butter. I never drank milk. There was a shed on Joe Costa's place where some of the families would bring milk and they would put it together to make a big, big cheese. They would take turns making it, and they would divide the cheese up.

We had chores to do. We carried in wood to fill the wood box in the wintertime. In the summertime we worked from morning till night, out in the fields. We picked up rocks. Every year we had to pick up wagon loads of rocks. That was the rockiest durn thing I ever saw.

I remember when the school burned [in 1927]. I hadn't started to school yet, but I remember seeing the black smoke about noon. Some of the boys stuffed the gutters with papers and set that on fire to warm their hands during the noon hour. I guess it drew the fire clear up to the roof, and that's what started the fire.

I completed the eighth grade. Some of the nuns I remember are Sister Albertine, Sister Angela [Corcoran], and Sister Loyola [Ryan], she taught me the last year I went to school. There was Sister Wilhelmina [Dower], Sister Vivian [McNally], and Sister deChantal [Devine]. Oh, and Sister Genevieve [Chafe], she was the ornery one.

We walked to and from school. For lunch we would take bread and jelly sandwiches, or sausage and cheese sandwiches. If it was cold we went to the basement and ate our lunch. If it was nice enough, we would go and play baseball or hide and seek out in the yard. We carried water from the pump to the sisters' back porch for them to carry upstairs to use in their bathroom. We washed dishes for Father Louis [Sittere]. We swept the church and the school.

Some of my best friends at school were Elizabeth and Josephine Bariola, Florence and Rosalie Pianalto, and Grace Maestri. Luciano Finn and Billy Pianalto used to bring me chewing gum.

I never had a job away from the farm. Oh, I did do my sister's laundry. They had five kids. I got 10 cents an hour. Scrub all day for a dollar!

I remember a store up on the southwest corner of the [Highway 412 and Barrington Road] intersection. Ernest Pianalto ran the store awhile, then Richard Ardemagni. The Peronas lived upstairs. There was Claude Morsani's store, and John Mollar's store. That was the main one. If we shopped anywhere, it was at Mr. Mollar's.

   MARGARET TALDO ROSO

I remember when the church blew down in 1934. Everything blew down except the sanctuary. The Blessed Sacrament was in the sanctuary, and after the storm, Father [the priest] went over and removed it. I don't know where they took it, I guess to Father's house. When they began to build the new church, everyone helped. I think my husband, Joseph, was about 15 years old. The younger boys would go up and make cement blocks, help mix the mortar.

The first grape festivals I remember were held on the old [Smith] school grounds, on the northwest corner of the [Highway 412 and Barrington Road] intersection, where the Ardemagni Mercantile building is now. The school building had a platform on the east side. They used to have music on that platform. I remember White River Red [a carnival game operator] would come and have her stand at the grape festival. She had stands with all these little bitty prizes. You'd spin the wheel and you'd get one of these little prizes. They weren't worth a darn, but that's where we spent half of our nickels, and we didn't have a whole lot of them to begin with. I remember saving my money from picking strawberries to spend at the grape festival. They sold soda pop and ice cream. They had a hamburger stand. They had swings. That was at the beginning, and then later on, we started having a little carnival.

The only thing I remember about Christmas as a child was what we did at school. We used to have a play, and then Santa Claus came and gave everyone a gift.

Our Easter family traditions were just like it is now: go to church, go to confession, and go to communion. The only other thing we did was to color Easter eggs, then roll the eggs. We would put them way down in a quilt, then we'd put something under the quilt on one side, and it would be like going downhill. They would roll down it, and I guess if we didn't break it we were lucky.

My husband, Joe Roso, and I grew up together, went to school together. We went to church every Sunday and in the evening we'd go to Benediction. That's what the dating was back then—going to church and walking home with the boys. A whole bunch of us would walk home together.

We married in 1940. Joe was drafted into the Army in 1945. He was in Korea after World War II ended. He drove a mail truck in Korea. After Joe got out of the service, we raised chickens, grapes, and cattle, to begin with. We milked cows. Later we went into the beef cattle business. We have three children, Ruth Ann, Tony, and Eddie, and six grandchildren.

I don't think the world is better today than when I was young. It's just too complicated. Too much traffic. You can't just walk somewhere. In fact, you can't even walk to the neighbor's house now without dang near getting run over. Of course, it's all right for younger people. But for old people that can't go out on the road, it's just really kind of rough.

Now television has taken over everything. I think they show too much on TV. Now you see every little thing they're doing. That's not good for people to be watching that stuff all the time. It may be good in some ways, I don't say it isn't. You learn a lot of stuff. Like that inter—what do you call it? Internet.

My hobbies are quilting and crocheting. I enjoy growing flowers. Joe and I had a nice life together. That's about as much as a person can say.

DELMO SABATINI

Delmo Sabatini was born in 1914 in Tontitown, Arkansas, to Aristide and Benedetta Taldo Sabatini. He was 88 years old when he was interviewed in 2002.

I don't know anything about my paternal grandparents. My maternal grandparents were John and Mary Taldo. They arrived in Tontitown with the original immigrants in 1898, accompanied by their eight children: Peter, Joe, Dick, Catherine, Anna, Luigia, Margaret, and Benedetta, who was my mother.

They never talked about the trip over to America, and they never talked about going back to Italy, because they weren't interested. They had such a hard time over there. Everybody was so poor they didn't even have enough to eat. But when they got here, they didn't find it much better because they couldn't get along with the Springdale people. They had it against the Italians, so they had it hard here.

The only thing I remember about my Taldo grandparents is that when my mother took me to visit them, I would hide under the table because they spoke to me in Italian. See, Mama and Dad never did speak Italian at home because they spoke different [Italian dialects]. My father was from Bologna, in northern Italy. Mother was from Venice, which was further south. They could understand each other when they spoke Italian but it was altogether different. If they were saying, "Shut the door," Mama would say, *"Sadda la porta,"* and Dad would say, *"Sadda qua luce."*

Here is how my father met my mother. Uncle Jim Brunetti was married to Mother's sister, Luigia. Uncle Jim was working in Oklahoma in the mines with Dad. On one of his trips back to Tontitown to see Luigia, Uncle Jim asked Dad to come with him, and that's when Dad met Mother. He fell in love at first sight.

Delmo Sabatini

There were eight children in our family: Dick, Geno, Johnny, Delmo, Virgil or Curley, Annie, Rosie, and Georgie. Rosie and Georgie were twins. There was a girl between Dick and Geno, she died. I think she was just a few months old.

When I was very young, we lived in Lutie, Oklahoma, about two miles from Wilburton. Dad and the older boys were working in the coal mines. Several of the guys from Tontitown worked in the mines. My brother Geno was killed in the coal mine when he was just 21 years old. Dad was going to have all of us boys work in the mines because there was no work in Tontitown back then. But whenever Geno was killed, Dad said, "That's it, no more," and he moved Mom and us kids to Tontitown. Then he went back to work in the mines. He came home once a year, so I didn't know him very well. When he got too old to work in the mines, he moved to Tontitown. By then, I was an adult and away from home.

I was seven or eight years old when Mother moved here with us kids. Rosie and Georgie, the twins, were less than a year old. I remember Uncle Joe Taldo coming to the train station and picking us up in his Model T. Ford. I didn't think we would ever get to where we were going. My mother with all these kids and no dad. She had a hell of a life.

Mother had a sense of humor. She whistled a lot. I don't know how she could be happy, but she seemed to be happy all the time, unless we got into trouble, which we did. She was like her brother, Uncle Dick Taldo. He whistled all the time, whether he was working or walking. You know, he had only one leg. I don't know this to be true, but the old timers said Uncle Dick was down at Tony Fiori's place, and there was a gun leaning up against the house. Somehow the gun fell over and discharged and hit Uncle Dick in the leg. Gangrene set in, and they had to cut off his leg above the knee. It did not clear up, so the second time they cut off a little higher. Then they still had to cut off more, until it was cut right up against the hip. The word was if that didn't clear the gangrene, there was nothing more could be done. It worked, and I'll tell you what, walking on those crutches didn't keep Uncle Dick from doing one thing. We used to go fishing down at Brush Creek, at Steele Hole, and Farish Hole, and he would always walk faster than I could.

The Taldos farmed and raised their own food. Uncle Joe planted berries and grapes. He also farmed and had an apple orchard. There was lots of timber back then. They would clear out the timber and plant strawberries. Strawberries do better in what they call "new ground." Uncle Joe had three different kinds of strawberries: Klondike, Aroma, and Blakemore. They didn't ripen at the same time, so there was always work to be done. He planted a lot of cowpeas. We picked cowpeas, and he had us working all the time. The berries were shipped out by train, and grapes went to Welch's Grape Juice Company in Springdale. The apples went to Felix Ardemagni's apple evaporator to be dried. It was located where the post office is now [on Barrington Road, north of the Highway 412 intersection]

Uncle Jim Brunetti was like a dad to us. When there was shopping to do, he would hook up the wagon and team and let me go with him. We went all the way to Springdale in a wagon, can you imagine? Springdale wasn't that big back then. One time I remember we got down there and he bought a cantaloupe and a loaf of bread. On the way back we crossed a little bridge, I don't remember if it was Spring Creek or Clear Creek, and we stopped and ate. You know, that was the best darn meal I ever had. You get sick of homemade bread. Bought bread was what I wanted. It tasted better to me.

For breakfast, Mother would fix us coffee and toast and jelly. We bought flour and sugar in 100-pound sacks. You would buy enough flour to last you all year, so we always had bread. Sugar was the same way. We went to Springdale for those items. I don't remember how they stored it, but the flour didn't get weevils.

We raised hens, and we had eggs all the time. Whenever a hen quit laying eggs, Mama would know about it, and she would kill the chicken and make soup out of it. She had a long wire hook attached to a long stick to catch the chicken with. First she would feed the chickens in the barn. They would come up to eat, and she would reach in with that hook and grab one by the leg and just pull it right on in. I know it sounds cruel, but she would get the chicken, put its head down on the ground, get a stick and lay it across the neck, step on each end of the stick, and just pull the chicken up by its legs. She would snap its neck. I tried several times, but I pulled too hard and pulled the head off. Mama didn't have that trouble. To clean the chicken, she would scald it in a pot of boiling water in the house, pick the feathers, singe off the pin feathers, gut it, cut it up, wash it, and cook it. We had no refrigeration, so she did that each time we had chicken to eat.

I didn't start school until we moved to Tontitown. We lived in Albano Maestri's house just east of the school playground. We walked to and from school. If you got wet on the way to school, you just stayed wet all day. This is the gospel truth—my mother didn't know nothing about school. We would go to school in the morning, and it would still be dark. The nuns would put us into bed up there before school started.

　　　　　DELMO SABATINI

We went too early, way before time for school to start. See, my mother didn't know.

At first the nuns weren't too strict, but as we got older and meaner, they got strict. Especially Sister deChantal [Devine]. She had been married at one time. Her husband died, and then she became a nun. She really had it out for me, Richard Roso, and Charlie Fiori. Even Jim Finn said she was mean.

I used to take care of the wood furnace for the school. Mr. Mollar paid me $5 for the winter months. I would get to school about one hour early, fill the furnace with wood, and start the fire so the school would be warm when the rest of the kids arrived. I emptied the ashes each morning before starting the fire. Whenever I'd put lots of wood in and the furnace would get real hot it would make a popping noise. Sister would get real scared when this happened, and send me down to see if everything was okay. Sometimes when I didn't feel like being in class too much, I'd go put extra wood in at recess or noon, so I could leave class and go check the furnace when it popped.

Some of the boys, when they had to go to the bathroom to urinate, they would go in the basement behind the furnace instead of going outside to the bathroom. When the furnace got real hot, the odor was terrible. Sister would always want to know what that smell was, and we would tell her it was just because of the heat.

One of the games we used to play at school was mumble peg. You play it with a pocket knife. You kneel down on the ground and open your knife. You flip the knife, and if it sticks in the ground, you keep going. You flip it from several different positions, and as long as it sticks in the ground, you keep going. The last step is to put the knife on your head with the blade open, and you flip it down toward the ground. If it sticks in the ground, you win the game.

Another game we played was shinny. Most of the time I played partners with Bill Fiori, because he was really good and I wasn't worth a darn. You had a stick like a hockey stick. We'd go out in the timber [to find a stick]. Hickory wood would be the best because it would last longer. You'd find a stick with a crook in it. If you couldn't find one with a crook, you could bend the end of a stick down and let it stay that way two or three weeks, and it would form a crook. Then you get these shinny sticks and any kind of a can. Two guys who were chosen would put the can down on the ground between them. You get your shinny stick and bring it up and touch his shinny stick, one guy on each side of the can. Put your stick back to the ground, come up and touch sticks—you do that three times. The third time after you touch sticks, you go down as fast as you can, and the guy who is the fastest hits the can first. You had a line drawn a quarter of a mile away and the one to get to the line first with the can won the game. Of course, we have all these opponents trying to knock the can back the other way. It was a fun game. You could play with a ball, but we didn't have the money to buy a ball, so we used cans. Lots of times a guy got hit with the can and it caused a pretty good bruise.

Bill Fiori was one of my best friends because we did a lot of stealing. Bill, Virgil Verucchi, Frank Verucchi, and the Penzo boys, we all used to play ball when the ball diamond was about where PAM Trucking's parking lot is now [near the southwest corner of the Highway 412 and Barrington Road intersection]. Anyhow, Bill said to me, "You want something to eat?" I said, "Oh yeah, what's up?" He said, "Come with me." Well, they stored items left over from the grape festival in the basement of the school. The Bastianelli girls lived across the street in the house where the Tontitown Museum is now. They always had their faces sticking out the window. Bill and I got to the school and a basement window was already open. Somebody had already broke in. We didn't break in, I'm positive. So we went in and got peanuts, Cracker Jacks, and cigarettes, went back to the ball diamond, and handed a lot of that stuff out, because we got more than we could eat.

Later, the sheriff, Hugo Pozza, came down to the house with a pistol strapped to his side. That's when my mother said, "Oh, Dio mio." He said, "Get in." I said, "What the hell's going on?" "Get in." It's a wonder he didn't put handcuffs on me. Well, Hugo took me up to the priest's house, and there was Uncle Dick Taldo, Albino Roso, Memo Morsani—who was the meanest guy around here—and five or six other mean-looking guys sitting out on the porch. They called me in first. I don't know why I had to go first, I guess they figured they'd get the truth out of me. They thought we broke in. I told the truth, that the window was already open. They had us thinking we were going to the reform school. They were really mad. At the end, they said, "Tell you what we

     DELMO SABATINI

are going to do. We are going to charge you all a dollar." I know we ate more than a dollar's worth of stuff, so we got by pretty clean.

You may not believe this, but back then we walked to church rain or shine. They bred that into you. It was a mortal sin if you missed Mass. You would go straight to hell if you missed Mass.

I remember when the grape festivals were held where the Tontitown Mercantile is now [northwest corner of Highway 412 and Barrington Road]. They just had a Ferris wheel. Hamburgers were 10 cents, with onions in the middle and pickles on top. Ice cream cones and Cracker Jacks were a nickel. They served spaghetti dinners in the school basement. Back then, they would go from house to house asking for donations, either money or food, for the festival—eggs, chickens, or anything to make the spaghetti. I thought a lot of Rosalie [Pianalto] even back then. I had one of those rubber balls on a long elastic string that you could flip it back and forth. Well, Rosalie was walking down to the school basement to go to work at the spaghetti dinner, and I flipped her on the butt with one of those balls, trying to get her attention.

I left home whenever I wasn't quite 18. I was picking apples for Clint Ritter, down by Elm Springs. I made $18 picking apples, and Pat Haney from Elm Springs asked if I wanted to go on a hobo trip. A hobo trip is when you take off and ride the rails. He had been on a hobo trip several times. I said, "Yeah, I'll go." I had $18 in my pocket. I knew I had to leave early in the morning because my brother Johnny found out I was leaving. He said he would just knock my damn block off if he found out I was going to leave, and he would have. He wanted me to stay and work on the farm. That is why I had to sneak off. I didn't even get to say goodbye to my mother.

Pat and I hitchhiked from Elm Springs to Watts, Oklahoma. That's where I caught my first freight train. You just run and jump on after the train is moving. You can't catch a freight train until they leave the switchyard because they have what you call "bulls"—they're something like cops. You had to wait till they were out of the switchyard to hop on. We went to Fort Worth, Texas. In Fort Worth, there was this guy who was running a game with soda pop lids and a ball. He would flip them all around, and you bet on which lid had the ball underneath it. Pat kept betting my money, and he finally lost it all. When we go to Phoenix,

Arizona, Pat decided to ditch me. He said, "There are two ways to get to California. I'll take one highway and you take the other one." I knew he was wanting to get rid of me, so I said, "Okay, you go ahead." I was out there in a hobo camp, and this guy came along and said he was a gold prospector. He asked if I wanted to come along with him. He knew where there was a camp where they would feed us. I was starving, so I went with him.

When I decided to leave that hobo camp, instead of coming home to Tontitown, I went to Oklahoma where my dad was. The mines were not working then, and I ended up going to work at a CCC camp in Idabel, Oklahoma. We worked on run-down farmland, building terraces so the water wouldn't wash away the ground. We planted bermudagrass and even did some rockwork to stop erosion. I stayed there two and a half years. The bad part about it was, I signed up in Oklahoma, so my dad got $21 a month, and my mother didn't get anything. I got $5. I wish my mother would have gotten the money.

Then I got this letter from my dad saying the family needed help on the farm in Tontitown. He wanted me to go home and put out a patch of tomatoes to help pay for the farm. I guess I was around 20 years old. Curley, Annie, Georgie, and Rosie all helped.

Charlie Fiori, Lawrence Pianalto, Ted Lynch, and I were the first ones around here who were called to join the service in World War II. We all went to Little Rock together. I was in the Army Coast Artillery in Alaska. I stayed there about a year and a half. When the Japanese got through destroying Pearl Harbor, we went to the Aleutian Islands. The first thing we did there was build an air strip for planes to land, which they couldn't do very often because it was so doggone cold. They had over 30 feet of snow there. We built barracks, and when we finished there, we came back to the States. We were going to Texas for training. That's when I went over the hill, AWOL, absent without leave. Yes, I did. It's on my discharge papers. I had asked for a three-day pass to come home. I wanted to come home and see Rosalie. They wouldn't give me a three-day pass, so I got a one-day pass to go to Brownsville, Texas. Instead of going to Brownsville, I caught a bus to Fort Smith. I managed to get all the way to Fayetteville and got to see Rosalie. I had to go back the next day, because I was AWOL. They knew I was gone, so when I got back to the base, the captain told my sergeant, "You keep

            DELMO SABATINI

that guy working all the time." I was in the Army 51 months, and they never would give me a three-day pass.

I never did date Rosalie before I went into the service. While I was in the service, I got a letter from my sister Annie telling me that one of Silvio and Emilia Pianalto's daughters had been burned in a fire. I thought it was Rosalie, so I sent her a card. That is how we got started. Instead it was Rosalie's sister Florence who got burned.

When I got out of the Army I stayed in Tontitown about a week. I think Rosalie and I dated twice. My brother was working in Michigan, so I left Tontitown and went there. The first job I had there was making seat springs for a car. Then I was laid off. Next I went to the Dodge factory, worked about two months, and was laid off again. My brother was working seven days a week at Bower Roller Bearing Company, where they were making aircraft bearings. I went there, and they put me on seven days a week.

Rosalie and I were married in Michigan, and we lived there about four years. Then we moved back to Tontitown and started raising broilers. We had four children: Barbara was born in Michigan; Shirley, Larry, and Rose Marie were all born in Tontitown.

I retired from actual heavy farming at age 63 and started drawing Social Security, rather than wait until age 65. I figured I wasn't going to last that long, anyhow. I kept raising chickens on the farm for two years. I had cattle also. Then we decided to just let our son, Larry, take over the farm. He bought it, and we have been happy ever since.

Rosalie always enjoyed raising flowers. Gosh-darn, she knew everything about flowers—gladiolas, peonies, jonquils. I had to chew her out a time or two because she planted flowers in the garden. I told her she had the whole yard taken up, so stay out of the garden!

Rosalie passed away in 1997. Now, I spend my time walking my dog, Rex. Depending on the season, I will work in my garden. After lunch I go to the bocce court, from 12:25 p.m. till about 3:00 p.m. Andy Franco, Riley Tessaro, Kenny Pianalto, Pete Pianalto, Gile Pianalto, Bob Sbanotto, Roger Pianalto—absolutely we play for money. Fifty cents per game.

Dorothy Fiori Sbanotto

DOROTHY FIORI SBANOTTO

*Dorothy Fiori Sbanotto was born in 1920 in Tontitown,
Arkansas, to Peter B. and Maria (Mary) Cortiana Fiori.
She was 82 years old when she was interviewed in 2002.*

My paternal grandparents were Domenico and Alene Fiori. Their
children were Joseph, Antonio, Rosa, John, Peter Beato, who was my
father, and Maria. Grandmother Alene died in Italy. Domenico came to
America with two of his children, Peter Beato or Peter B., and Antonio
or Tony.

Domenico Fiori was a horticulturist and a winemaker. When it was
legal to sell wine in Tontitown, Dominico had a bell tower in his front
yard. This was used by people who stopped by to purchase wine. They
would ring the bell if Domenico wasn't in the house. He was usually in
the vineyard. He kept a *tina* [vat] on the front porch and two or three
barrels of wine in the front room.

My maternal grandparents were Eustacchio and Lucia Strobe
Cortiana. Grandmother Lucia died in Italy. Eustacchio brought the
children [to America] from Italy. The children were Domenico or Dick,
Virginia, Giuseppe or Joe, Luigia or Louise, Maria or Mary, who was
my mother, and Celeste or Cel.

Along with farming his vineyard, Eustacchio Cortiana was a cob-
bler. Mom said that as children, in the winter they skated on the ice in
wooden shoes made by their father, Eustacchio. Mom also said that
Eustacchio walked with his children to Mass at 7:30 a.m. every day without fail—hot, cold, rain, or snow.

Mom said when they first came to Tontitown [in 1898 with the original group of settlers from Sunnyside], there was a *casotto*—a two-story
house—northwest of the intersection [of Highway 412 and Barrington

Road]. There was a well there that had lots of water. Several people had cows, and they would bring their cows up to this well for water. In the beginning a lot of people stayed there in that home. There was one boy there about 19 years old. Evidently, his caretaker couldn't afford to keep him any more, so he jumped out of the second story window, broke his neck, and died.

Mom didn't talk much about the bad things. She did tell us some funny things that happened. Her sister, Virginia, being the oldest, was the mother, so to speak. Virginia's boyfriends would come to the house to visit. She would tell her brother Cel to behave, because he was always passing gas. One night some boyfriend was there and it was real cold. Cel opened the door. Virginia told him to shut the door, and Cel said, "Well, you told me not to fart in the house."

Mom completed the fourth grade in school. When she was 10 years old, she was sent to Oklahoma to work for a family who owned a grocery store and butcher shop. She stayed there a year. When she left home, she had just a small sack of clothing, and when she returned, she had a whole big sack full. The family in Oklahoma treated Mom just like one of their own children. They bought her lots of clothes. She must have gotten lonesome, because she said she could hear her sister Louise calling her. So the family in Oklahoma called Mom's family and said that she needed to come back home. Miss [Bernadette] Brady, the schoolteacher at the time, went to Oklahoma and got Mom.

My parents, Peter B. and Mary Cortiana Fiori, were married in Tontitown in 1912. Their children are William or Bill, Clara, Charlie, Dorothy, twins Virgil and Virginia, and Elsie Mae. Virgil was drafted into the Army during World War II and was killed at Anzio, Italy, in 1944. He was 22 years old.

We lived in a four-room house. Elsie Mae came after some of us were gone, but before that, the three girls slept in a bed downstairs, the three boys slept in a bed upstairs, and Mom and Dad had a bed downstairs. We also had a room upstairs we called the "big room." Dad had made a hanging shelf in the big room to store flour, sugar, and food supplies. Every time Mom would get something she really prized, she would put it in the big room to keep it safe.

Mom sewed most of our clothes. She made this one dress for me out of a sugar sack. She didn't have a pattern. She would just say, "Come

here and let me try this on you." She had me try it on and try it on until
the dress was finished. Then she dyed it purple. It was the prettiest dress.
I just loved it.

Mom ironed sitting down. She had phlebitis in her ankle, and
almost died from it. She walked with a limp for the rest of her life. It
hurt her to walk or stand for very long, so she did many jobs sitting
down. She loved to dance, but she and Dad had to quit going to dances.

Dad had other jobs besides farming. He helped build Highway 68
[present-day Highway 412]. He was a dynamite man in construction.
He worked for awhile during the Depression with the CCC Camp at
Devil's Den. He also kept a vineyard. At one time he went to St. Louis
and was a cook, along with Mrs. Kate Frizzo, for a man who owned a
quarry. Dad took my brother, Bill, with him. Mom was home with the
rest of us kids, so he took Bill to St. Louis to make it easier on Mom.

I used to follow Dad around all the time when he was home. He
had a little rotisserie that he would cook birds on out in the yard. He
built a little fire and I got to turn the crank. He would say, "You got to
turn it slow, Dorothy." He would sit there and baste it while I turned the
crank. Dad used to furnish shells to Pete Penzo to go out and kill him
some birds. Pete loved to hunt, so it was a good deal for both.

Dad raised our own hogs, and he and Joe Bariola butchered every
year. Joe would go from house to house in the wintertime and butcher
hogs for people. After Joe died, Lino Bariola, his nephew, inherited his
tools and did butchering for a long time. There is a real art to butchering. You'd be surprised how clean they keep things. They scald everything. When you butchered, you always wanted a big fat hog, the fatter
the better. They cut away the excess fat and cooked it. Mom usually
cooked hers in the house until it cooked down to nothing but liquid
and chitlins [pieces of hog intestines]. We stored that in a large eight-
gallon crock jar in the cellar. This was our lard jar. Mom would use out
of that crock all winter for frying, making spaghetti sauce, or whatever
she needed lard or salt pork for. We had salami. You sure can't get that
good salami anymore.

Dad always had a hen with chicks following her. We were never
without chicken. We had a cow, and sometimes a goat. As for beef, once
in awhile some farmer from the Harmon community would butcher a
beef, load it in the back of his truck, and go from house to house selling

beef. There was no refrigeration then, so you just looked in the back of the truck and he would cut off what you wanted, weigh it, and sell it to you.

There was a cheese factory on the Pete Tessaro property [northeast corner of Highway 412 and Tessaro Lane]. The reason they had a factory is because no one family would have enough milk at one time to make a large cheese. People would bring milk to the factory every day. The milk was weighed, the weight written down for each family, [and the cheese would be distributed accordingly]. The collected milk was heated in a large container. Rennet was added to make it clabber. After the milk clabbered, the liquid was drained off of it and the curd was placed in a round wooden frame to form a wheel of cheese. They used their hands to press the moisture out of the curd. When all the moisture was out of the cheese, folks would take it home. Dad hung a special shelf in the cellar to dry our cheese. It was a long board hung from the ceiling with four wires. This was to keep the mice from getting into the cheese. Dad would rub salt onto the surface of the cheese for several days. Next, they covered the cheese with a cloth and left it to cure. This cheese was very bland at first, but became sharper as it aged.

Mom could cook real well. She cooked just enough [for a meal] because there was no refrigeration. She cooked every meal, every day, morning, noon, and night. When we canned tomatoes, Mom cooked them outside in the black kettle. We would strain it, put it through a sieve outside, then bring it inside to bottle it. She canned so much stuff. Our cellar was full for the winter—sweet potatoes, potatoes, onions, cheese, sausage, salami, lard, and salt meat made from the hog that Dad raised and butchered. Also a barrel of wine, sometimes two. Our cellar was a stone building in back of the house. In the upstairs over the cellar, we stored things like grape baskets.

We had a cistern and hand pump on the back porch to catch rain water. We did not drink this water. We'd use it for other things— washing clothes, taking baths, scrubbing floors or walls. To make a cistern, you dig a hole on the order of a well, but not as deep. You line the hole with concrete to hold water. We put things we needed to keep cool in a bucket and lowered the bucket by rope into the cistern.

They only taught through ninth grade at Tontitown, but Father [Francis] Dollarton and Sister Loyola [Ryan] taught tenth grade, so I was

 DOROTHY FIORI SBANOTTO

given credit for that and entered Mount St. Mary's Academy [in Little Rock, Arkansas] as a junior. Mount St. Mary's was a boarding school. I wanted to attend high school, and I knew if I stayed [in Tontitown], I could not go because we had no vehicle and I had no way to get to Springdale [to go to high school]. Sister Loyola encouraged and helped me go on to high school.

I remember the results of one school prank my brother Bill pulled on one of the nuns. He put a mouse in her desk drawer. Several years later, when I went to high school at Mt. Saint Mary's, this nun said to me, "Your name is Dorothy Fiori. Do you have a brother named Bill? I hope you are not as mean as he was." That was my welcome to Mount St. Mary's.

Some of my best friends in grade school were Josephine Perona and Grace Maestri. They lived close by so we were always together. We played ball. We played hopscotch. We rolled a wheel with a stick—you get a wheel, you put a board at the bottom of a stick, and you just roll that wheel around in the dust.

I remember the tornado that destroyed the church [in 1934] because we lived directly across Barrington Road from the church. It was a stormy night, so of course Mom wanted all us kids in the bedroom with them. The storm picked our house up, straight up, and then sat it back down. Dad said, "It's gone," and that's when the church blew down. We had a well in the front yard with a bucket and chain. It picked up the chain and bucket and sat it down in the middle of the yard. Mom had some wicker chairs on the front porch and it blew them way down in the vineyard north of the house.

At Christmas, we always went to Midnight Mass. We sang in the choir. All of the kids had a chance to sing. Mr. Mollar played the organ in church and for all the school plays. Between him and the nuns, they taught us to sing. Santa Claus came to our house on Christmas morning. I suppose we had a special meal, but as kids you don't remember the meals. Santa, we remembered.

My parents were not all that strict about us fasting at Easter. We didn't eat meat on Friday, of course. We would bring fugassa and boiled eggs to the church on Holy Saturday to have them blessed. You were supposed to eat the eggs the first thing on Easter Sunday.

The first grape festivals I remember were on the [northwest corner of Highway 412 and Barrington Road]. The parishioners would sell hamburgers and ice cream cones. There was a Ferris wheel. Cap Tiller would come with a movie projector and show movies. Vendors would come in and sell trinkets to the kids. A paddle attached to a ball by a rubber band was always good! Fortune tellers would come. John Mollar would play piano before some speaker—usually a politician—would talk. I remember singing a song with Mary Natale one year. I don't know when they started serving the spaghetti dinners. They were held in the school basement, but I do know if they served 98 people, they were happy.

The grocery stores I remember in Tontitown are Albano Maestri's, Claude Morsani's, Frank Perona's, and Richard and B. Ardemagni's. There was a blacksmith shop. At one time the Felix Ardemagni family owned an apple dryer and sold dried apples. Apples were already here when our people arrived, so they had apples before they had grapes.

Sometimes on Sundays, we would get in the wagon and go to Aunt Louise Gaiche's house. They lived almost all the way to Gentry. We just loved to go there because they lived by a spring. We would play in the water and have the best time. They wouldn't know we were coming, because we didn't have a phone. They would go out, kill a chicken, and make polenta and umido. Polenta is just a cornmeal dish. You boil water and add cornmeal, cook and stir it a long time until it becomes thick, add a little salt. Umido is just chicken, or any meat, with tomato sauce. Mom would start with a little bit of fatback, brown some onions, and add whatever seasoning you want. She would add the meat, cover it, and cook it in the oven. You put the umido over the polenta.

One day when I was in high school at Mount St. Mary's, I was looking through a magazine and saw a picture of a nurse's capping ceremony. That did it for me. I decided I wanted to become a nurse. After high school, I went into nurses training in El Dorado, Arkansas. I worked at the hospital there until I joined the Air Corps. I don't know why I wanted to go into the service. We were at war, and I just wanted to. When you joined the armed services as a nurse, there was no basic training, you just went to a hospital and started working. I reported to Barksdale Field in Shreveport, Louisiana. They asked for volunteers for air evac duty, because they were getting ready for the big invasion in Japan. They were expecting lots of casualties. I volunteered for air evac

          DOROTHY FIORI SBANOTTO

training and was sent to Randolph Field in San Antonio, Texas. Then we were sent to Fort Dix, New Jersey. Normally they trained six months for air evac, but because of the war, they pushed us through in three. But by the time we completed our training, they had dropped the atomic bomb and the war was over. They sent us to Miami Beach, Florida. Most of the hotels along the beach were converted into hospitals. Many of the troops from overseas were sent there for physicals before being discharged, so that's what we did. I was in the service for two and a half years. When the war was over, I got my discharge.

My husband, Harry Sbanotto, and I knew each other from the time we were kids on up. We were in the same grade. Harry went to high school in Springdale. He rode his bicycle to and from school for almost two years. He was determined to get an education. Luckily during a really bad spell one winter, his sister Mabel let him use her car. He finally bought a pickup truck from Lino Bariola.

Harry and I didn't date each other as teenagers. Maybe we did a few times, not much. We would go to dances sometimes. Gildo Mantegani had a dance hall across from the Venesian Inn. We all went there to dance whether we had a date or not. If I was dancing with the wrong guy, my brother Charlie would come by and say, "Don't dance with him anymore." I was always afraid of Charlie, but he was really the best kid of the family, I think.

After graduation, Harry went to St. Louis. His brother and sister-in-law, Roy and Vicki Sbanotto, were living there, and Roy helped Harry find a job. Harry joined the service in St. Louis. We were writing and calling each other, and he would come down to see me at Barksdale Field once in awhile when he could. We were both in the service when we got married in 1943. We were never stationed near each other. After we were married, I would go to Columbus, Ohio, to visit him occasionally.

After our discharges, Harry started school at University of Arkansas. Our first home was in Fayetteville. I worked at City Hospital in Fayetteville while Harry attended college. He was interested in aeronautical engineering, but he really wanted to get back to farming, so we moved back to the Sbanotto homeplace in Tontitown. Harry's mother, Pierina Sbanotto, lived with us there for quite awhile. Not all the time, sometimes she would stay with her daughter, Emma Sbanotto Verucchi.

Harry used to tell of a Sunday ritual involving his mother, Joe

Franco, and some of the folks who lived near Sbanottos. They would all walk to church, and on the way home they would stop by the Sbanotto home to have a cup of coffee. Harry's mother, Pierina, would say, "Hey *vecchio* [old man], do you want some *grappa* [grapejack or brandy] in your coffee?" "Oh, just a teaspoon," he would say. Pierina would pour directly from the bottle, much more than a teaspoon.

My dad, Peter B. Fiori, died in 1948. He, his brother Tony, and Pete Tessaro had been playing cards at Hugo Pozza's house. They were walking home along Highway 68 [Highway 412] and he was struck by a car.

Harry passed away in 1998. He and I had seven children: Betty, Pete, Harry Jr., Tony, twins Dennis and David, and Bob. Harry was mayor of Tontitown from 1955 to 1978. He also served for many years as an alderman, and as water superintendent. I still live here on our farm, and hope to remain here as long as I can.

LENA MANTEGANI STOCKTON

*Lena Mantegani Stockton was born in 1918 in
Tontitown, Arkansas, to Cesare and Rosa Fiori Ceola
Mantegani. She was 85 years old when she was inter-
viewed in 2003.*

My mother arrived in Tontitown with the original settlers [from
Sunnyside] in 1898. At the time she was married to Marco Ceola and
they had a son, Augusto or Gus. They had two more boys, Joe and Dick,
before Marco died. Then my mother married Cesare Mantegani, who
was my father. He came to Tontitown in 1904. Their children were
Norina, Cesarina, Gemma, Gildo, Albina, Lena, and Palma or Beba. My
parents never talked about their lives when they were younger. They
just took life as it came.

My father farmed and was a stonemason. He used to get rocks,
bust them with a hammer, make the shape, then build a wall. He helped
make all the cement blocks that were used to build the church [that
was dedicated in 1942] and also the school. They made the blocks right
there. All the forms were made by hand. They mixed all the cement
by hand, poured it in the forms until it dried, and then they took them
out. My father also helped build Father Bandini's memorial altar at the
cemetery. They used to get my father to fix the plaster in the school
because nobody else could get it to stick.

When I was growing up, we had a vineyard and strawberries. We
hoed strawberries from one season to the other. We picked beans. Mom
always had a big garden. We canned all our stuff back then. We ate a lot
of wild greens. We went out and picked them in the field. My mother
would cut the greens up and put salt and pepper and vinegar and oil on
them, like a salad. Mom made pasta, and she made cheese.

Lena Mantegani Stockton

We had a few chickens. Mom would just get out there in the chicken house and catch one with her hands. Then she wrung its neck, just kind of twisted and pulled its neck. She could pull its neck and break it. I never could. The more I pulled, the longer the neck got. Next we would scald it, pull all the feathers off, burn all the little hair off of it, and then cut it up. When we ate chicken, everybody got one piece and that was it. Stuff wasn't plentiful like it is now, where you eat part of it and throw the rest away. Back then you ate every bit of it.

People would get together and help each other butcher a hog. We worked with the Bariolas, Fioris, and some of the Pianaltos. We always had salami. We canned any beef that we had. We cooked it, cut it up, put it in jars and covered it with grease. The grease kept it [from spoiling].

Mom made lye soap when we butchered hogs. You take all the grease from the hog and you boil it for so long, and then you put lye in it. You cook it until a certain stage, and then cook it some more. Mom boiled it in a large black pot outside. When it reaches a certain stage, it gets hard. We cut it into blocks a little smaller than a brick. We used it for laundry soap.

When we were kids, we slept three in a bed. We milked cows before we went to school. We had milk and coffee for breakfast with biscuits. I still like that. We fixed our own lunch for school, mostly jelly on home-made bread.

Mom made home brew in the cellar. Sometimes at night you could hear some of the bottles blow up. We also made wine in the cellar. The revenue men came out one time. Gus [Ceola] had sold a quart of wine to the sheriff. Gus didn't know who he was. The sheriff came out and raided the place. They poured out all the wine, all the beer, everything. They opened the barrels and wine ran all down the hill. The Lazzaris were also making wine, and they got scared and tried to move theirs. They got caught moving the wine.

Later, Dad built a big building behind the house and started the Mantegani Winery. The Granatas built a winery, Lazzaris had one, and Joe and Dick Taldo had one. Gildo or Beba and I delivered our wine. We delivered in Arkansas only. We couldn't go to Oklahoma because we couldn't take it out of state.

Dad built the Luncheonette, a little café and tavern directly across the highway from where the Venesian Inn is today. There was a little stand out in front of the café where they sold wine. He also built a large platform behind the Luncheonette where they would have dances. Local people usually provided the music. Dick Fiori played for a long time. There was a bocce court there too.

I completed the eighth grade in school. We went to school in Tontitown until Dad got mad at the nuns who were our teachers, and he transferred us to the school at Harmon. Later we went back to school in Tontitown. I remember that if you didn't know your catechism, you got whipped.

The earliest grape festivals I remember were around that old building [Smith schoolhouse, on the northwest corner of Highway 412 and Barrington Road]. Sometimes we got a nickel to buy an ice cream. The first time we got a quarter we thought we were rich. We walked the festival grounds about 50 times before we spent our money. I don't think they had spaghetti dinners back then. They just had the carnival. They had a cage with an alligator in it.

At Christmastime, we always got together and ate. Santa Claus came Christmas morning. For Easter, Mom always made fugassa. It takes quite a while to make. You make it like bread, only you add lots of eggs and sugar, and nuts if you want to. You have to let it rise overnight.

I met my husband, Woodie Stockton, at a dance at the VFW Club in Springdale. Woodie was playing with the band that night. When we were dating, Woodie would walk all the way from Springdale out here to see me. Once in a while we would borrow Dad's truck to go on a date. We went to Springdale or to a dance. That was about it. There weren't many places to go.

We were married in 1941 here in Tontitown. We stayed with my sister Norina for a while. Woodie was drafted into the Army in 1942. He served in Italy, France, and Germany. He was in the Army about four years. During that time, I moved back home with Mom and Dad.

After Woodie returned from the Army, we lived with Mom and Dad until we bought a house that my brother-in-law, Mano [Gasparotto], had built. Woodie farmed for a while, and then he drove a truck for Willis Shaw Express. In the early 1950s, we built a tavern called "Woodie's Place" next to our house. We ran the tavern together. Woodie passed away in 2003.

Our children are Donald, Ronald, Glenda, and Janet. None of them were born in a hospital. They were all born at home. We have five grandchildren.

About my doll collection—I don't know how I got started with that. I never had a doll when I was little, and I always wanted one. So I started out with one, and then the first thing you know, I got another one. I don't have a favorite. I like them all.

LORINE PIANALTO TALDO

Lorine Pianalto Taldo was born in 1928 in Tontitown, Arkansas, to Silvio and Emilia Taldo Pianalto. She was 74 years old when she was interviewed in 2002.

My maternal grandparents, Dionisio and Rosa Pianalto, came from Italy to Sunnyside. They had three children: Catherine, Silvio, who was my father, and Dionisia, who we called Nisia. Dionisio died in Sunnyside when a tree fell on him. Rosa then married Joseph Verucchi. Joseph, Rosa, and the three children arrived in Tontitown in 1898 with the original group of settlers from Sunnyside. After they settled in Tontitown, Rosa and Joseph had Floyd, Virgil, Egedio, Alma, Helen, and Evangeline.

I remember Grandmother Rosa. She was a pretty woman. She had beautiful hair. She loved flowers. Her whole life was flowers. She had flowers all over the yard. And she limped. Later in life I found out she had tuberculosis of the bone.

My dad told me very little about his childhood. I think it's sad that they never did talk about Italy. They never did have anything nice to say about Italy. That is the reason I never wanted to go to Italy. I never did care to go, but I learned so much when I did go. I met a lot of relatives. I was in the house where my dad was born. It was cement and rock, all handmade.

Dad only completed the third grade in school. He mostly farmed, but at one time he worked with the WPA. At one time he was in Niles, Ohio, and he was gone six months at a time. He had to do this during the Depression so he could send money home so the family could live.

My maternal grandparents were James and Clementina Costa Taldo. Their children were Emilia, who was my mother, Joseph [Joe Jack], Blanche, Edward, Irma, Argie, Rita, Margaret, and Olivia. Mother

Lorine Pianalto Taldo

talked like they had it pretty rough when she was growing up. Her dad was very strict. When they had to be punished with a switch, he would send them after it. One of the good things she told about was baking bread in the outdoor oven. They would put the bread right on the coals. She said it was the best bread in the world. She taught us a game they played called *trea*. They drew lines on the back of a tablet, and you had to get three in a row somehow. When we played it, we used buttons or corn [as game pieces].

I remember my mother telling me that as a child, she was petrified of the nuns, because they would beat the children. There was one boy who was not very bright, and he got whipped so many times by the nuns. At that time, you didn't contradict what the priests or nuns said, so his mother sewed papers inside his pants so it wouldn't hurt him so bad.

I don't know how my parents met, but there were married in Tontitown. Their children, including the ones who have died, are Rosalie, Florence, Albert, Henry, Lorine, Helen, Pauline, Richard, Bob and Harvey. Henry is the one that died, and Mother had one stillborn child.

Dad worked so hard, and he could build anything. He built our kitchen table and the benches we sat on. There were only two chairs in the kitchen—one was Mom's and one was Dad's. The rest of us sat on a bench. We didn't slide back and forth too much because we may have had a problem with splinters.

The house we lived in was on blocks. Well, it wasn't on blocks, it was on stumps. When Dad started raising chickens, no, I think it was before he started raising chickens, I think he sold grapes, and he got hold of a little money. He bought a jack and jacked the house up, one section at a time, dug a foundation, and filled it with cement. Our house had two long porches, and we had three rooms and nine kids. So Dad closed in these porches, extended the kitchen, and eventually put in a bathroom and a utility room. Then on the outside of it, he put tar paper with a brick design. When my mother and dad moved out of that house, it looked like a palace compared to what it looked like when they moved into it.

When we were children, they put a new floor in the house and the wood was green, so it shrunk. I remember a knot hole falling out of the wood floor. Dad took the lid off a tin can, fixed it so it wouldn't cut our feet, and nailed it over the hole.

We had an old Model T Ford, and we always had to get out and push it when we went up that hill by Joe Ranalli's house. Dad would say to us kids, "Okay, everybody jump out and push!" I'm sure my mother was petrified.

We raised our own pork, but never had beef. Once in a while, a peddler would come by and we would buy a little piece of beef. Besides sausage, we only ate meat one day a week, and that was on Sunday. We had chicken for Sunday dinner.

Mother was an excellent cook. She made the best lemon and coconut cream pies. She would never let us skip a meal, even if you were sick. She had it in her head that you had to eat, sick or not. We had to eat bread with every meal.

We usually had homegrown foods, potatoes, carrots, beets, everything that was raised in the garden and canned. Dad would buy sugar and flour when he sold the grapes, enough to last a whole year. He would buy it in huge bags, and he built a platform for the bags in one of the bedrooms. We set mouse traps under the platform so mice wouldn't get into the bags.

We kept our milk and butter cool by placing it in a shallow creek behind our house. We put it in a gallon or half-gallon jar, and we had a certain place where we had dug out the gravel so it would be a little deeper there. We would anchor the jar with a big rock.

Mother made cheese. Dad fixed a board for her, it was a one-by-six or a two-by-six, on a slope so that all the whey would drain out of it. It was my job to wash the cheese every day. You had to put it in water, and be real gentle with it. It really was good cheese. It finally aged, but sometime it would get these tiny worms. Some of the older Italians would pick up a handful of worms because they were the same color as the cheese. Some of the people would pick up the bugs and eat them just like cheese.

We had caffè latte for breakfast and for supper in the evening. This is [warm] milk with some sugar, colored with a little coffee and some homemade bread. My brothers would take their spoon and put it down in the loaf of bread, then pour the caffè latte right down the spoon. Coffee would get into the loaf and they would eat this whole big loaf of bread. I also remember my brothers putting jelly on their spaghetti. I was told by one of the older Italians that they inherited that taste because the old Italians used to pour wine over their spaghetti, or over their minestra.

With nine children, Mother washed a lot of clothes on the scrub board. She made all of our underclothes—panties, slips, everything— out of blue shirt material because it didn't show the dirt so bad. I didn't like it a bit. I wanted little pink clothes just like everybody else. I could probably wear my slip a week before any dirt would show. My mother said I was so wild that I used to jump over the barbed wire fence instead of going under them.

Mother used to hide things. She hid her money in an empty jar in the cellar. One night somebody broke into the cellar, probably to steal some wine. They took some wine and jelly, but didn't find the money Mother had saved.

One time, one of my sisters got into some raisins that Mother had hidden away. Well, I suppose because she wouldn't give me any, I went and told on her, so my sister took off her shoe and threw it at me. She hit my glasses and broke them and cut my face right below my eye. I remember being so petrified that my father was going to find out about that. I dodged him. I didn't look at him because I knew I was going to catch it when he found out my glasses were broken, because he didn't have the money to replace them. When Dad found out, even though my sister had thrown the shoe, I got bawled out for it. That same sister pushed me against a window one time. We were fighting, and she pushed me with her foot and I fell back through the window and just shattered it, and I got in trouble because of it. I was always the one in trouble. I felt like I took the blame for a lot of things, even when I was innocent. There was a lot of sibling rivalry in my family. If I could get one of my sisters in trouble, I was in my glory. They were the same about me. See, there were three of us girls in a row, Helen, me, and Pauline. That's just the way we were.

I completed seventh grade in school. At that time, my mother had surgery and I was the oldest one living at home, so she kept me out of school for two weeks to help her. Then when she wanted me to go back to school, I wouldn't go. Let me tell you about school. I disliked it. When they would tell us about the old school burning down [in 1927], I would sit at my desk and think, "Why doesn't this building burn?"

We had nuns as teachers. I remember Sister Bernaldo [Kaelin], Sister Madonna [Hall], Sister Adrian [McGrath] and Sister Bernadine [Lake]. Sister Bernaldo was my first teacher, and I really loved her. Sister Madonna was a different story. If you missed a spelling word, she would stand there and make you hold out your hands, and I mean stiff, and she would whack you right across the palm of your hand with her ruler. When you were spelling, you had to stand with your hands behind your back. You couldn't fidget the way kids do today. I was always a good speller. To this day, I can spell almost anything, so I guess she did something for me. There were nuns who came back for a visit in later years, and I never did care if I saw them or not.

Olivia Pianalto, Lucy Piazza, and I were all about the same age. We walked to school and back together. At recess we played games. We would choose sides. I never was very popular in school. There were always those who were the leaders. When they chose sides, I was always the last one chosen. That grows up with you and gives you an inferiority complex.

I took bread and jelly for lunch. I got so sick of bread and jelly. Sometimes Mother would mix cocoa and sugar, stir in milk to make a paste, and slap it on a piece of bread. If I ever had an apple or orange in my lunch box, I couldn't wait for lunch.

I remember the church that was destroyed by the tornado [in 1934]. I remember all the red velvet drapings in it. It was very picturesque, I thought. I was about 7 or 8 years old the night the tornado hit. It looked terrible out, so Mother took us up to the Cunningham farm. They had a storm cellar. It was raining so hard, and water was running in all over the place. The next morning, we found out that the church was gone.

Albino Roso told me that the men made all those cement blocks that were used to build the new church. That is something that Tontitown should be very proud of. They made all these cement blocks and put them all together, so they had to be pretty smart to do that.

The early grape festivals were held around the old [Smith] schoolhouse [on the northwest corner of Highway 412 and Barrington Road] where the Tontitown Mercantile building is now. I remember when Joe Mussino won the pie-eating contest. He ate more pies faster than anybody. They had sack races and things like that. It was all our own people, nobody from out of town.

We had Christmas after Christmas that we never did get anything. My older sister told us that we never did get anything because we were too mean. But we made do like everybody did back then. For dolls, we would go out to the woodpile and get a stick of wood with a knot hole in it. That would be the baby's face. Then we would wrap it in a tea towel or a rag, and we carried it around like a baby.

My first job, other than picking strawberries when I was young, was at the City Hospital in Fayetteville. I was very young. I don't remember how much I was paid, maybe $20 a month, after they took out our room and board. I lived in the nurse's quarters. My mother always preached to save your money, so when I got married, I had a little money. In 1948, $1,000 was a lot of money.

My husband, Fredie Taldo, and I grew up together. When we dated, we went in groups. Everywhere we went, half of Tontitown was there. Fredie didn't dance, so I was really glad we went in groups, because I was one of these ornery people who thought that if there was a loose man around, and music that I liked to dance to, that man wouldn't be sitting down very long. Let me tell you something else about that. We went to Bella Vista to the cave [Wonderland Cave]. They used to have dances there. You could dance all night and never get overheated, because it was underground and always cool in there. We went there a lot.

Fredie and I were married in 1948 in Tontitown. The first year we lived in an apartment in Springdale, and then we bought the old Mary and Aldo Maestri farm. We bought the house and 27 acres for $5,500. Fredie sold furniture and TVs for 41 years. We have four children: Philip, Kenneth, Marilyn and Curtis, and we have ten grandchildren.

I taught myself how to sew. I have sat up many a night until one o'clock sewing. I made the boys' shirts and Marilyn's dresses. I even designed and made my own things. I would take a basic pattern and completely disfigure it. I would cut the sleeves and add a piece in the middle of the sleeve of a contrasting color. I would cut the skirt off and put another color. I got to the point where I would lay in bed at night and think of what colors I could put together.

A funny story happened one Halloween that involved Rachel Franco, Joe Taldo, and a bunch of other people. We were in bed sound asleep when we heard all this commotion on the front porch. Screaming, yelling, and going on. Fredie went and got his shotgun. Now this could have been a tragic thing because we were scared half out of our wits. Fredie went into the kitchen and flipped on a flood light that we had out back. He recognized Joe's car, so then he knew that his brother was behind it. When we opened the door, here were all these adults dressed in costume. I fixed them all a drink and we had a lot of fun.

I think the world is a better place today than when I was a child. People today are living better than they ever did. I think God has blessed us abundantly.

John Zulpo

JOHN ZULPO

*John Zulpo was born in 1930 in St. Louis, Missouri, to
Henry and Edith Pesselato Zulpo. He was 74 years old
when he was interviewed in 2004.*

My Zulpo grandparents, Tomaso and Mariana Brunialti Zulpo
came to Tontitown from Sunnyside in 1898 with the original group of
settlers. They came with five children: John, James, Adolpho, Ernest,
and Theresa. They also had a daughter who died in Italy, and a daughter
who died aboard the *Kaiser Wilhelm*, the ship that brought the Zulpos
to America.

One of Tomaso's brothers, Pietro Zulpo, died in Tontitown in 1899.
He is buried in St. Joseph's Cemetery. Pietro Zulpo's wife, Catherine,
then married John Pesselato and moved to St. Louis.

My father, Henry Zulpo, was born to Tomaso and Mariana Zulpo
in Tontitown in 1904. Mariana died six months after Dad was born. The
Maestri family helped raise my dad. Grandpa would take Dad to the
Maestri home in the daytime and pick him up in the evening.

I'm going to tell you how my story is so intertwined with Tontitown.
When Nonno Tomaso Zulpo got sick here in Tontitown, who do you
think came to take care of him? It was Catherine Zulpo Pesselato,
Tomaso's former sister-in-law. When Catherine came to help Tomaso,
she brought along her daughter, Edith. That's how my parents, Henry
Zulpo and Edith Pesselato, met.

Dad never talked much about his childhood in Tontitown. He told
me picking up rocks on the farm. He grew to adulthood in Tontitown,
and moved to St. Louis, Missouri, when he was about 21 years old.
Pacifico Pianalto went with him. The way Dad explained it, he, his two

brothers Adolph and John, and their dad, Tomaso, were going to haul a wagon load of apples up near the depot. Dad and Pacifico timed it just right, so Dad would be going past the depot about the time the train was leaving for St. Louis. Pacifico got two train tickets and was waiting for Dad at the depot. Dad jumped off the wagon, said goodbye to his father and brothers, and jumped on the train. One of the brothers said, "Where are you going, Henry?" Dad said, "St. Louis. I'll see you," as he waved goodbye.

Dad and Pacifico went to St. Louis to look for work. They made it to the east end of Dago Hill [an Italian neighborhood in south St. Louis] and stayed with a family there. Then they went to meet Dad's aunt, Catherine Pesselato, and her family. Catherine was the widow of Dad's uncle, Pietro Zulpo, who died in Tontitown in 1899.

My parents married in 1927 in St. Louis. They had two children: my sister, Dolores, and me. Dad didn't get back to Tontitown too often. The first time I came with him to Tontitown was in about 1947. We stayed in a motel next to the Venesian Inn. We visited Dad's sister, Theresa Zulpo Franco, his brother, Adolph Zulpo, and his sister-in-law, Ida Brunetti Zulpo. Once when I came for a visit, Rachel and Tom Franco took me to [Wonderland Cave] in Bella Vista. It was a nightclub in a cave, and it was built like a deck of cards.

Betty and I married in St. Louis in 1951. We have three children: John Jr., Patricia Linda, and Dennis. If I want to stay connected to my Zulpo side of the family, Tontitown is it. It's not up in St. Louis. My children are not married, so they are the end of the Zulpos in St. Louis.

In 1956, Dad came to Tontitown for the funeral of his sister, Theresa Zulpo Franco. While he was here, Rachel and Tom Franco gave Dad a homemade salami seasoned by Albert Pellin. Dad came back to St. Louis with that salami, and we couldn't wait to open it. When we did, we saw that the salami was green and had all this mildew on it. We wiped it off, cut it, fried it, and ate it, except for Betty, who said there was no way she would eat it.

One time Betty and I took my parents and met my Tontitown cousins, Jack and Leon Zulpo, at Lake Norfork in Arkansas. This was about 1960. We were waiting at the cabin, and here comes this black Cadillac. It's Jack, driving a black Cadillac he bought from Sisco Funeral Home

　　　JOHN ZULPO

[in Springdale]. Jack gets out of the car, and he doesn't have any shoes on. Dad said, "Damn, Jack, you don't have any shoes." It was about 110 degrees in the shade. Leon got out of the car and said it was so hot outside that it felt like a shotgun had hit him. Then they opened the trunk of the car, and there was a full bar set up in the trunk!

Leon Zulpo

LEON ZULPO

Leon Zulpo was born in 1928 in Tontitown, Arkansas, to Adolpho and Theresa Sbanotto Zulpo. He was 76 years old when he was interviewed in 2004.

My paternal grandparents were Tomaso and Mariana Brunialti Zulpo. They came from Italy to America with five children: John, James, my father, Adolpho, Ernest, and Theresa. They were part of the original group of Tontitown settlers who came here from Sunnyside in 1898. After they settled in Tontitown, Tomaso and Mariana had another child, Henry.

My maternal grandparents were Antonio and Pierina Tessaro Sbanotto. They were also with the original Tontitown settlers. Their children were Roy, Harry, Dora, Emma, Connie, Mabel, Helen, and my mother, Theresa. I miss Nonno Sbanotto. He would always tell me, "You're going to speak Italian." Whenever he spoke to me, he said, "You could answer me in Italian." Mother and Daddy spoke Italian among themselves, but never where I had a chance to learn. Nonno was my only chance, but he passed away suddenly.

Dad was quiet. He never did talk much. In fact, for several years I didn't know that Dad was with his brother [James Zulpo] when James was killed in World War I. They were right there side by side. Dad said they were walking back from a battle. Uncle James told Daddy, "I'm going to lean up against this tree and read my letter from home." Daddy walked off, and while Uncle James was leaning up against the tree, a mortar shell hit him and killed him. After that happened, Daddy had the chance to get a discharge and come home because he lost his brother, but he said, "I came in to serve my time in the war and I'm going to stay until my time is up." Dad had to write a letter to Mary Bastianelli telling her that Uncle James had died. Uncle James was the only man Mary Bastianelli ever dated.

My parents married after Dad returned from the war. My brothers and sisters are Jack, Zelma, Mabel, and Antoinette. I remember when Antoinette was born. Dr. Cooper from Elm Springs came to our house and delivered her.

Dad had 10 acres of vineyards and also raised apples and peaches. Later on, he had two or three little chicken houses. We raised milk cows. We used to process our own beef and hogs. We made our own sausage. Daddy would get Uncle Virgil Verucchi to come in and they would kill a couple of hogs, then Dad would go and help Uncle Virgil kill a couple. They would work together.

People never kept a male cow to breed their cattle. Dick Piazza—they called him Minco Piazza—he had the male. Daddy used to send me down to Minco's house with our cow when she was in heat. Here I would go, walking with this cow across the highway and down the road past the cemetery to Minco's house. We would turn the cow in with the male and get her bred, and I'd walk her back home. I did that time and time again.

We had two hired hands, Bill and Charley, who used to live at our place. They picked grapes for us and for Gene Ardemagni. Bill couldn't say Gene's last name. Bill would tell my dad, "We will pick for you today, Adolph, and then we'll go to Gene Godalmighty's tomorrow."

I remember taking a load of corn in our wagon to the Johnson Mill to make cornmeal. Daddy made polenta every Sunday. That was his job after church. We also had corn ground up for our hogs. Mother had large cans with lids that we poured the cornmeal in. Daddy had cans in the barn that he put ground corn for his horses and his hogs.

In the mornings before school, I had to run my box traps to see if I caught any rabbits. After school, I would come home, get the wheelbarrow, and go to the garden and pick turnips to feed to the cows. I dumped them in the barn lot and chopped them up so the cows wouldn't choke on them.

I always made sure there was wood in the house. Mother had a woodstove to cook on, and we had a heating stove that also used wood. I would carry the wood in, and the girls would help.

We had a wooden refrigerator in the house. I would hang a sign out on the front porch for the ice man that said 25–50–100 pounds. When the ice man stopped, Mom would tell me how many pounds she wanted, and the ice man would carry it in and put it in the refrigerator. We had a well where we kept butter and cream. We would send the butter and cream down so many feet in a bucket, tie it, and leave it down there where it was cool.

Mother did not work outside the home. She stayed home and cooked for Daddy and the hired hands. She loved to work in the garden. A few ladies would come to the house to make quilts. They would sit around [a quilt frame] and quilt, then roll the quilt up [and pull the frame up to the ceiling] where it was out of the way.

I went through the ninth grade in Tontitown. The nuns were our teachers. I remember Sister Adrian [McGrath], Sister Bernadine [Lake], Sister Jerome [Nash], Sister Quintilla [Halter], and Sister Madonna [Hall]. Sister Bernadine made it pretty hard on me, because she thought I was Sister Adrian's pet.

At lunchtime, all I had to do was jump the fence to go home, so I would go home to eat lunch, and then I would come back and play. We played ball. We had a swing. We used to go down in the field and dig up this grass they called chow chow. We would dig it up and eat it. We used to get in trouble over that.

I had lots of friends in school—Mary Frances Tessaro, Patsy Taldo, Hugh West, Abraham Pianalto, Rudy Costa. I had lots of fun with Josephine and Catherine Piazza. They wore long underwear to school. In Sister Adrian's room, there was a stepladder up to the attic. One time Josephine was up on the ladder, and I was looking up to Josephine. Sister Adrian caught me and really raised cane. I said, "She's got long underwear on!"

Josephine is still a character with me. I love her because she sends me a birthday card every year and she signs it, "Guess Who." The next Sunday when I see her at church, Josephine will say, "Did you get my card?" I'll say, "No, I didn't get one from Josephine, but I got one from Guess Who." We used to have good times in school. We never got into any trouble.

After I finished the ninth grade, I attended Springdale High School. Hugo Pozza wanted me to drive his automobile to school because his daughter, Annabelle, couldn't drive. So during my first year of high school, I drove Hugo's car and took Annabelle to school. Rudy Costa, Sarah Mitchell, and Jim Aimerito also rode with us. The next year I drove my red pickup with a camper on it. For three years I drove those kids to school.

I remember when the tornado came through and destroyed the church [in 1934]. Our house was just north of the church. A tree blew right in the window of the bedroom Jack and I shared. The church was gone. I remember going barefooted with Dad to see the church the next morning, and he told me to go get some shoes on. Right away, that same day, everybody got together and started salvaging everything they could at the church. After they got everything cleaned up, they made all the blocks and started rebuilding. Everybody donated their time. Tontitown was wonderful about helping. They built the church back.

At Christmas we always went to Midnight Mass. That was something that just had to be. We hung stockings. I remember Mother telling us to go to bed at a certain time because Santa Claus was going to come. It was nothing like it is today, but it was fun.

Lent was a big deal for us. We always gave up candy. We would put it in a jar, take it upstairs, and hide it. There was no insulation in the walls, so we would put the jar in there. A lot of times the jar would slip all the way down the wall.

There was no such thing as not going to church. I don't care if it was 110 degrees outside, Dad wore a jacket to church. He would leave the house with a necktie on, carrying his jacket, and he walked to church. When he got there, he would put his jacket on. It made it so respectful. Mother always wore a bandana or some kind of hat. It's something that has fallen away today.

I was drafted into the Army in 1950. In 1951, the day before we were supposed to leave for Germany, my dad had a stroke. Father [Thomas] Kennedy called where I was stationed, and they held me over. I went ahead and got an honorable discharge to come home and take care of my father, because nobody was at home but he and Mom. I went back into the milk business and also raised some chickens. I stayed in the reserves for five years after that to serve out my time.

Geraldine Rose Sally Verucchi and I dated for three years and three months. We got married in 1952, when Sally turned 18. Our first home was on top of Frank Perona's store. Mr. and Mrs. Perona lived there

   LEON ZULPO

too. Their apartment was in the back, and ours was in the front. I was still working on my parents' farm. Later Sally and I operated a service station and restaurant up in Gateway, Arkansas. We did that for a little over a year, and then we moved back to Tontitown. Our children are Linda, Adolph, Laura, Lydia, Doug, Lisa, Mike, and Ben. Sally passed away in 2001.

What I really remember about my childhood days in Tontitown is how people helped each other. If someone got sick, everyone would get together and go to that farm, and if it was grape picking time, they would take care of the vineyard. They would help put up hay. They would stay all night at home with the sick. And folks always had time to visit, which we don't have today. Today people hardly know their neighbors. They don't visit anymore. I can remember that so well—people would find time to go to one of their neighbors, play a couple of hands of pitch, and visit. I thought that was so great. Neighbors helping neighbors. That is the way I grew up.

INDEX

Page numbers in italics indicate pages with photographs.